JEREMIAH TOWER'S
NEW AMERICAN CLASSICS

JEREMIAH TOWER'S

NEW AMERICAN CLASSICS

PHOTOGRAPHY BY ED CAREY

1817

Harper & Row, Publishers, New York
Cambridge, Philadelphia, San Francisco, Washington
London, Mexico City, São Paulo, Singapore, Sydney

FIRST EDITION

Design by Walter Sparks and Jeremiah Tower

Styling by Noreen Lam and Jeremiah Tower

Library of Congress Cataloging-in-Publication Data

Tower, Jeremiah.
  New American classics.

  Includes index.
  1. Cookery, American.   I. Title.
TX715.T739   1986   641.5973   86-45155
ISBN 0-06-181878-X

86 87 88 89 90 WAK 10 9 8 7 6 5 4 3 2 1

Contents

RECIPES BY CATEGORY
4

PREFACE
12

PERSONAL FAVORITES
14

SAUCES & RELISHES
25

EGGS, CHEESE, PASTA, & GRAINS
43

FISH & SHELLFISH
69

POULTRY, RABBIT, & GAME
103

MEATS & OFFAL
133

VEGETABLES & FRUIT
159

DESSERTS
187

STANDARD PREPARATIONS
216

ACKNOWLEDGMENTS
225

GENERAL INDEX
227

RECIPE INDEX
227

To Elizabeth David, Richard Olney,
and the staff of my restaurants

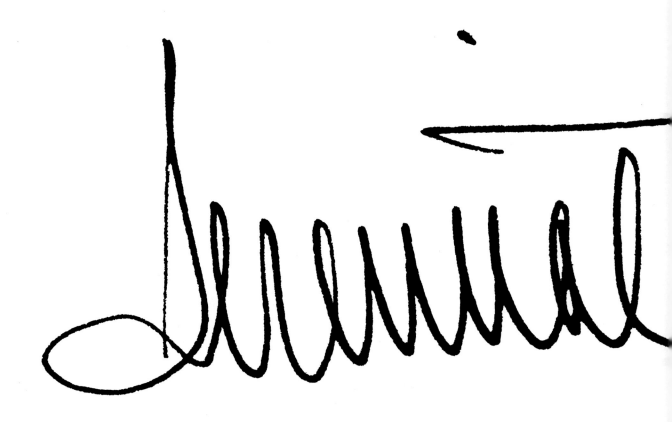

To Larry,   fellow chef —
A pleasure to meet you —
best luck in your career —
my warm regards —
Jeremiah Tower

Tower

Recipes by Category

SAUCES

Salsa, page 28

Steven Vranian's Mission Fig–Mint Relish, page 28

Steven Vranian's Mango–Chili Salsa, page 28

Fresh Cherry Chutney, page 28

Tomatillo Salsa, page 29

Tomato Chutney, page 29

Garlic Puree, page 30

Ancho Chili Puree, page 30

Black Bean Sauce, page 30

Vinaigrette, page 32

Tomato Vinaigrette, page 32

Raspberry Puree, page 32

Raspberry Sauce, page 32

Yellow or Red Bell Pepper Puree, page 32

Cilantro–Lime–Ginger Butter, page 34

Montpellier Butter, page 34

Mayonnaise, page 36

Herb Mayonnaise, page 36

Black Bean Mayonnaise, page 36

Aioli, page 36

Rouille, page 36

Hollandaise, page 38

Sauce Mousseline, page 38

Sauce Maltaise, page 38

Sauce Noisette, page 38

Tomato Hollandaise, page 38

Hollandaise with Essences, page 38

Sabayon, page 40

Béarnaise, page 40

Mint Béarnaise or Sauce Poloise, page 40

Sauce Béarnaise with Meat Glaze, page 40

Barbecue Sauce, page 222

COLD FIRST COURSES

Eggs Rémoulade Creole, page 50

Eggs in Hell, Texas Style, page 51

Pickled Herring with New Potatoes, page 74

Seviche, page 76

Shrimp Salad with Three Mayonnaises, page 78

Tartare of Salmon and Tuna, page 82

Squab Mousse with Field Salad, page 116

My Steak Tartare, page 141

Bündnerfleisch with Vegetable Salad, page 142

HOT FIRST COURSES

Grilled Goat Cheese in Leaves,
page 53

Squash Blossoms with Goat Cheese,
page 54

Stuffed Chilies with Black Bean
Sauce, page 57

Polenta with Wild Mushroom
Sauce, page 58

Risotto with Prawns, page 58

Truffled Sweetbread Ravioli,
page 59

Cornmeal Blinis with Smoked
Sturgeon and Caviar, page 63

Blue Cornmeal Pancakes, page 63

Grilled Calamari with Lobster
Mayonnaise, page 85

Fish "Sausage" with Sorrel and
Lobster Sauce, page 92

Soft-Shell Crabs with Tomato and
Basil, page 96

Mixed Shellfish Plate, page 99

Grilled Spiced Shrimp with Pearl
Onions, page 99

Brioches with Marrow, Lobster,
Poached Garlic, and Chervil,
page 100

Fish Paillard with Ginger, Garlic,
and Tomatoes, page 100

Grilled Duck Leg with Endive
Salad, page 115

Grilled Duck Sausage with Polenta,
page 116

Duck Livers with Andouille
Sausage, page 118

Grilled Ham Hocks with Rocket
and Mustard Aioli, page 147

Warm Vegetable Stew, page 167

The Black Bean Cake, page 175

Artichoke Bottoms Stuffed with
Fava Bean Puree, page 177

Mushroom Caps with Bone
Marrow, page 178

Warm Salad of Black-Eyed Peas,
page 180

French-Fried Eggplant with Florida
Guzpachy Sauce, page 182

SOUPS

Lobster Gazpacho, page 77

My Favorite Fish Soup, page 84

Tarpon Springs Soup, page 96

Duck Soup, page 112

Cream of Corn Soup with Crayfish
Butter, page 170

Borscht with Pickled Mushrooms
and Cucumbers, page 170

Chilled Sorrel and Herb Soup with
Tomato Cream, page 172

Garlic Soup with Sage and Ham
Butter, page 172

Cucumber Vichyssoise with
Crayfish Cream, page 173

My Black Bean Soup, page 175

Minestrone with Artichokes,
Sausage, and Pistachios, page 182

FISH AND SHELLFISH SALADS

Shrimp Salad with Three
  Mayonnaises, page 78

Belgian Endive Salad with Lobster,
  page 78

Lobster and Rocket Salad, page 79

Warm Salad of Crayfish with
  Cucumbers and Dill, page 80

Warm Salad of Lobster and
  Avocado, page 81

Grilled Calamari with Lobster
  Mayonnaise, page 85

Warm Salad of Artichokes and
  Grilled Prawns, page 176

Grilled Radicchio and Smoked Eel
  Salad, page 178

MEAT AND POULTRY SALADS

Warm Duck Salad with Turnip
  Pancake, page 112

Warm Squab Salad with Okra,
  page 122

Warm Chicken, Sweetbread, and
  Pepper Coleslaw Salad, page 123

PASTA SALADS

Pasta Salad with Baked Eggplant
  and Tomatoes, page 60

Warm Pasta Salad with Smoked
  Duck and Radicchio, page 60

Pasta with Rabbit and Chanterelles,
  page 64

FRUIT AND VEGETABLE SALADS

My Aunt's Coleslaw, page 15

Belgian Endive Salad with Lobster,
  page 78

Warm Salad of Lobster and
  Avocado, page 81

Warm Cabbage Salad with Duck
  Fat, page 110

Warm Grilled Vegetable Salad with
  Texas Ham, page 165

Roasted Bell Pepper Salad with
  Anchovies, page 167

Fresh Fig and Mint Salad, page 168

Watermelon and Onion Salad,
  page 168

Avocado, Papaya, and Rocket
  Salad, page 169

Mango and Avocado Salad,
  page 169

Warm Salad of Artichokes and
  Grilled Prawns, page 176

Warm Salad of Black-Eyed Peas,
  page 180

Okra, Tomato, and Basil Warm
  Salad, page 180

GREEN SALADS

Garden Salad with Salmon Caviar
  Croutons, page 165

Avocado, Papaya, and Rocket
  Salad, page 169

LUNCHEON OR LIGHT MAIN COURSES

Scrambled Eggs with Truffles, page 17

Sea Urchin Soufflé, page 23

Poached Eggs with Mushrooms, page 50

French Scrambled Eggs with Smoked Salmon, page 51

Spinach, Sorrel, and Ham Frittata, page 52

Noreen Lam's Lamb Hash, page 52

Grilled Goat Cheese in Leaves, page 53

Raclette with Radicchio, page 54

Polenta with Wild Mushroom Sauce, page 58

Risotto with Prawns, page 58

Pasta Salad with Baked Eggplant and Tomatoes, page 60

Warm Pasta Salad with Smoked Duck and Radicchio, page 60

Pasta with Rabbit and Chanterelles, page 64

Timbale of Macaroni and Sweetbreads, page 65

Shrimp Salad with Three Mayonnaises, page 78

Belgian Endive Salad with Lobster, page 78

Warm Salad of Crayfish with Cucumbers and Dill, page 80

Warm Salad of Lobster and Avocado, page 81

Grilled Calamari with Lobster Mayonnaise, page 85

Fish "Sausage" with Sorrel and Lobster Sauce, page 92

Grilled Scallops with Tarragon Sauce, page 93

Mixed Shellfish Plate, page 99

Grilled Spiced Shrimp with Pearl Onions, page 99

Fish Paillard with Ginger, Garlic, and Tomatoes, page 100

Brioches with Marrow, Lobster, Poached Garlic, and Chervil, page 100

Duck Skin Omelet, page 110

Duck Confit, page 113

Grilled Duck Leg with Endive Salad, page 115

Duck Livers with Andouille Sausage, page 118

Grilled Chicken Paillard with Ancho Chili Butter, page 118

Rabbit Chili, page 131

Chopped Lamb Steak au Poivre, page 141

My Steak Tartare, page 141

Grilled Whole Lamb Kidneys with Potato Pancakes, page 143

Grilled Spicy Lamb Sausage with Oysters, page 146

Grilled Ham Hocks with Rocket and Mustard Aioli, page 147

The Chili Recipe, page 150

Artichoke Bottoms Stuffed with Fava Bean Puree, page 177

Warm Salad of Black-Eyed Peas, page 180

Eggplant and Zucchini Timbale Soufflé, page 184

SANDWICHES

Chicken Club Sandwich, page 19

Toasted Lobster Sandwich, page 82

Toasted Chicken and Ancho Chili Sandwich, page 123

MAIN COURSES

Roast Beef, page 16

Country Ham, page 23

Fish Stew with Fennel Aioli,
    page 74

Mark Franz's Calamari with Sweet
    and Hot Chilies, page 85

Grilled Calamari with Lobster
    Mayonnaise, page 85

Grilled Salmon with Cucumbers
    and Black Bean Sauce, page 88

Salmon Stew with Artichokes and
    Rose Peppercorns, page 88

Mussels in Cataplana, page 89

Grilled Swordfish with Rosemary
    Mayonnaise, page 90

Grilled Dungeness Crab, page 92

Grilled Scallops with Tarragon
    Sauce, page 93

Poached Turbot with Lobster,
    page 94

Catfish with Black Bean Sauce,
    page 95

Soft-Shell Crabs with Tomato and
    Basil, page 96

Grilled Spiced Shrimp with Pearl
    Onions, page 99

Fish Paillard with Ginger, Garlic,
    and Tomatoes, page 100

Duck Confit, page 113

Duck Breast with Wild Rice and
    Mango-Chili Salsa, page 114

Grilled Duck Leg with Endive
    Salad, page 115

Grilled Chicken Paillard with
    Ancho Chili Butter, page 118

Roast Quail with Pumpkin Seed
    Sauce, page 119

Smoke-Roasted Squab, page 120

Smoked Duck with Belgian Endive,
    page 120

Grilled Squab Marinated in Berry
    Puree, page 121

Stars Gumbo, page 124

Saddle of Rabbit with Black and
    Rose Peppercorns, page 127

Braised Rabbit with Leeks and
    Prunes, page 127

Capon with Wild Mushrooms and
    Mint Béarnaise, page 130

Poached Duck with Duck Sausage
    and Horseradish Sauce, page 130

Grilled Whole Lamb Kidneys with
    Potato Pancakes, page 143

Grilled Sweetbreads with Chili
    Butter, page 144

Grilled Sweetbreads with
    Mushroom Butter, page 144

T-Bone Steak, Cowboy Style,
    page 146

Braised Lamb Shanks, page 148

Lamb Stew with Artichokes,
    page 148

The Chili Recipe, page 150

Ham with Black Beans, Oranges,
    and Lime Cream, page 150

Poached Beef Fillet with Vegetables,
    page 153

Fricassee of Veal with Crayfish,
    page 152

Coulibiac of Sweetbreads, page 156

Roast Pork Loin Stuffed with Ham
    and Rosemary, page 156

Braised Sweetbreads in a Sealed
    Casserole, page 157

GRILLS

Grilled Goat Cheese in Leaves,
  page 53

Grilled Calamari with Lobster
  Mayonnaise, page 85

Grilled Salmon with Cucumbers
  and Black Bean Sauce, page 88

Grilled Swordfish with Rosemary
  Mayonnaise, page 90

Grilled Dungeness Crab, page 92

Grilled Scallops with Tarragon
  Sauce, page 93

Mixed Shellfish Plate, page 99

Grilled Spiced Shrimp with Pearl
  Onions, page 99

Grilled Duck Leg with Endive
  Salad, page 115

Grilled Duck Sausage with Polenta,
  page 117

Grilled Chicken Paillard with
  Ancho Chili Butter, page 118

Grilled Squab Marinated in Berry
  Puree, page 121

Grilled Whole Lamb Kidneys with
  Potato Pancakes, page 143

Grilled Sweetbreads with Chili
  Butter, page 144

Grilled Sweetbreads with
  Mushroom Butter, page 144

T-Bone Steak, Cowboy Style,
  page 146

Grilled Spicy Lamb Sausage with
  Oysters, page 146

Grilled Ham Hocks with Rocket
  and Mustard Aioli, page 147

Grilled Vegetable Salad with Texas
  Ham and Aioli, page 165

Grilled Radicchio and Smoked Eel
  Salad, page 178

Mushroom Caps with Bone
  Marrow, page 178

FAST FOODS

Pizza with Three Cheese, Tomatoes,
  and Herbs, page 18

Chicken Club Sandwich, page 19

Black-Truffled Hamburger, page 20

Pasta Salad with Baked Eggplant
  and Tomatoes, page 60

Warm Pasta Salad with Smoked
  Duck and Radicchio, page 60

Toasted Lobster Sandwich, page 82

Fish Paillard with Ginger, Garlic,
  and Tomatoes, page 100

Toasted Chicken and Ancho Chili
  Sandwich, page 123

Chopped Lamb Steak au Poivre,
  page 141

T-Bone Steak, Cowboy Style,
  page 146

ACCOMPANIMENTS

Squash Blossoms with Goat Cheese,
  page 54

White Cheese with Roasted Garlic,
  page 56

Stuffed Chilies with Black Bean
  Sauce, page 57

Polenta with Wild Mushroom
  Sauce, page 58

Grilled Spiced Shrimp with Pearl
  Onions, page 99

Grilled Duck Sausage with Polenta
  and Tomato Chutney, page 117

Grilled Spicy Lamb Sausage with
  Oysters, page 146

Warm Vegetable Stew, page 167

Mushroom Caps with Bone
  Marrow, page 178

Eggplant and Zucchini Timbale
  Soufflé, page 184

CHUTNEYS AND RELISHES

Salsa, page 28

Steven Vranian's Mission Fig–Mint Relish, page 28

Steven Vranian's Mango–Chili Salsa, page 28

Fresh Cherry Chutney, page 28

Tomatillo Salsa, page 29

Tomato Chutney, page 29

FRUIT

Warm Berry Compote, page 193

Pears in Red Wine with Basil, page 193

White Peaches with Raspberry and Blackberry Sauces, page 194

Russian Raspberry Gratin, page 195

Figs in Red Wine with Walnut Cream, page 195

Turtle Cay Bananas with Passion Fruit Sauce, page 196

Summer Pudding, page 196

Raspberry Soufflés with Sabayon, page 198

Apricot and Lemon Mousse, page 198

Mango Mousse with Coconut Sauce, page 200

Tropical Fruit Compote, page 201

Caramelized Apple Tart, page 204

ICE CREAM AND ICES

Black-and-White Ice Cream Soda, page 23

Fresh Plum Ice Cream, page 200

Cross Creek Tangerine Ice, page 202

Nougat Ice Cream, page 213

CAKE/PASTRY

Shortbread with Apples and Apricot Sauce, page 202

Plum Napoleon with Sabayon, page 203

Trifle, page 204

Pecan Puff Pastry with Chocolate Sauce and Sabayon, page 206

Pumpkin Gingerbread with Rum Cream, page 207

Polenta Pound Cake with Madeira Cream, page 207

Saffron Brioche with Pear Glaze, page 209

Bourbon Pecan Tart, page 209

Bittersweet Chocolate Torte, page 210

Chocolate Paradise, page 210

Three Custards, page 212

DESSERT SAUCES/ PUREES/CREAMS

Raspberry Puree, page 32

Raspberry Sauce, page 32

Walnut Cream, page 195

Passion Fruit Sauce, page 196

Coconut Sauce, page 200

Chocolate Sauce, page 206

Rum Cream, page 207

Madeira Cream, page 207

Chocolate Cream, page 210

Custard, page 213

Chantilly Cream, page 214

Sabayon Mousseline Sauce,
    page 214

STAND-BYS AND STANDARD PREPARATIONS

Pizza dough, page 19

Vinaigrette and variations
    (hazelnut, tomato-herb), page 32

Purees (garlic, ancho, bell pepper),
    pages 30–32

Basic butter with herbs (and
    variations), page 34

Mayonnaise (and variations),
    page 36

Aioli (and variations), page 36

Hollandaise (and variations),
    page 38

Shellfish essence (and variations),
    page 221

Sabayon mousseline sauce,
    page 214

Quick puff pastry, page 217

Sugar syrup, page 216

Tart pastry, page 217

Shortbread, page 202

Creme Chantilly, page 214

Fish stock, page 218

Fish velouté, page 221

Chicken stock, page 220

Beef, veal or lamb stock, page 220

Court bouillon, page 221

Tomato concasse, page 220

Velouté, page 221

Pasta dough—white and green, 219

Basic tomato sauce, page 220

Polenta, page 219

Herb oil, page 222

Mirepoix, page 127

Preface

I started my cooking career in 1972 as chef of Chez Panisse restaurant in Berkeley, California. After two years I had landed on my feet and, looking around for ways to challenge the restaurant, I started a series of special monthly dinners, each one featuring a menu from a region of France. When, after a year, most of the regions had been used up, I turned to Morocco (we did two of those) and finally to Corsica, with great difficulty in finding anything Corsican that anyone wanted to eat. In those days Chez Panisse was a French restaurant, if with the stirrings of the as yet unborn California movement. So it was not unusual for me to be reading French or a book like *The Epicurean,* a "Franco-American Culinary Encyclopedia" by Charles Ranhoffer, which contains recipes he used at Delmonico's in New York from 1862 to 1894. There I saw the title of a soup, *Crème de maïs verte à la mendocino*—Cream of Green Corn à la Mendocino. What struck me about the recipe was that it took its name from a town up the coast from San Francisco. What, I wondered, were chefs in New York doing thinking about Mendocino in the 1890s? And then, like a bolt out of the heavens, the realization came to me: Why am I scratching around in Corsica when I have it bountifully all around me here in California? I looked further into the chapter on soups and saw the words "Cambridge" and "Portland," and next to "Dubarry" and "Sévigné" I saw "Franklin" and "Livingstone." We used to live in General Livingstone's house in Brooklyn Heights, and could the "Franklin" be Benjamin?

The recipe for the green corn soup was breathtaking in its simplicity, elegance and informality. One took some fresh young corn, cooked it, mashed it to a puree, added broth, sieved it, reheated almost to a boil, stirred in an egg yolk–cream liaison to thicken the soup, and at the moment before serving, stirred in a "fine crayfish butter." The soup was garnished with cooked shrimp tails cut in small pieces. I immediately revised the recipe, using less crayfish butter in the soup and drizzling a crayfish cream over the top.

It was American food using French cooking principles. I could not contain my exhilaration over

what I beheld as the enormous doors of habit swung
open onto a whole new vista. And I began to compose
an American regional dinner—California, not Corsica.

•

Tomales Bay Bluepoint Oysters on Ice
1973 Schramsberg Cuvée de Gamay

•

Cream of Fresh Corn Soup Mendocino Style, with Crayfish Butter
1973 Mount Eden Chardonnay

•

Monterey Bay Prawns Sautéed with Garlic, Parsley, and Butter
Preserved California-grown Geese from Sebastopol
1974 Ridge Fiddletown Zinfandel

•

Fresh Caramelized Figs from Sonoma
1974 Harbor Mission del Sol

•

Walnuts, Almonds, and Mountain Pears from the San Francisco
Farmers' Market

•

The restaurant and I—and several others—were
never the same again. I put the menus in English and
gave up the regions of France, except for visiting and
for inspiration.

Since then I have gone on, through Ventana in Big
Sur, the Balboa Cafe in San Francisco, the Sante Fe Bar
and Grill, and Stars, to develop a style of cooking
which, in its influence and scope, drawing on bar and
grill, bistro, brasserie, and classical restaurant food, has
become a new American classic.

Personal Favorites

When I read Elizabeth David's *French Provincial Cooking* in 1970, I was enthralled and totally inspired by the essays at the front of the section called "The Cooking of the French Provinces." Among them Mrs. David offers a description, in his own words, of "Escoffier's Shooting Week-end Fifty Years Ago," translated from a 1912 issue of *Le Carnet d'Épicure.* The simplicity of the food he described is still an inspiration to me. He tells of the kind of food that cannot be improved upon, food one could eat every day, the epitome of successful cuisine then and today, and of the maxim *"faites simple."* At the end of the passage, after complimenting the beauty of the countryside and the hospitality received, Escoffier says, "For my part, I have never forgotten the sauce of horseradish and walnuts." I looked to see if Mrs. David had let such a tantalizing statement go by, and she had not. There is a recipe for *sauce raifort aux noix,* and I used it in preparing the next week's menus at Chez Panisse.

But it is not so much the sauce recipe that stays with me as Escoffier's personal devotion to the "simple" pleasure of that one element in a glorious few days.

So when I think of the years of indulging myself beyond the usual share, I wonder what were my favorite experiences with food, what are the dishes that I can't do without, or won't. I remember a hot afternoon in Marrakesh in midsummer. I had wandered around trying to decide where to have lunch. No restaurant looked suitable: too crowded, too expensive, too empty, too everything. By two-thirty, no one would serve me anyway, since afternoon nap time was fast approaching, and I walked back to my hotel outside the center of town, in the European district. By the time I reached the hotel, the only noises in the whole area were the barking of dogs, the hum of flies, and the slight tinkling of a plastic fountain. I woke the owner of the converted private house that served as a five-room hotel, and he graciously explained that at three o'clock there is no food. I asked if I could use the kitchen, a request that so horrified him that, suddenly wide awake, he told me to sit in the garden.

Half an hour later, he appeared with a bucket of ice studded with beer bottles dripping with condensation in the 110-degree heat, a bottle of olive oil, a plate of salt, a loaf of bread, and a huge platter of sliced tomatoes that he had just picked from the garden, and which still smelled as if they were ripening in the blazing summer heat. Hot from the sun, they were covered in chopped herbs and freshly ground pepper. He shuffled off to sleep in his slippers and left me under the shade of the trees, completely alone, the whole city asleep, the only sound that of the fountain, to crack open one and then another of the ice-cold beers, eating the summer tomatoes, dipping my bread first in olive oil and then in salt. I felt satisfied, and immensely privileged, like a prince in a tiny but momentarily perfect kingdom.

A setting that was as special to me as the Moroccan garden, but one that I visited many times and that was the origin of much of my inspiration with and teaching about food, was the apartment of my aunt and Russian uncle in Washington, D.C. It was there that I drank hundred-year-old Madeira, there that I discovered flavored vodkas frozen to oily smoothness, there that I learned to eat blinis—the fire-and-ice vodka first, then the rich, buttery, caviar-laden blinis. I ate guinea fowl braised in 1907 Malmsey served on a bed of kasha and wild rice, the sauce made from the braising juices, and the wine was an 1891 Sercial. I was fifteen. Despite all these riches and indulgences, it is the memory of the simple food that most vividly conjures up every detail of the lost moments—the flavors, attitudes, and quietly deeper satisfactions. I remember the lobster served with my aunt's coleslaw, the potato chips and beer. Perhaps the best part was, as an adoring adolescent, to partake in the conversations, endless ones: about the various potato chips on the table, one of which had to be decided upon as the winner, the others banished; about beer being the best drink with boiled lobster and butter. And with the hot lobster dripping the butter into which

I had mashed the tomalley and the coral, we ate the cold tomato and cabbage coleslaw.

My Aunt's Coleslaw

The whole key to the success of this dish, I was firmly but very gently told, is to cut the cabbage and tomatoes in large pieces and to soak the cabbage in ice water in the refrigerator for four hours. Then you have to peel and seed the ripe tomatoes, and the dressed slaw has to sit in the refrigerator for a couple of hours to achieve perfect flavor and texture.

1 head	*white cabbage*
4 large	*ripe tomatoes*
½ cup	*mayonnaise (page 36)*
½ cup	*sour cream*
1 tablespoon	*finely chopped fresh ginger*
1 teaspoon	*powdered ginger*
1½ teaspoons	*dry mustard*
	salt and freshly ground pepper

Serves 4 to 6

Discard any of the outer leaves of the cabbage that are wilted or discolored. Cut the cabbage in half from top to bottom and cut out the core. Put each half, cut side down, on the cutting board and cut into ½-inch slices. Put the cabbage in a large bowl, cover with cold water and ice cubes, and refrigerate for 4 hours.

Peel and seed the tomatoes; cut each tomato half into 6 pieces. Mix the mayonnaise, sour cream, fresh and powdered gingers, and mustard in a bowl. Drain the cabbage very well and mix thoroughly with the sauce. Season with salt and pepper, add the tomatoes, and toss lightly. Refrigerate covered for 2 hours. Serve very cold.

In that same apartment in Washington, I sat over a Russian Easter dinner with Sergei Cheremetev, whose family had been the richest in Russia and who told stories of his father, who thought the Romanovs were upstarts and would barely speak to the czar; with a classmate of my uncle's who was the pretender to the Polish throne; and with my uncle and my aunt, who that night was wearing her set of copies of imperial emeralds. With that group the conversation soon turned to which wine was superior, Burgundy or Bordeaux, and then, white or red? My aunt would drink only Scotch, Cognac, and very old first growths in prime condition. The rest of us drank anything good. My uncle had saved a dozen or so bottles of various esoteric things from before the revolution. He had been saving them for years, to teach me the immense difference between excellent and the very best possible. Talk of excellence divided the diners on the question of whether it is achieved through austerity or indulgence, purity or excess.

Inevitably the subject of decadence arose, with everyone invited to define it. My aunt disapproved of the entire conversation, and said so. The Polish prince smiled elegantly. My uncle deferred to Cheremetev, who said the best definition came from his boyhood friend Prince Youssoupof. The story involved Youssoupof and a French count. When the question of what is decadence came up, the French count said something lyrical about beautiful women. Youssoupof said, "Nonsense, my dear fellow, the epitome of decadence is to drink Château d'Yquem with roast beef." I think my mouth must have fallen open (not necessarily in expectation of this combination being consumed) and my aunt gave me a threatening frown. There was a silence as we all tried to conjure up, unsuccessfully, the dangers of that combination.

Years later, while an undergraduate at Harvard, I experienced the almost breathtaking beauty of drinking Château d'Yquem with cold roast goose in the suffocating afternoon heat of Boston in August. Spurred by its success, I decided to hold a summer test of the Youssoupof theory. I invited only my closest friends, those who would not seek vengeance if they became sick or pushed over the edge. Remembering my aunt—who was a modest dresser in public, but with me and her husband, or with intimates, wore silk everything, and her fabulous emeralds—I asked everyone to dress to the hilt. It was ninety degrees and the kitchen was over a hundred. The taste of Château d'Yquem with the rich, aged, perfectly cooked roast beef was indescribable. And "taste" does not adequately convey the sensation, because what happens to you, as I see it now, is like something out of recent space films—travel at space-warp speed through the stars. Only, with the wine and beef there is very little noise, unless it is the sound of someone going over backward in his chair and hitting the floor.

Years later, after I had moved to the West Coast and was the chef and co-owner of Chez Panisse restaurant in Berkeley, the story and the experience still haunted me, so I put on a Sauternes Dinner. It caught the attention of a number of people, including food writer Charles Perry. After I told him the beef story, we wondered if perhaps it had been the heat that actually devastated all of us. Charles said, Let us do it again. In San Francisco, there was no problem with the heat. I think it was the usual fifty degrees outside. The rest of the menu is not important, because when the beef was served, and the wine was poured, when I demonstrated the necessary ritual of chewing the beef and taking a draft of the wine, chewing twice and swallowing, there followed the familiar silence, the almost agonized sighs and rapturous smiles.

Roast Beef

The success of roast beef depends on the best-quality beef, with very good marbling and about twenty-one days' dry-aging. Use a large rib roast from the loin end. The two controversies about roasting (baking) beef are whether to salt the meat first, and at what temperature to cook it. It is said that if you salt the beef before putting it in the oven, all the juices will come out. I have never seen that happen, and if you do not salt the meat first, or at all, it has little taste. Some say to salt the meat halfway through the cooking process—very difficult and dangerous. I believe in salting before cooking, which produces the best flavor and a salty crust. Should you start with a hot oven and then turn down the temperature? Or use the low-temperature method throughout the cooking? The low-temperature method produces very tender but tasteless mush, so I believe in searing the beef and then turning down the temperature. That way, you get wonderful crisp fat and "outside" pieces, as well as a range of meat cooked well-done to rare.

1	*beef rib roast of 5 to 7 ribs*
½ cup	*vodka*
3 tablespoons	*salt*
1 tablespoon	*freshly ground pepper*
12	*bay leaves*
4 slices	*stale bread*

Serves 8 to 10

Rub the rib roast all over with the vodka. This begins to break down the fat and makes the meat very flavorful and tender. Rub in the salt and pepper. Cut some small pockets evenly in the fat and slip in the bay leaves. Let sit at room temperature for 2 hours.

Heat the oven to 425°F.

Put the beef in a roasting pan and roast for 30 minutes. Then turn down the heat to 325° and cook 12 to 15 minutes per pound for rare to medium rare, at which point the juices will run slightly pink when you stick a skewer or fork into the meat. When the beef is cooked, it is very important that it sit in a warm place (on the oven door or in the oven with the door open) for 30 minutes, so that the meat can soften and reabsorb all the juices that, if the meat were cut now, would run out.

Place the bread slices under the roast before carving and serve the juice-soaked bread with the beef.

Another dish that one does not get to try very often but that is definitely an old favorite is scrambled eggs done the French way, cooked slowly over hot water, incorporated with a good deal of butter and a little fresh cream, so that they have an ethereal texture and flavor quite unlike the rubber-mat, dry "egginess" of short-order scrambled eggs. A recipe for a version with smoked salmon appears on page 51. My all-time favorite variation of this dish, though, first served to me by Richard Olney in a house perched in an old, terraced olive grove above the village of Solliès-Toucas (near Toulon), is made with black truffles. With those eggs we drank a tired, old Bordeaux, making a memorable marriage of the wine, the eggs, and the earthy, fallen-leaves perfume of the truffles.

Truffles

Truffles are best when fresh, but unlike anything else except pastry, meat and fish essences, and ice cream, they do very satisfyingly well when frozen. While they are at their peak of freshness, wrap each truffle separately in two layers of odorless plastic wrap, then in aluminum foil, and put in a sealed, dated container in the freezer. The secret to using frozen truffles is to put them in whatever they are flavoring while *still frozen* and leave them there for an hour or two, for maximum flavor penetration. Only in this way do the truffles retain their crisp texture and their flavor, and impart all their perfume to what surrounds them. Truffles preserved in Madeira make superb truffle-flavored liquid but soft truffles. Canned truffles are a total waste of money. Despite their reputation, truffles are not expensive when used effectively. A whole egg-size black truffle, costing twenty to thirty dollars, will provide six people with a special-occasion feast they will never forget.

Scrambled Eggs with Truffles

If the truffle is frozen, cut it into thin "matchsticks" while still unthawed and put in a bowl. Add the eggs and leave *unbeaten,* covered, at room temperature for two hours.

1½ ounces	*fresh white or black truffle*
8 large	*eggs*
4 tablespoons	*unsalted butter, room temperature*
4 tablespoons	*unsalted butter, chilled*
	salt and freshly ground pepper
2 tablespoons	*heavy cream*

Serves 6

Coat the bottom and side of the top pan of a double boiler with 2 tablespoons of the soft butter. Heat water in the bottom pan to simmering. Beat the eggs just until well mixed and add the seasonings and the remaining soft butter. Fit the top pan into the bottom and stir the eggs with a wooden spoon for about 8 minutes, making sure to scrape all the surfaces of the pan, especially the corners. Never stop stirring or let the eggs stick to the pan. If the eggs start to thicken too quickly, remove the top pan from the water for a minute or so. When they are nearly done, stir in the cream and cook 30 seconds more. Turn off the heat and stir in the chilled butter; this will stop the cooking as well as enrich the texture and taste of the eggs.

Spoon the eggs onto 4 hot plates and serve immediately with non-sour country bread or grilled brioche.

The first time I ever saw a small individual pizza was in California in 1974. Its appearance was gratuitous and accidental. As chef I was faced with what to serve at Chez Panisse's third-birthday celebration, planned as an all-day open house. I was looking through a favorite textbook of those days, *La Cuisine du Comte de Nice,* by Jacques Médecin, and saw on page 76 a recipe for something called, aptly enough, "Les Panisses." Excitement caused haste, and I did not read the recipe carefully, noting only that it was a flat pancake type of thing with something boring on top which I knew I could improve upon. I wrote the menu—

Menu for 3rd Birthday
28 August 1974

HORS D'OEUVRES VARIÉS
PANISSES
SALADE VERTE
GLACE DE FRUITS
DEMI CARAFE DU VIN
$5.00 COMPRIS

—and sent it over to David Goines of St. Hieronymous Press for printing into a poster. Soon the day arrived for me to tell everyone what a "panisse" was and to order the ingredients. I rushed back to the book and found the recipe called for chick pea (garbanzo bean) flour, the end result being fried gruel. Few things to me are more repugnant than chick pea flour, so I assured everyone, "It's just like a little pizza; don't worry about it."

Money was very scarce in those days, and I knew the walk-in refrigerator would contain all kinds of left-over fresh ingredients from the night before, as well as hams, cheeses, and vegetables. The previous evening's menu had featured bouillabaisse, so I had available clams, prawns, squid, crab, onions, saffron, garlic, and fennel. It was not difficult to determine what would go on those little pizzas, which came out of the oven all day long, changing slightly every hour depending on what was left. They caused a sensation and later, a lot of press.

The success of the pizza, the experience of eating at Tommaso's famous pizzeria in San Francisco, which has a wood-fired brick oven, and a subsequent trip to Italy by my partners Gerry Budrick and Alice Waters, aroused in Gerry an almost messianic mission to build a brick oven. It was to be part of the café he and I proposed to build upstairs at Chez Panisse to promote cash flow. Gerry and I fought for the café and lost. Two years later, the idea was resurrected, the brick oven was built, and pizza hit the stage again, going on to another culmination at Spago in Los Angeles and Stars in San Francisco.

Pizza with Three Cheeses, Tomatoes, and Herbs

Many pizzas are more exotic or more esoteric than this one. But when the dough is really perfect, one should never lose track of its glory and the deep, simple satisfaction of biting into it and having its hot, yeasty flavors float up one's nostrils, with the ingredients never overpowering the dough. This pizza is really the foundation for all good pizza, both simple and more architectural versions.

1 recipe	*pizza dough (recipe follows)*
½ cup	*coarse cornmeal*
4 tablespoons	*olive oil*
4	*ripe tomatoes, peeled, sliced*
	salt and freshly ground pepper
12 leaves	*fresh basil*
1½ teaspoons	*fresh marjoram leaves, chopped*
1½ teaspoons	*fresh thyme leaves, chopped*
4 ounces	*Fontina cheese, thinly sliced*
4 ounces or ½ cup	*Parmesan cheese, grated*
4 ounces	*fresh mozzarella cheese, thinly sliced*

Serves 4

Heat the oven to 500°F. Put a sheet pan or pizza stone in the oven to get it very hot.

Divide the dough into 4 pieces. Roll each piece into a 6-inch circle. Stretch each circle another 2 inches in diameter by turning and pulling it round and round in your hands. The edge should be slightly thicker than the middle.

Sprinkle the heated pan or stone with cornmeal before putting on the circles of dough. Bake for 3 minutes.

When you take them out of the oven, brush each circle with 1 tablespoon oil. Place the tomato slices on the dough and season with salt, pepper, and the herbs. Layer first the Fontina, then the Parmesan, then the mozzarella, on the dough. Bake until the cheese is melted and the dough is cooked, about 5 minutes.

Easier than pizza, but just as satisfying, is the bacon-lettuce-and-tomato sandwich, and particularly its apotheosis, the toasted chicken club sandwich.

Ever since I was old enough to order champagne, the combination of the club sandwich and a great, slightly old, yeasty champagne has been the perfect palliative for many trying moments: I have just arrived in a hotel, too tired or late to go out for dinner; I've been out to dinner in a strange city, the food was bad, I return and call room service for this perfect combo; I've been out all night, the sun is rising over Hong Kong harbor, the Mandarin Hotel has world-perfect twenty-four-hour room service; or yet another business lunch is to be followed by a heavy dinner, and the understanding restaurant has put a BLT or chicken club on the menu. The sandwich will not tolerate too many frills, but avocado and bacon or pancetta were made for each other; some mild Chinese black bean mayonnaise drifts along with the champagne or beer; some fresh-roasted pasilla chilies drive away heavy-morning or late-night blues; or some mushroom duxelles butter used on the toast comes close to wonderfully excessive. Whatever or wherever, the BLT and the club are the traveler's and the night owl's companion.

Chicken Club Sandwich

Every element being best in quality and at its freshest is the secret of sublime success with this sandwich. The bread is especially important. Ideal is the circular one-pound San Francisco sourdough loaf. Or it could be French or Italian country style. (American sliced bread doesn't work.) The slice should be cut across the loaf, parallel to the bottom, ¼ inch thick, so two round slices, cut in half, serve as one large sandwich.

(continued)

Pizza Dough

1 package (¼ ounce)	active dry yeast
1¼ cups	warm water
½ cup	olive oil
1 pound	bread flour
1 teaspoon	salt

Soften the yeast in water. Stir in the oil, then the flour and salt. Knead until the dough is smooth and elastic, 15 to 20 minutes. Place in a plastic bag and refrigerate for 1 hour.

6 thin slices	*bacon or pancetta*
4 large slices	*bread (see headnote)*
2 tablespoons	*butter*
¼ cup	*mayonnaise (page 36)*
1 whole	*chicken breast, poached, skinned,*
	shredded by hand
	salt and freshly ground pepper
4 pieces	*green leaf or curly leaf red lettuce,*
	washed, dried
6 slices	*ripe tomato, ¼ inch thick*

Serves 2

Lay the bacon or pancetta out in flat strips and broil or bake in the oven until crisp.

Grill, broil, or toast the bread until just golden. Immediately butter the bread; then spread the slices with mayonnaise. Put the chicken on the mayonnaise and season with salt and pepper. Place the lettuce on top of the chicken, then the tomato slices, the bacon, and then the remaining bread. Cut each sandwich in half and serve with potato chips.

My once-a-year sandwich is a variation on a private passion: the hamburger—a supremely satisfying and nutritious quick meal, easy for anyone to achieve with perfection. I love lambburgers with cracked black pepper; hamburgers with poached garlic cloves and mint aioli (the J. T. Burger); hamburgers with salsa, avocado, and bacon; with basil or sage mayonnaise, tomatoes, and lettuce; or with horseradish cream sauce. But the ethereal one, my Christmas Eve or New Year's Day lunch, is a:

Black-Truffled Hamburger

Hamburgers are best in English muffins, a *baguette,* or a firm, dense hamburger roll. The bread must be buttered and toasted for that final sensual "push." The fitting drink with this sandwich, and one without which the burger falls short of its overwhelming effect, is a luscious, old-fashioned, deep red, rich and powerful Burgundy—a La Tâche, any wine made by Roumier (his own or Comte de Vogüé), or a Morey-Saint-Denis—in a large balloon glass, so the perfume of the wine and the truffled beef hit one's brain at the same time. If you are using a charcoal grill, the beef should have 22 percent fat; if using a flat-top griddle or frying pan, only 18 percent fat.

1 2-ounce	*fresh black truffle*
2 pounds	*ground beef chuck or ground*
	sirloin
¼ cup	*mayonnaise (page 36)*
2 teaspoons	*salt*
1 teaspoon	*freshly ground black pepper*
4	*English muffins (Thomas' type)*
3 tablespoons	*butter*

Serves 4

Chop the truffle finely and mix three-quarters of it into the beef by hand. Cover loosely and let sit at room temperature for 4 hours, so that the truffle perfume permeates the meat.

Mix the remaining truffle into the mayonnaise. Refrigerate it covered for a few hours.

Season the truffled burger meat and form into 4 patties by hand, making neat edges but handling it as little as possible. Do not compact the meat.

Split the muffins. Fry, griddle, or grill the hamburgers, seasoning them a little more on the outside as they cook. Toast or grill the muffins and butter each half. Put the burgers on the muffins, spoon 1 tablespoon of the mayonnaise on top of each burger, top with the other muffin half, and serve at once.

Another great brain food, for cold-night eating and only for the brave, is blinis (see page 63). My Russian uncle and his roué pals explained to me many times, with nostalgic tears in their eyes, how to judge how much butter one should use with blinis: enough, they said, so that when one picked up a blini or a piece of coulibiac, the butter should run down the soft inside of one's wrist, through the ruffles and into the shirt sleeve. I always took it for granted that the vodka took care of any ensuing butter discomfort throughout the rest of dinner.

To put that assumption to the test, I held a twenty-first-birthday party for an undergraduate friend in Cambridge, Massachusetts, in 1970, while I was studying graduate architecture. He had never been to my uncle's manhood initiation lunches, and needed, so I thought, some old-fashioned Russian training. Among those present were the guest of honor, John McSween, blond, all-American, but with the inner workings of Southern heritage; an illegitimate grandson of Edward VII; Philip Core (already starting his publishing and painting career); some ballet students; and some old New York family inheritors.

To this day there are as many versions of the end of the party as there were guests, but there was unanimous agreement that three blinis are the maximum and no amount of butter is too much.

Even now it takes weeks to train cooks to use enough clarified butter on a blini. I have to say "More . . . more," as their eyes grow larger and whiter.

The most satisfying way to eat them is with frozen vodka. One "shoots" the vodka down whole, waits *just* until the burn starts in the back of the throat, then pops the whole, caviar-laden, buttery, creamy hot blini into one's mouth. This exercise needs large napkins and a seat for everyone.

When I look back at personal favorites, at the momentary passions that have happened sometimes by accident and can be repeated, I remember the terrace of the Oliver Messel suite at the Dorchester Hotel in London one pink and blue evening in 1958, and a cocktail party given in anticipation of my return to America. That is when I discovered gin and tonic and canapés. To this day, on a hot evening of a harried day, a tall Waterford crystal glass filled to the brim with ice, a full measure of dry gin, the pulp of half a ripe lime, cold Schweppes tonic water (and a few violets) can bring, for a while, perfect peace.

In the category of memorable drinks I would also place the margaritas in Yelapa, a little fishing village near Puerto Vallarta, where I had gone for some severe recuperation after the first year at Chez Panisse. I would lie in a hammock and watch the day boat arrive and leave, a process that consumed about six margaritas. They were perfection: freshly squeezed lime juice, ordinary tequila, and sugar syrup, with no salt on the glass, and very, very cold. The salt was supplied by the occasional dip in the turquoise ocean; coming back to the hammock with the salty tropical water still dripping down my face, I'd be handed a fresh cold margarita, and a minute portion of the seawater on my lips became incorporated in the cocktail.

I remember great moments of a huge and cold Scotch and soda after dinner instead of brandy, or freezing champagne after working in the garden all day in summer or the perfect smoked salmon at the Hyde Park Hotel in London in the fifties (salmon of that quality is very rare these days). My taste for that cold-smoked salmon made from fresh fish (not frozen), and sliced paper-thin at a long, shallow angle, placed together with the dark meat from beneath the skin on a plate in a symmetrical pattern, was formed on a voyage on the *Queen Elizabeth* from New York to Southampton, when I ate it three times a day. I serve it now with grilled brioche or bread. Some black pepper freshly ground and maybe some lemon are all it needs—dispense with the capers, onions, or any other garnish.

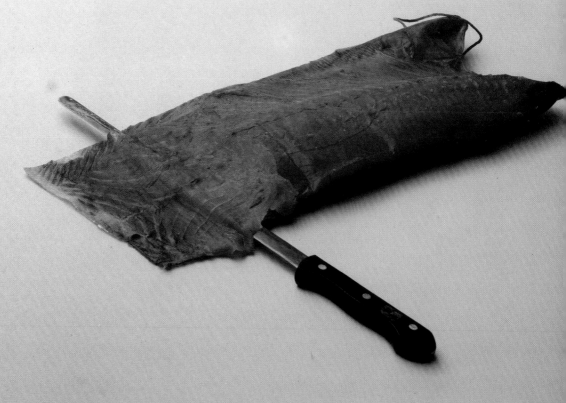

Some simple dishes take a great deal more work than salmon or blini, however, and often they are not so obviously appealing visually. A great such favorite of mine is fish soup, the *soupe de poisson* of the south of France. In *French Provincial Cooking,* Elizabeth David says, "I don't think it is possible to make the soup without all those odd little Mediterranean fish, which are too bony to be used for anything except *la soupe,*" but I made it for her with great success in London in 1979 for a dinner with Richard Olney and Sybille Bedford. The soup takes two days and costs a fortune, but the reward comes when the tureen is brought to the table and one sees a faded but deep coral-pink liquid, the hue of worn Mexican tiles, and smells the rich aroma. The taste is as broad a spectrum of flavors and essences as anything I know. If you have ever loved the sea and fish and shellfish, that bowl of simple liquid holds their entire mystery. For the recipe see page 84, and if you are in the south of France go to the restaurant Bacon in Antibes.

Whereas the fish soup is fairly insignificant in appearance (except as it can evoke one's memory and nostalgia), a very simple dish that also looks stunning is one that I first cooked for James Beard in the mid-

seventies, a soufflé of sea urchin cooked and presented in its spiny shell. I had never cooked for Mr. Beard, except at Chez Panisse. Even though it was there he told me that if he had to choose four restaurants in the United States to revisit, they would be The Four Seasons, The Coach House, Tony's, and Chez Panisse, I was very nervous to be cooking for him, let alone at home, with no backup staff or professional equipment. Up to the morning of the day of the dinner, I could not decide what to serve. I wandered around Chinatown in San Francisco, looking for inspiration by way of available supplies. I saw several deep-sea urchins, each the size of a large grapefruit. I knew I must have them, whatever their preparation or place in the meal. When I faced them in the kitchen that afternoon, from somewhere came a memory of a recipe for sea urchin sauce that referred to using the sauce as the basis for a soufflé. "Right," I thought aloud. "Soufflés they will be." It was too late to buy individual soufflé dishes, so the shells just had to do. At the moment of opening the oven door, my heart held by cold hands, I saw that the scheme had worked. The spines were intact, a wonderful ocean smell began to waft into the kitchen, and best of all, the soufflé mixture had risen above the craterlike openings in the shells, puffy, pink-beige, and beautiful. I rushed them to the table. Jim tried a spoonful. No word was said. He looked up slowly, aware of the theatrical effect, rolled his eyes slowly, and said, "My God, that is the best thing I have ever tasted."

Sea Urchin Soufflé

4 large	sea urchins
2 ounces	butter
2 tablespoons	flour
1 cup	fish stock (page 218)
2	egg yolks
4	egg whites
	salt and freshly ground pepper

Serves 4

Using scissors, cut a hole around the inside perimeter of the underside of the sea urchin. Discard the cut shell and clean out the inside of the remaining shell, leaving only the orange-colored roe that sticks vertically to the shell. When the shell is perfectly clean, scoop the roe into a bowl. When all the roe is out, clean the shells thoroughly and dry the inside surfaces. Puree the roe.

To make the soufflé base, melt 1 ounce of the butter in a saucepan. Add 1 tablespoon of the flour and cook over low heat for 5 minutes, stirring all the time. Heat the fish stock, add to the butter-flour mixture, and whisk until smooth. Cook over low heat for 30 minutes, whisking every 5 minutes and skimming off any scum that rises to the surface. Let cool to room temperature.

Heat the oven to 400°F.

Stir the egg yolks and the pureed roe into the soufflé base. Rub the insides of the shells with the remaining butter and dust with the remaining flour. Beat the egg whites until stiff. Fold them into the soufflé base and spoon into the shells. Cook until the soufflés have risen and are slightly browned on top, about 20 minutes. Serve immediately.

Country Ham

When one remembers Jim Beard, the image of huge platters of sausages and steaming boiled meats, especially pork, is usually conjured up. In those photographs where he is standing in front of a mound of sausages, looking slightly pink and stuffed himself, there tends to be a ham. Jim and I talked for hours and hours on the subject of hams, and the proper way to cook a Smithfield. We decided on the following: Wash the ham off with a stiff brush to remove the pepper, then soak it overnight in enough water to cover it. Then, in a pot large enough to hold it vertically, submerge the ham in enough water to come right up to the shank but not above it, and poach it with carrots, onions, celery, and bouquet garni, until the ham shank or hock is flexible to the point of breaking off, five to six hours depending on the size of the ham. Remove the ham and let it cool; remove the skin and trim down the fat until there is half an inch left overall. Put the ham in a baking dish, pour over two glasses of madeira, cover with foil, and bake in an oven at 350 degrees for 30 minutes. Let the ham cool while still covered. The ham is then ready for carving in the thinnest possible slices, and serving with almost anything, like stuffed dates and Sauternes or figs and Madeira.

Black-and-White Ice Cream Soda

Hardly a great culinary triumph, but a memory no less intense for being everyday simple, is the black-and-white soda of American soda fountain fame. I remember hot, humid days in Manhattan, walking along hoping I would pass a Schrafft's so that I could nip into the air-conditioned room, sit at the cool marble counter, and order a black-and-white. In those days the ice cream was good, the chocolate syrup was real, and the soda had big, lasting bubbles. The bite of the soda water against the sweetness of the chocolate was what battling the heat was all about. To make a black-and-white soda, use the best chocolate sauce you can find, get some good Italian ice cream and very lively soda water. Put the syrup in the bottom of a tall glass, add scoops of ice cream, pour in the soda, and stir briefly with a long-handled spoon just enough to mix the chocolate and soda so that the whole thing is frothy and marbled. Drink through a long straw and then scoop up the last of the ice cream with the spoon. A few contented sighs, and then out onto the streets again, able to face anything, wearing the invincible armor of pleasure.

Sauces and Relishes

What I would like to say about sauces is that sometimes they are the greatest pleasure, and sometimes there is nothing more satisfying than to have in front of one food that has no sauce at all. What can be more miserable than to be on a long trip, eating out every night and sometimes afternoons too, in restaurants where all the food is sauced—and usually heavily—and then having to face yet another menu of sauces? And yet if one is hungry and has been looking forward to a rather grand dinner, what can content the soul more than a great bordelaise sauce, the perfectly clean roasting or braising juices reduced with a little wine, with the soft, unctuous, pale-rose glistening rich nuggets of bone marrow just waiting to dissolve in one's mouth against a bite of grilled, rosemary-scented double lamb chop? Or the awesome *périgueux* sauce, with its fresh black truffles, Madeira, and meat glaze? In fact, there is hardly a sauce that I don't like, except for Cumberland sauce, but I do object to the attempts to keep certain sauces alive when their day has passed. *Financière,* for example, which is not a sauce so much as a garnish, continues to appear on menus. Even if it is made correctly, no one can afford to serve it anymore with its real Madeira sauce, veal quenelles, wild mushrooms, cocks' combs, cocks' testicles, chicken livers, and fresh black truffles.

The secret to sauces is balance: How many to have in a dinner and which ones. Can there be a sauce on every course without killing everyone's digestion and ruining the dinner? What range and types of sauces are acceptable if one is going to have more than one sauce in a meal? Here are some menus that help answer these questions.

A 1971 summer lunch I prepared for poet Michael Palmer was cold poached salmon with an herb mayonnaise (page 36), followed by strawberries from the garden. I put some reduced salmon-poaching liquid into the mayonnaise to whip it into velvety consistency and bring the two elements of fish and sauce closer together. The only other sauce in the meal was the juices of the strawberries mixed with a little red currant jelly, which colored the strawberries and brought out their flavor. It was so simple a menu that I could and did serve gobs of the mayonnaise with the fish, content to "overdo" just that one sauce.

In 1972, I served "My Very Last Dinner on the East Coast" in Atlantic City. The meal included vegetables from the garden served with the hot bath of creamed anchovies and white truffles called *bagna cauda* (very rich); Westphalian ham with pears; *le gâteau de foie blond de poularde de Bresse au coulis de queues d'écrevisses* from Lucien Tendret's book *La Table au Pays de Brillat-Savarin,* which is a chicken liver "mousse" with, again, a very rich sauce of crayfish essence; asparagus in olive oil; "Prior's" chocolate cake with raspberry ice cream; coffee; and walnuts. The dinner was supposed to be a bit overboard because of the occasion, and the carefully paced sequence was to be rich sauce, no sauce, rich sauce, light sauce, no sauce, with hot and cold alternating as well. It was very successful.

In February of 1970, I was given, upon my return one evening from Harvard Design School, a two-hour notice by some dancers who were my houseguests that the ballet stars Margot Fonteyn and Richard Cragun were coming to dinner. There was no food in the house and no time for sauces except fast ones. We rushed off to the store and the menu became salmon rillettes with toasts, roast ribs of beef with Escoffier's spinach cream, green salad, raspberry and lemon sherbets, cookies, coffee, and Cointreau. The sauce with the salmon was a mayonnaise (very fast to do) with the fat from the skin of the salmon in it and lots of black pepper, and the sauce for the beef was merely its roasting juices, defatted and reduced with some stock that I had in the freezer. That sauce, which mixed with the cream from the spinach on the plate, was all that was needed—or possible. The sherbets acted as a cleaning element (as did the salad) following the rich roast beef, and needed no sauce.

Recognizing the problem of producing sauces on the spur of the moment and realizing that most people are either not sauce-makers, or feel inadequate about making them, I have presented in this chapter the bases and purees from which an endless range of sauces can be made, along with a limited collection of sauces that can be used in an infinite number of ways. I have started with salsas because they are so easy and require no cooking, just chopping, so any guest can be commandeered into helping. I have always enjoyed *salsa fresca,* the traditional Mexican fresh sauce, but it became an addiction at the Santa Fe Bar & Grill in Berkeley in the early eighties. Because salsa takes only a half hour to make, we used it to garnish just about everything in the first months of the restaurant. Served on grilled fish, salsa became a rage, and the restaurant achieved money and success for the first time. The subsequent avalanche of salsas, relishes, and chutneys, some quite esoteric, that came out of the kitchen launched a style of garnishing grilled foods that became popular across the country.

We were well into our salsa mania when mango sauces first landed on fish at the Santa Fe Bar & Grill, probably because one day we just had too many ripe mangoes. A basic sauce was developed, and then many variations (based on additions of cilantro, mixed chilies, avocado, sesame oil, garlic, chipotles, etc.); mango sauce reached its apogee after grill chef Steven Vranian visited Guadeloupe and discovered the Caribbean mirepoix that was in every kitchen on that island: a mixture of chopped onions and green chilies that are "sweated" down in oil and kept in big jars to add to almost everything—very handy and delicious. You can also make a smooth, warm version of this sauce by pureeing the final product in a food processor, and whisking in 4 tablespoons of butter over heat.

Another spur-of-the-moment invention was cherry chutney. Cooked cherries, other than in compotes and pies, first appeared at the Santa Fe Bar & Grill when a cook of Italian origin became slightly crazed and tried, in my absence, to do fettuccini with fresh cherry sauce. He was prevented, but cooked cherries stayed in his mind, and he started to prepare cooked chutneys for sauces with grilled lamb and pork dishes. Other fruits— pears, apples, slightly unripe papayas, pineapples, and so on—can also be used in chutneys, either alone or in combination.

Clockwise from top left: Fresh Cherry Chutney; Tomatillo Salsa; Mission Fig-Mint Relish; Mango-Chili Salsa; basic Salsa (recipes on pages 28–29).

Salsa *(pictured on page 27)*

4 cups	tomato concasse *(page 220)*
1	red onion, peeled, finely chopped
2	fresh serrano chilies, stemmed, seeded, finely chopped
½ cup	fresh cilantro, stemmed, chopped
1 teaspoon	salt
2 to 4 tablespoons	fresh lime juice
1 tablespoon	olive oil

Serves 6 to 8

Mix the tomatoes, onion, chilies, and cilantro in a bowl. Add the salt and 2 tablespoons lime juice. Mix well, taste, and then add the remaining lime juice, as needed.

Let the salsa sit for an hour before using. If it has gotten too watery, drain it. Stir in the oil and serve.

Steven Vranian's Mission Fig–Mint Relish

(pictured on page 27)

8	fresh ripe Mission figs, finely chopped
2	fresh serrano chilies, stemmed, seeded, finely chopped
½ cup	fresh mint leaves
¼ cup	fresh lime juice
1 teaspoon	salt
1 teaspoon	freshly ground pepper

Serves 6 to 8

Combine the figs and chilies in a bowl.

Blanch the mint leaves in boiling water for 1 minute. Cool in ice water, drain, squeeze dry, and finely chop. Add the mint leaves to the figs and chilies.

Add the lime juice, salt, and pepper to the mixture, stir well, and let sit for 1 hour before serving.

Steven Vranian's Mango–Chili Salsa *(pictured on page 27)*

4	mangoes, peeled, sliced, cut into ½-inch cubes
1 medium	red onion, peeled, finely chopped
2	fresh serrano chilies, stemmed, seeded, finely chopped
1	fresh red chili, stemmed, seeded, finely chopped
¼ cup	peanut oil
2 tablespoons	water
1 cup	fresh mint leaves
¼ cup	fresh lime juice
1 teaspoon	salt
1 teaspoon	freshly ground pepper

Serves 6 to 8

Put the chopped mangoes in a mixing bowl.

Mix the onion, chilies, oil, and water in a pot. Cover and cook over very low heat until the onion is transparent, about 10 minutes. Do not let the mixture brown. Cool and add to the mango.

Blanch the mint leaves in boiling water for 1 minute. Cool in ice water, drain, squeeze dry, and finely chop. Add to the onion and mango mixture. Stir in the lime juice, salt, and pepper. Let sit for 1 hour before serving.

Fresh Cherry Chutney

(pictured on page 27)

8 cups	ripe fresh cherries, pitted
½ cup	red wine vinegar
½ cup	dark brown sugar
¼ cup	molasses
4 cloves	garlic, peeled, chopped
3	bay leaves
3	fresh chilies, serrano or jalapeño— stemmed, seeded, chopped
6 whole	cloves
1 tablespoon	green peppercorns
1 teaspoon	ground cinnamon
½ teaspoon	freshly ground nutmeg
1 teaspoon	salt
½ teaspoon	freshly ground pepper

Serves 8

Combine all the ingredients in a stainless-steel pot. Cook covered for 30 minutes over low heat, stirring every 15 minutes. Uncover and continue to cook, stirring often, until the mixture is the consistency of jam, about 30 more minutes. Always keep ¼ inch liquid on the surface. If the chutney starts to dry up or stick to the pot, add ½ cup water at a time.

Tomatillo Salsa *(pictured on page 27)*

12 medium	tomatillos, outer husks removed, rinsed, finely chopped
1 small	red onion, finely chopped
2 to 3	fresh serrano or other small green hot chilies, stemmed, seeded, finely chopped
½ cup	fresh cilantro leaves, chopped
1 tablespoon	virgin olive oil
1 teaspoon	white wine or champagne vinegar
1 teaspoon	salt

Serves 6 to 8

Mix all the ingredients together and let sit for 30 minutes to allow the flavors to blend.

Tomato Chutney

4 cups	tomato concasse (page 220)
¼ cup	capers, rinsed, drained
2 tablespoons	finely chopped fresh ginger
4 cloves	garlic, peeled, finely chopped
¼ cup	olive oil
1 teaspoon	salt
1 teaspoon	freshly ground pepper

Serves 6 to 8

Heat a nonstick pan. Put in the concasse and stir over medium heat until all the liquid evaporates, about 10 minutes; turn up the heat for the last minute.

Add the capers, ginger, and garlic and cook another minute. Put in a bowl over ice to stop the cooking. When just cool, stir in the oil, salt, and pepper. Let sit 1 hour. Serve at room temperature.

Ancho Chili Puree

Ancho chilies are the most commonly found large dried chilies in California. They are in fact the ripened and dried poblano chili, which is sometimes labeled "pasilla" in California. They are mild, with a full and complex flavor.

From the first days of the Santa Fe Bar & Grill in 1981, this puree was a mainstay in sauces. Make a lot at one time, for it will keep in a sealed jar in the refrigerator up to two weeks. It is also an excellent marinade for grilled fish.

10	ancho chilies
1 tablespoon	fresh lime juice
½ cup	olive oil or good-quality peanut oil
	salt

Makes 1 cup

Put the chilies in a bowl and add water to cover. Weight them with a plate so they are all submerged and let them soften overnight.

The next day, remove and discard the stems and seeds. Puree the flesh with the lime juice in a food processor and push through a fine-mesh sieve or food mill into a bowl. Whisk in the oil. Season to taste with salt.

Black Bean Sauce

When soaking Chinese fermented black beans, you are faced with the same problem as you are with salt cod: If you didn't like the saltiness of the product, you wouldn't be eating it in the first place. So don't soak out all the flavor. Yet the beans can be terrifyingly strong, and you do not need a lot of them. More often than not, you will find this sauce is best as an accent "drizzle" sauce, for both color and taste contrasts. Poached fish with a lobster cream sauce and black bean sauce drizzled over, served with fresh fava beans in butter, makes a meal that is an ideal balance of flavors.

½ cup	fermented salted Chinese black beans
1 cup	fish or chicken stock, depending on the final use
½ pound	unsalted butter, cut into 1-ounce pieces
	freshly ground black pepper

Makes 2 cups; serves 4 as a sauce, 6 to 8 as a drizzle

Rinse and then soak the beans in water, changing the water twice, for 2 to 3 hours, depending on your fondness for the taste and the use for the sauce.

Drain the beans, rinse under running water, and put in a blender. Add the stock and blend to a fine puree.

Put the puree in a saucepan and bring to a boil. Reduce the heat and simmer 5 minutes. Remove from the heat and whisk in the butter one piece at a time. Season to taste with pepper and keep in a warm place.

Garlic Puree

When garlic is cooked it loses its raw, fiery effect and aftertaste and becomes mild, to be eaten as whole cloves or pureed for sauces. Garlic can be broken up into unpeeled cloves and poached in chicken stock or salted water until soft, then put through a food mill or sieve, making a mild white puree for thickening roasting juices to put over chicken, or to add to cream for a pasta sauce, or to make garlic soup. The puree holds in the refrigerator in a sealed jar for a week. Spread on toast or mixed into a salad dressing, it is spectacular.

But for grilled meats and fish, or simply for serving with some cheese and bread, beer or crisp white wine for lunch or snacks, whole roasted garlic heads are my favorite. I started serving them at Chez Panisse in Berkeley in 1976, another first I owe to Richard Olney. At the Santa Fe Bar & Grill, the puree was the basis for many compound butter sauces for the grill.

The garlic should be as fresh as possible and firm, with no mildew. The most glorious garlic is the first crop in the spring, when one wants to poach or bake them whole, pour butter or olive oil over them, squeeze out the puree from each clove, and spread it on bread or roast lamb.

8 heads	garlic
¼ cup	olive oil
4 sprigs	fresh thyme
	salt and freshly ground black pepper

Makes 1 cup

Heat the oven to 300°F.

Rub the garlic heads with the oil. Spread the thyme out in a heavy baking dish just large enough to hold the garlic in a single layer. Place the garlic on the thyme; season with salt and pepper. Cover with foil and bake until the garlic cloves are just soft when you squeeze them, or 30 to 45 minutes.

Take the garlic out of the baking dish. Eat whole or put them through a food mill to make a puree. Discard the skins. Any unused portion stored in the refrigerator will keep for a week. Be sure to cover puree tightly.

Clockwise from top: Black Bean Sauce; Garlic Puree; Raspberry Puree (recipe on page 32); Ancho Chili Puree; Bell Pepper Puree (recipe on page 32).

Raspberry Puree *(pictured on page 31)*

Berry purees can be a base for simple dessert sauces (see below) and marinades (for squab), added to butter (for grilled meats), folded into mousses and sabayon sauces, or used to make ethereal soufflés (especially of wild strawberries). Whatever the use, the berries have to be pureed by hand. The best method is through a fine-mesh nylon or stainless-steel sieve or a food mill fitted with the finest mesh disk. Once berries are subjected to the violence of a food processor or, worse, a blender, color, flavor, and texture deteriorate. Put through a sieve, berries will produce a puree with body, which is very important when you have to add other liquids and do not want a thin sauce. Strawberries really need a food mill, since they are difficult to put through a sieve by hand. Blueberries should be cooked for 10 minutes and then pureed.

>   1 pint   fresh raspberries
> 1 pinch   salt

Push the raspberries through a sieve or food mill into a bowl. Discard the seeds. Stir the salt into the puree. Cover and refrigerate until needed.

Raspberry Sauce

To make this simple dessert sauce mix 1 cup raspberry puree with ½ cup light syrup (page 216). These proportions will work approximately for all berries as long as you take into account the varying water content of different berries, which can also be affected by the time of year.

Yellow or Red Bell Pepper Puree *(pictured on page 31)*

This puree is not a sauce by itself, but added to mayonnaise, sour cream, whipped cream, sabayon, olive oil, or butter, or mounted with stock and butter, it becomes a sauce for salads, soups, and grilled fish and meats prepared in countless ways. If you want dice or strips of pepper for salads, garnishes or sauces, follow the process up to the step to puree, then chop or julienne the peppers.

>   6 large   yellow or red bell peppers
> 3 tablespoons   olive oil

Makes 1½ cups

Preheat the oven to 350°F.
  Rub the peppers with the oil and put them in a baking pan. Cover with aluminum foil and cook until soft, about 45 minutes. Remove from the oven and let stand, still covered, until cool.
  Remove the skin from the peppers and discard the stems and seeds. Puree the peppers in a food processor and pass through a fine sieve or food mill.

Vinaigrette

Most recipes for oil and vinegar dressing call for 3 parts oil to 1 part vinegar. These proportions make a very acid sauce, too strong for most salads. For a delicate butter lettuce, for example, the proportion should be 5 to 1.

The types of vinegar and oils used depend also on the nature of the salad ingredients. The endive family and bitter field greens taste best with strong vinegars and heavy oils like Italian green extra virgin oil.

Always add the salt and freshly ground pepper to the acid, stir to dissolve the salt, then whisk in the oil. It is very important to make an emulsion so you don't get the disparate textures and tastes of the two liquids in the salad. Only with asparagus on a plate do the separate rivers of oil and vinegar look and taste wonderful.

> 2 tablespoons   vinegar
>   ½ teaspoon   salt
>   ½ teaspoon   freshly ground black pepper
>   ½ cup   olive oil

Serves 4

Put the vinegar and salt and pepper to taste in a bowl and stir to dissolve the salt. Whisk in the olive oil and continue to whisk until a smooth emulsion is formed.

Tomato Vinaigrette

This sauce can be an obsession. It is easy to make, and on warm pasta, pasta salads, grilled fish hot or cold, asparagus hot or cold, meats, and grilled garlic bread as a snack, it's sublime. The explosion of herb perfume when poured over hot vegetables or pasta is for me what summer is all about.

Do not assemble the sauce until you are going to use it. The sauce is better very loosely mixed, not as an emulsion.

>   1 cup   tomato concasse (page 220)
>   ¼ cup   mixed herb leaves, such as basil,
>   marjoram, tarragon, thyme, or fennel,
>   coarsely chopped
>   ¼ cup   fresh lemon juice or vinegar
> 2 large   shallots, peeled, coarsely chopped
>   1 cup   extra virgin olive oil

Serves 4

Put all the ingredients in a bowl and stir briefly.

Pasta with Tomato Vinaigrette.

Simple and Compound Butters

These butters are particularly appropriate for grilled or roasted fish, meats, and birds. With a crisp duck skin or perfectly grilled lamb chop, for example, a liquid sauce would destroy their effect by making the cooked surface soggy.

Simple butters have one or two elements, like anchovies, caviar, tarragon, mustard, paprika, or pistachios. Compound butters—such as Bercy (shallots, parsley, marrow), and the great Montpellier butter—have several ingredients or more than one step in the making.

The classic maître d'hôtel butter is a "simple" one of chopped parsley, lemon juice, salt, and pepper mixed to a creamy texture and divine on grilled sole. It becomes a "compound" butter if you mix in chopped tarragon leaves and meat stock reduced to a syrup with Madeira.

I had always used flavored butters at Chez Panisse, but at the Santa Fe Bar & Grill they really came into their own and encouraged the widespread use of them in restaurants throughout the United States, sometimes to an almost lunatic degree.

Taking tradition and a huge grill with no place to make pan sauces, and an aversion to ready-made restaurant sauces sitting around in hot water all day, we came up with relatively conservative butters like ancho chili, sorrel, orange–cilantro, or tomato–rocket. Then with several cooks working, the dam of invention suddenly burst, and there was born roasted chili–duck liver butter; red Anaheim chili–sesame; roasted fennel; roasted garlic–red onion; ginger–garlic–chili; ginger–cilantro–tequila; ginger–scallion; roasted peanut–scallion–chili, and so on. All butters should be left for two hours to develop their flavors.

Cilantro-Lime-Ginger Butter

½ pound	unsalted butter, at room temperature
2 teaspoons	grated fresh ginger
10 sprigs	fresh cilantro, stemmed, chopped
2 tablespoons	fresh lime juice
½ teaspoon	salt
¼ teaspoon	freshly ground pepper

Serves 6 to 8

Combine all the ingredients in a food processor and puree until smooth. The butter should be silky. Let sit 2 hours. Serve at room temperature (never cold), so that it melts easily over the food.

Montpellier Butter

This greatest of all butters is traditionally made in a mortar with a pestle, but a food processor will do. It is very good with cold poached fish, especially salmon, but is equally delicious with hot grilled fish. Spooned between slices of cold roast veal or pork, the slices reassembled, left for a day, and served at room temperature, it creates a lifelong memory.

6 leaves	spinach
½ bunch	watercress leaves
2 tablespoons	fresh parsley leaves
2 tablespoons	fresh chervil leaves
2 tablespoons	chopped fresh chives
1 tablespoon	fresh tarragon leaves
2	shallots, peeled, chopped
2	cornichons
4	salted anchovy fillets, soaked, drained
2 tablespoons	capers, rinsed
1 clove	garlic, peeled
½ teaspoon	salt
¼ teaspoon	freshly ground pepper
¼ teaspoon	cayenne
3	hard-cooked egg yolks
2 large	raw egg yolks
¼ pound	unsalted butter, room temperature
½ cup	olive oil
1 teaspoon	white wine vinegar

Makes 1 cup

Blanch the spinach, watercress, herbs, and shallots in boiling water for 1 minute. Drain, refresh under cold water, and squeeze dry. Put them in a mortar or food processor. Add the cornichons, anchovies, capers, garlic, salt, pepper, and cayenne. Work with a pestle or process to a smooth paste. Add the egg yolks and the butter and process again until thoroughly mixed. Put through a food mill, fitted with the fine-mesh disk, into a bowl or back into the mortar and whisk in the oil *by hand*. The mixture should be glossy and as smooth as velvet. Beat in the vinegar and taste to see if it needs more salt and pepper.

Calamari with Montpellier Butter.

Mayonnaise

Whereas flavored butters lend themselves to food processors, the closer mayonnaise gets to a machine, the less good it is. A rewarding cooking and taste experience is to make mayonnaise in a bowl by hand and then compare it with mayonnaises made in an electric mixer, a food processor, and a blender. Each mayonnaise tastes, feels, and looks different. The hand-whisked sauce will be silkier, smoother, lighter, and more delicate-tasting, and sit easier in the stomach.

Use a light, high-quality olive oil, and have your ingredients at room temperature. Italian green extra virgin oil will make a good mayonnaise, but it will overpower most foods.

3 large	*egg yolks*
½ teaspoon	*salt*
4 tablespoons	*fresh lemon juice*
1 to 1½ cups	*olive oil*

Makes approximately 1½ cups

Put the yolks, salt, and half the lemon juice in a bowl and whisk until smooth. Whisk in the oil very slowly at first, increasing the flow at the end. If the mayonnaise gets too thick to beat, add droplets of water and continue adding oil. (The amount of oil will depend on the consistency of mayonnaise desired.) Whisk in the remaining lemon juice and taste for salt.

Herb Mayonnaise

For herb mayonnaise, blanch 1 packed cup mixed herbs (tarragon, parsley, chervil, thyme, marjoram, and basil in equal proportions, for example), 4 spinach leaves, and 3 tablespoons watercress leaves for 30 seconds in boiling water. Drain, squeeze dry, and very finely chop or coarsely puree them. Stir into 2 cups mayonnaise and let sit several hours for the flavors to develop.

Black Bean Mayonnaise

To make a mayonnaise flavored with Chinese black beans, stir ¼ cup bean puree (page 30) into 1 cup mayonnaise.

Aioli

The most dramatic difference between hand- and machine-made mayonnaise can be tasted in aioli (garlic mayonnaise) made in a mortar and pestle (not the smooth chemist's variety but one of semi-rough marble). The texture is like velvet, the flavors are subtle, and the result is more digestible.

It was Richard Olney who showed me the best way to make aioli. Later I made the red pepper version, rouille, for Julia Child in her house at Plascassier in the south of France in 1978, when a group including the English novelist Sybille Bedford, Richard Olney, and other friends gathered and Julia let me cook. Put in the fish soup, the rouille was a sensation. Yet another version of aioli can be made by adding sea urchin puree (page 23)—the result is transcendental.

4 cloves	*garlic, peeled*
2	*egg yolks*
¼ cup	*fresh white bread crumbs*
½ teaspoon	*salt*
4 tablespoons	*fish or chicken stock, depending on final use*
2 cups	*olive oil*

Makes 2½ cups

Work the garlic, egg yolks, bread crumbs, salt, and a little stock in a mortar or food processor to a paste. When the paste is smooth, start adding the oil slowly, working it all the time. Add as much oil as it will take without breaking; then add stock to thin it to the right consistency.

Rouille

Work ⅓ cup red bell pepper puree (page 32) and 1 teaspoon cayenne (or more) into the initial garlic paste of the Aioli recipe.

Vegetables accompanied by (from left) Rouille, Aioli, and Herb Mayonnaise.

Hollandaise

"Hollandaise" was the first French word I could remember and pronounce, asparagus with hollandaise sauce being an early passion. It is a pure sauce, and I feel purist about it: lemon juice, salt, pepper, butter, and egg yolks are its proper components.

The sauce is made with five to seven yolks (depending on egg size) per pound of butter, and the question of whether to use clarified or whole butter is easy to answer, to my mind. Clarified-butter usage comes from nasty habits of restaurants and hotels, which have endless vats of clarified butter on the backs of their stoves; it also produces hollandaise more quickly, but the result is oily in texture, less fresh in taste, and not very digestible.

Here are the secrets to a successful hollandaise: Make a sabayon-like base first by beating the yolks with the lemon juice and then cooking slightly over simmering water; never let the sauce get too hot or you will have scrambled eggs; add the butter gradually and keep the sauce slightly warm when finished. If the sauce breaks, start the process again with a couple of yolks and add the broken sauce gradually; a tablespoon of hot water does wonders for critical moments (breaking sauce) and texture (too thick).

Make this sauce with imported French butter and you will become an addict.

5 large	*egg yolks*
3 tablespoons	*fresh lemon juice*
½ teaspoon	*salt*
1 pound	*unsalted butter, at room temperature, cut into tablespoon-size chunks*
1 pinch	*cayenne*

Makes 3 cups

Put the egg yolks, lemon juice, and salt in a stainless steel, enamel, or other noncorrosive bowl over simmering water and whisk until foamy; continue to whisk until the yolks thicken and increase in volume like a sabayon. Remove from the heat and whisk in the butter one piece at a time. After the first 2 pieces of butter, return the sauce to the water and continue whisking in the butter. If you think the eggs are getting too hot, remove the bowl from the water and let them cool a bit. After all the butter has been added, remove the sauce from the heat and season with the cayenne. Check to see if it needs more salt or lemon.

Sauce Mousseline

This is hollandaise with whipped cream folded in. Eating it is like living in the clouds. It is a lighter, richer sauce, with a less pronounced taste, and is perfect with fresh poached fish. Whip ½ cup heavy cream until soft peaks are formed. Fold it into the hollandaise just before using the sauce. The seasoning in the hollandaise should be more pronounced because the cream will dilute the flavors.

Sauce Maltaise

This sauce, wonderful with asparagus and other hot steamed or blanched vegetables, is made by adding the juice of 2 to 3 blood oranges and the grated zest of 1 of the oranges in place of the lemon juice in the hollandaise recipe. Meyer lemons or Rangpur limes make a superb alternative. The sauce can be made mousseline by folding in whipped cream.

Sauce Noisette

This is a hollandaise to which 4 tablespoons butter heated to the nut-brown stage is added instead of the last 4 tablespoons of the ordinary butter. Use it for poached salmon or sole.

Tomato Hollandaise

Use 1 cup tomato concasse (page 220), and 4 tablespoons chopped fresh herbs if you want, and fold into the hollandaise at the last moment. It is very good with fish or eggs.

Hollandaise with Essences

If you are saucing fish, like a poached sole, reduce some fish fumet and add that to the eggs in the beginning. This pulls the sauce and the fish closer together.

Béarnaise

Sauce béarnaise is really a hollandaise that uses a reduction of shallots, vinegar, and wine instead of lemon juice, orange juice, or fish stock. There is a whole family of béarnaise, depending on which additive is used—tomato, meat glaze, or various herbs.

As with hollandaise, the sauce should be made in a noncorrosive saucepan or bowl. Do not try to get the sauce very hot when serving; the food it accompanies (grilled meats, etc.) should be hot and the sauce warm.

½ cup	tarragon sprigs, tightly packed
⅓ cup	dry white wine
⅓ cup	white wine vinegar
4 tablespoons	shallots, finely chopped
5 large	egg yolks
2 cups	unsalted butter, at room temperature, cut into tablespoon-size chunks
½ teaspoon	salt
	freshly ground pepper

Makes 3 cups

Stem the tarragon sprigs. Put the wine, vinegar, shallots, and tarragon stems in a stainless-steel or enamel pan and reduce over medium heat by half. Strain and use the liquid with the egg yolks and butter as you would for the hollandaise. Season the sauce with salt and pepper and throw in the tarragon leaves.

Mint Béarnaise or Sauce Paloise

Make the same way as the tarragon béarnaise but substitute mild mint for the tarragon. Use the sauce on grilled pork loin.

Sauce Béarnaise with Meat Glaze

This sauce uses the same principle as that of adding a fish fumet reduction to hollandaise for fish. In this case, one adds ⅓ cup (or less) of a meat reduction to the completed sauce; even better, the juices (completely defatted) from the grill pan can be stirred into the sauce after the meat is cooked. Any sauce that is to be diluted must be made thicker in the first place.

Sabayon

Apart from the Italian zabaglione dessert sauce, I had never come across sabayon until a lunch I arranged in 1969 at the great Albert Stockli's restaurant Stonehenge in Connecticut. Stockli brought in a huge silver platter one-half-inch deep in melted butter, through which were swimming four large "blue" trout, mouths agape, only minutes from swimming around the pond we could see out of the window. He passed separately at the table a sabayon made with fish stock, in which he had incorporated whipped cream to give the sauce the texture of cumulus clouds. Spooned over the delicate poached trout flesh, it formed one of the best combinations I had ever tasted.

6	egg yolks
1 cup	dry white wine (or ½ cup wine plus ½ cup fish or chicken stock)
½ teaspoon	salt
1 small pinch	cayenne

Makes 4 cups

Choose a pan in which a stainless-steel (or other non-corrosive) bowl fits halfway down and fill the pan a third with water. Bring the water to a boil. Put the yolks, wine, and salt and cayenne in the bowl and whisk vigorously for 5 minutes. Put the bowl on top of the pan and whisk until the mixture thickens to the consistency of thick whipped cream. Do not let the mixture boil or you will have scrambled eggs. Have ready a bowl of ice and water (in case you overheat the sabayon) and cool the bowl in that, if necessary.

If you are going to serve the sauce cold, it *must* be whisked over the ice-water bath until cold. If left to cool by itself, it will lose its volume and separate.

Sweet Sabayon

For a sabayon to be served with desserts or over fresh fruit, follow the above recipe but substitute a sweet white wine and omit the cayenne.

Berries with Sweet Sabayon.

Eggs, Cheese, Pasta, and Grains

I used to hate eggs as a child, as I sat at the breakfast table and watched the adults wolf down fried eggs with uncooked whites hanging from their forks. Nothing filled me with greater dread than the anticipated Sunday-morning trial by egg. Appreciation of this intimidating food was one of the many mysteries of adulthood.

It took me years to grow to realize how versatile eggs are, taking their place in dishes as massively complex as *oeufs Carème,* which takes a staff of five two days to make, as refined as the recipe from *Le Cuisinier Royal* of 1839 that calls for the pressed juices of twelve spit-roasted ducks to be poured over fifteen poached eggs, or as simple as the dishes I shall present here.

Without eggs there would be no pastry-making or, worse, no pasta or, even worse, no egg yolk and cream sauce to pour on top of fresh noodles. Pasta could take up several books of recipes, and all I can do here is present my feelings about the nature of pasta and how it can accommodate both everyday cooking and grand

special events. Pasta is a more valuable commodity than the current craze for fresh pasta would allow; the convenience and quality of dried pasta, which can be used in the simplest fast food to the most splendid concoctions, receive acknowledgment on pages 60 and 65.

There is a hue and cry that the lifestyle evolving in the United States today leaves no one the time to cook at home. But what could be simpler than to return from the office, put a pot of salted water on the stove, pour oneself a cocktail or glass of wine; and by the time one has taken a shower the water pot is boiling, and all one has to do is throw in some pasta. The next step is to peel and seed some tomatoes (using the same boiling water to dunk the tomatoes), chop them up, mix them with chopped fresh herbs, virgin olive oil, and lots of freshly cracked pepper, and to mix the whole lot over the hot drained pasta at the table. All that's left is to grate some Parmesan or dried goat cheese or crumble some blue cheese or fresh goat cheese on top, to smell

the herbal and olive oil perfumes as they rise off the table, to enjoy some crusty bread and fresh young wine with the pasta. The whole operation takes thirty minutes, with a shower thrown in. Pasta means there is no excuse for being deprived of convenient dinner at home.

Not wanting to be a slave over the kitchen stove is nothing new. Just because one's grandmother or grandmother's cook started baking pies at five in the morning does not mean she enjoyed it. In an 1878 housewives' companion from Ohio, the dedication is "To the Plucky Housewives, who master their work instead of allowing it to master them." When I see the richness and detail coming back into American food, and when I see that so much of it involves women professionally—like Sadie Kendall and her goat farm in Atascadero, California—I am reminded that the first professional cooks in America were women. It was they who cooked from sunup to sundown, and the sensual richness they brought to the food of nineteenth-century

America is something we are trying to recapture now. The great tradition in any bountiful rural area, and especially in the Middle West, of the groaning board, the harvest dinner, the hospitality of the farm, is something to look to, not merely out of nostalgia, but because they ate well *and* simply.

Farms mean to me eggs, butter, and cream. Whereas I like cream to be as rich as possible—whether the sublime Jersey or Guernsey cream of England, which I have by the spoonful whenever I go back there, or the *mascarpone* of Italy, eaten with wild strawberries or raspberries—I like fairly austere cheeses, which is why I highlight goat cheese. There have always been goats around somewhere throughout my life. In Mexico, my parents had Nubians the color of Irish setters. In England, I had twins that were pure white and ate themselves practically out of the country. At my farm in Manchester, Massachusetts, our Australian fainting goats produced milk but would keel over in a dead faint at the sight of a milking pail.

In California, I tried to use the first goat cheeses that were imported (about 1973), but they had been wrapped in plastic and been on the shelf too long, since no one was buying them in those days. Then I put them in the center of a mixed garden greens salad with walnut oil and was able to sell them, starting a movement that culminated in a craze for goat cheese. Crottin de Chavignol with a little age is the aristocrat of goat cheeses for me, but fresh goat cheese has its place. In Burgundy, the fresh cheese is formed in pyramid molds and served after the main course, either as a cheese course with *crème fraîche,* salt, and pepper, or as a sweet course with wild strawberries and berry puree. Fresh cheeses, from which the American cottage cheese came, are definitely easier on wines than very high or powerful aged cheeses.

If you buy cheeses that are wrapped in plastic, immediately remove the wrapping and let the cheeses dry off. The best place for keeping cheeses is a very slightly damp, cellar-temperature place, free of insects, with some air circulation. In Richard Olney's house, nestled in the hillside in Solliès-Toucas, there is a little cave off the kitchen with his cheese storage box, which over the years has accumulated a family of cultures. One day after placing a day-old goat cheese there, I could see the cream-colored folds of mold starting to form. It became an education to try and match which day the cheese was at its peak in relation to the wine we were going to have with it. To buy a *cuvée spéciale,* especially La Migoua from Domaine Tempier in Bandol, owned by the Lucien Peyraud family, and to sit out on a terrace under the grape arbor in the late

summer afternoon with this wine, grilled country bread, salt, olives, rich butter, and a selection of week-old goat cheeses of different shapes—it is enough to make time stand still.

In Atascadero, I asked Sadie Kendall, while standing in the moist aging room of her goat farm, surrounded by racks of almost pulsating living cheeses, why the same curd, made into different shapes, has different tastes. It's something to do with the mass and volume of the shape in relation to the amount of bacteria in the cheese. I have also spent many dinners talking with the doyenne of cheese-making in America, Marie-Claude Chaleix of the Coach Farm, Gallatinville, Dutchess County, New York, and am constantly amazed at the complexity of cheese-making.

Eating cheese is much simpler, and if goat cheese is

the best part of a summer afternoon, raclette in the winter—in front of a fire, a crashing storm outside, frozen vodka, good small potatoes, and the fire-roasted crisp crust of the raclette melting in the heat of the flames—is another great way to eat cheese. Or a great aged Stilton wrapped majestically in a napkin, the top cut off so that you can see the crust giving way to the old marble yellowing, that color moving into the off-white and blue veins at the center of the cheese. Stilton and port, of course, with walnuts are traditional, but try both with undyed pistachios heated in the oven for ten minutes, an idea given to me by Belle and Barney Rhodes of Bella Oaks in Napa Valley.

Eggs Rémoulade Creole

An almost infallible way to "hard cook" eggs is described below.

6 large	eggs
2 cups	mayonnaise (page 36)
¼ cup	whole-grain mustard
2 teaspoons	tarragon vinegar
1 teaspoon	paprika
1 teaspoon	Tabasco sauce
½ teaspoon	cayenne
¼ cup	capers, rinsed, finely chopped
1 tablespoon	finely chopped fresh parsley
12	cornichons, finely chopped

Serves 4

Put the eggs in a small saucepan, cover with cold water by 1 inch, and bring to a boil over high heat. The moment the water boils, remove the pan from the heat, cover it, and let stand 10 minutes exactly. Then cool the eggs under cold running water.

Mix the mayonnaise, mustard, vinegar, paprika, Tabasco, cayenne, capers, and parsley. The mayonnaise should be thick enough to nap the eggs (coat evenly without falling off).

Peel and cut the eggs in half lengthwise. Put the halves in the center of a plate. Spoon just enough sauce over the eggs to nap them. Spoon the cornichons around the eggs and pass the remaining sauce.

Poached Eggs with Mushrooms

1 pound	domestic mushrooms
2 tablespoons	olive oil
½ cup	heavy cream
1 cup	reduced veal stock
½ cup	Madeira
9 tablespoons	butter
1 teaspoon	salt, plus additional to taste freshly ground pepper
8 large	very fresh eggs, chilled
12 slices	cured ham (Westphalian, Texas, prosciutto), very thinly sliced
1 tablespoon	chopped fresh parsley

Serves 4

Chop the mushrooms very fine. Heat the oil in a sauté pan over medium heat. Add the mushrooms and toss and stir until they start to give off juices. Cook over high heat until all the liquid is reduced. Add the cream and cook until the mixture is thickened.

Mix the veal stock and Madeira in a small saucepan and reduce over high heat to ¼ cup. Turn the heat to low and whisk in 8 tablespoons of the butter, one tablespoon at a time. Do not let the sauce boil. Season with salt and pepper. Strain and keep warm in a double boiler over low heat.

Fill a shallow saucepan or frying pan with enough water to cover an egg. Bring to a bare simmer and add 1 teaspoon salt. Break the eggs one at a time directly into the water. Cook until the whites have congealed but the yolks are still runny. Remove the eggs carefully from the water and trim them. Blot them on towels to remove the excess water.

Reheat the mushroom mixture (duxelles) and stir in the remaining 1 tablespoon butter. Have ready 4 warm plates and arrange 3 slices of ham on each plate. Spoon the duxelles in the center of each plate. Put 2 eggs on top and pour over the sauce. Garnish with parsley.

French Scrambled Eggs with Smoked Salmon

These eggs are one example of the French method of scrambling eggs, called *oeufs brouillés* or a brouillade. Made with black truffles (page 17), they are beyond sublime. I eat them every Christmas Eve, with an old, lesser, red Bordeaux.

8 large	*eggs*
¼ pound	*unsalted butter, cut into pieces*
½ teaspoon	*salt*
½ teaspoon	*freshly ground pepper*
2 tablespoons	*heavy cream*
8 ounces	*smoked salmon, boned, skinned, julienned*
½ cup	*hollandaise (page 38)*
8 slices	*smoked salmon*
2 tablespoons	*chopped chives*

Serves 4

Beat the eggs just until well mixed. Coat the bottom and sides of a saucepan with some of the butter. Add salt and pepper and 2 tablespoons of the butter to the eggs and put in the pan. Put the pan into the simmering water of a water bath and stir the eggs with a wooden spoon, making sure to scrape all the surfaces of the pan, especially the corners. Never stop stirring or let the eggs stick to the pan. If the eggs start to thicken too quickly, remove the pan from the water for a minute or so. When the eggs are nearly done, stir in the cream and the julienned salmon.

Remove from the heat, and stir in the remaining butter, which will halt the cooking as well as enrich the texture and taste of the eggs. Put the eggs on 4 warm ovenproof plates and spoon over equal amounts of the hollandaise. Broil for 1 minute to glaze the sauce.

Place 2 slices of salmon on each plate and sprinkle with the chopped chives as shown.

Eggs in Hell, Texas Style

This is a dish I invented for the Texas dinner in the series of American regional dinners we gave at the Santa Fe Bar & Grill in 1982.

4 large	*eggs*
1 tablespoon	*olive oil*
1 cup	*red bell pepper puree (page 32)*
	salt
½ cup	*barbecue sauce (page 222)*
24 leaves	*cilantro, for garnish*

Serves 4

Put the eggs in a small saucepan, cover with cold water by 1 inch, and bring to a boil over high heat. The moment the water boils, remove the pan from the heat, cover it, and let stand 10 minutes exactly. Then cool the eggs under cold running water.

Peel and cut the eggs in half lengthwise. Whisk the oil into the red pepper puree. Add salt if necessary.

Make a round pool of the red pepper sauce in the center of each plate and place 2 egg halves, cut side down, in the center of each pool of sauce. Spoon the barbecue sauce over the eggs so that they are napped perfectly, swirling the sauce out from the eggs toward the rim of the plate. Garnish with the cilantro leaves.

Spinach, Sorrel, and Ham Frittata

Don't think a frittata has to have these ingredients. Almost anything will do, even something as simple as potato and left-over pasta.

1 cup	*stemmed spinach leaves, washed, well drained*
½ cup	*stemmed sorrel leaves, washed, well drained*
2 ounces	*cured ham (prosciutto, Texas, Smithfield, or Westphalian)*
4 ounces	*mushrooms, thinly sliced*
4 tablespoons	*olive oil*
4	*eggs*
½ teaspoon	*salt*
½ teaspoon	*freshly ground pepper*
8 leaves	*fresh tarragon or basil*
½ cup	*tomato chutney (page 29)*

Serves 2

Cut the spinach, sorrel, and ham into a fine julienne.

Sauté the mushrooms in 2 tablespoons of the olive oil until tender, about 5 minutes; then set aside to cool.

Beat the eggs with salt and pepper in a bowl. Add the spinach, sorrel, ham, mushrooms, and tarragon, and beat well.

Heat a large omelet pan over medium heat, brush with a tablespoon of olive oil, and pour the egg mixture into the pan.

Reduce the heat to low; cook until the bottom is set and lightly browned and the omelet moves freely in the pan. Flip the omelet over and cook another minute, until the omelet is set and slightly puffed.

Slide onto a warm platter and top with the tomato chutney. Drizzle the remaining olive oil over the top.

Noreen Lam's Lamb Hash

Don't be put off by lamb. This is a *winner*, a rage on Sunday morning at the restaurants.

1 tablespoon	*freshly grated or prepared horseradish*
½ cup	*sour cream*
½ teaspoon	*fresh lemon juice*
¼ teaspoon	*freshly ground pepper*
4 medium	*russet potatoes, peeled, cut into ½-inch dice*
¼ cup	*olive oil*
1 large	*onion, coarsely chopped*
3 thick slices	*bacon or pancetta, cut into ½-inch pieces*
4 cloves	*garlic, minced*
2 cups	*cooked lamb (preferably from braised lamb shanks), cut into ½-inch dice*
1 teaspoon	*finely chopped fresh thyme*
1 teaspoon	*finely chopped fresh marjoram*
¼ teaspoon	*ground cumin*
pinch	*ground turmeric*
	salt and freshly ground pepper
½ cup	*heavy cream*
4 large	*fresh eggs*
1 tablespoon	*chopped fresh parsley*

Serves 4

Combine the horseradish, sour cream, lemon juice, and pepper and let stand to develop the flavors while you make the hash.

Rinse the potatoes and pat dry between towels.

Heat the oil briefly in a large heavy-bottom frying pan, preferably nonstick, over medium heat. Add the onion and bacon and sauté until the onion is translucent but not brown, about 5 minutes. Add the garlic and cook 2 minutes more; then add the potatoes.

Continue to cook over medium heat, stirring often, until the potatoes are three-quarters cooked. Mix in the lamb, thyme, marjoram, cumin, and turmeric and season with salt and pepper. Cook, stirring once or twice more, until the potatoes are done, about 5 minutes more. Add the cream and turn up the heat to thicken the cream and form a light brown crust on the bottom. Flip the hash and brown the other side for 3 minutes.

While the hash is cooking, poach the eggs, drain, and trim. Divide the hash between 4 warm plates. Put a spoonful of the horseradish cream in the center of each serving and top with a poached egg. Sprinkle with the parsley.

Grilled Goat Cheese in Leaves

The best equipment for grilling these wrapped cheeses is a hinged grill—a good cheap investment because it makes grilling anything easier, and makes turning things, like little fish, mushrooms, bread, or vegetables, a snap.

Set up the hinged grill on top of another grill, or if you are cooking in your fireplace, build up a few bricks to support the grill, take out some coals, and set the grill on the bricks. Wonderful for grilling flattened-out little birds, sliced green tomatoes, or thick slices of Parmesan cheese marinated in fresh thyme or sage.

4	*grape leaves*
4 leaves	*radicchio*
8 2-inch rounds	*fresh goat cheese*
1 tablespoon	*thyme leaves, finely chopped*
1 cup	*olive oil*
12 slices	*country bread, ⅛ inch thick*
1 clove	*garlic, peeled*
	salt and freshly ground pepper

Serves 4

Cut the stems from the grape leaves. Cut the thick cores from the bottoms of the radicchio leaves.

Put 4 of the goat cheese rounds in the center of the grape leaves and 4 in the radicchio leaves. Sprinkle each round with thyme and 1½ teaspoons of the olive oil. Fold the leaves over the cheese and turn the packages over so that the leaves stay closed.

Brush the outside of the cheeses with ¼ cup of the olive oil and marinate for 2 hours.

Start the fire or heat the grill.

Brush the bread with ¼ cup olive oil. Put the cheeses on the grill and cook over medium heat for 4 minutes on each side, until the goat cheese is soft and warm. Some color on the edges of the leaves is inevitable, but do not let the leaves burn.

When the packages are cooked, put them on a hot platter and grill the bread lightly on each side; then rub the bread with the garlic clove.

Serve the bread at once with the cheese. To eat it, spread the cheese on the bread and season with salt, pepper, and the remaining olive oil. Eat the radicchio but discard the grape leaves.

Raclette with Radicchio

Raclette served this way (you can use an infinite range of ingredients for the base of the dish) is fast, delicious, and easy. Use a broiler or the top of a very hot oven. Have the raclette sliced from a quarter of a wheel when you buy it, in pieces 1/16 inch thick; they will be about 6 inches long and 4 inches wide. If you don't have radicchio use Belgian endive, curly endive, cooked leeks or scallions, or rocket.

16 slices	raclette cheese
6	new potatoes
2 small heads	radicchio
2 tablespoons	fresh lemon juice
¼ teaspoon	salt
2 pinches	freshly ground pepper
⅓ cup	olive oil
1 cup	cherry chutney (page 28)

Serves 4

Heat the broiler or the oven to 450°F.

Remove the rind, if there is any, from the cheese. Cook the potatoes in salted water until they can be easily pierced with a fork. Drain the potatoes, let cool, and then cut in half. Cut the cores from the radicchio and tear each leaf in half.

Mix the lemon juice, salt, and pepper in a bowl. Whisk in the oil. Toss the potatoes and radicchio leaves in the dressing.

Put 3 potato halves on each of 4 ovenproof plates and divide the radicchio equally among the plates. Put 4 slices of cheese over the potatoes and radicchio so that they are entirely covered. Broil or bake until the cheese is just but completely melted, about 1 minute. Remove the plates and put 1 tablespoon of chutney in the center of each plate. Serve immediately with the rest of the chutney.

Squash Blossoms with Goat Cheese

Squash blossoms can be stuffed with olive puree, chopped cooked eggplant, lentils, cheeses—a whole range of ingredients. They can be covered with raclette and broiled, or served with ancho chili mayonnaise, or the salsas or relishes mentioned in the previous chapter (pages 28–29). Here I have used the combination (some might consider it perverse) of mayonnaise and vinaigrette, a mixture I adore and which works very well in this case with the herb and tomato flavors. The more the blossoms are cooked, the worse they look and the better they taste, so choose your compromise. Use a fresh goat cheese, like a French Montrachet or bulk goat white cheese.

1 tablespoon	fresh thyme leaves or flowers
2 cups	fresh goat cheese
1 teaspoon	freshly ground black pepper
16 large	fresh squash blossoms
⅓ cup	olive oil
1½ cups	tomato vinaigrette (page 32)
1 cup	herb mayonnaise (page 36)

Serves 4

Chop the thyme very fine and mix the thyme, cheese, and black pepper well. Let sit covered for 1 hour to allow the flavors to mingle. Cut the stems and hard bases from the blossoms, but do not cut away so much that the flowers fall apart.

Heat the broiler.

Oil a sheet pan to go under the broiler.

Put a spoonful of the cheese mixture in each blossom. Gently fold the opening of each flower over, pat it into shape, and put it on the sheet pan. Brush the flowers gently with oil. Broil until the cheese starts to melt and the flowers are just turning crisp, 5 to 10 minutes.

Serve immediately, with the tomato vinaigrette spooned over the blossoms and the herb mayonnaise on the side.

White Cheese with Roasted Garlic

In the introduction to this chapter I mentioned the little pyramids of fresh white cheese served in France with fruit, cream, or just salt and pepper. You don't have to have a pyramid mold to make this dish; in fact, the cheese could just be spooned out on the plate. Here I have used the fresh curds of goat cheese packed into a cheesecloth-lined mold, weighted down for a day to compact the cheese, and unmolded onto the plate. The best garlic to use is the very fresh, new-crop spring garlic, and the best accompaniments are crusty bread and Niçoise olives.

Heat the oven to 350°F.

Cut each head of garlic in half horizontally. Brush each half with ½ tablespoon oil and sprinkle with salt and pepper. Pull half the leaf clusters off the thyme or marjoram sprigs and put between the cut surfaces of the garlic. Put the garlic halves back together and wrap in aluminum foil. Bake until they are soft, about 30 minutes.

Put the cheeses on plates, pour the remaining olive oil over them, and sprinkle with the remaining thyme flowers and leaves. Serve with the baked garlic. Squeeze the garlic onto bread; then spread the cheese on the bread. Eat with olives and lots of cool white wine.

4 heads	garlic
1 cup	virgin olive oil
	salt and freshly ground pepper
4 sprigs	thyme or marjoram
4 whole	fresh goat's- or cow's-milk white cheeses
1 tablespoon	fresh thyme flowers and leaves

Serves 4

Stuffed Chilies with Black Bean Sauce

Chilies can be stuffed with a variety of vegetable or meat or cheese mixtures, as long as the stuffing is moist and a softer texture than the chilies. In this recipe the Fontina gives a melting texture, the goat cheese gives body and flavor, and the Parmesan a sharpness and bite. Any kind of fresh peppers—even bell peppers— can be used, as long as they are big enough and not too hot. I have used pasilla chilies here, which have more heat than, say, an Anaheim or yellow Hungarian. The best way to skin the peppers is to deep-fry them, but this is very impractical unless you are deep-frying something else, so an alternative method is given here.

8 fresh	*pasilla chilies*
¼ cup	*oil*
1½ cups	*fresh white goat cheese*
¼ cup	*grated Fontina cheese*
¼ cup	*finely grated Parmesan cheese*
6 tablespoons	*heavy cream*
½ teaspoon	*freshly ground pepper*
1 cup	*black bean sauce (page 30)*
½ cup	*salsa (page 28)*
12 to 16 sprigs	*cilantro*

Serves 4

Heat the broiler.

Coat the chilies with the oil and put them in a baking pan. Broil, turning the chilies often, until the skin is browned and the chilies are just tender. Remove from the broiler, cover, and let stand for 15 minutes. Peel the chilies, slit them down the side, and remove the seeds.

Heat the oven to 400°F.

Mix the cheeses, cream, and pepper in a bowl. Stuff the chilies with the cheese mixture and put them on an oiled baking sheet. Bake until the cheese starts to melt, about 15 minutes. While the chilies are baking, heat the black bean sauce in a double boiler. Then pour the sauce equally onto hot plates and put the chilies on top. Garnish with the salsa and cilantro.

Polenta with Wild Mushroom Sauce

This is a dish whereby to enjoy one of the best comforting foods, polenta, in small quantities and in a light way.

2 tablespoons	mixed fresh herb leaves, finely chopped
1 cup	sour cream, crème fraîche, or mascarpone
1 cup	polenta meal
2 to 3 cups	water
¼ pound	butter
2 pounds	combined fresh wild and domestic mushrooms, sliced
2 tablespoons	chopped garlic
	salt and freshly ground pepper
½ cup	chicken stock
2 tablespoons	chopped fresh parsley

Serves 4

Mix the herbs into the sour cream and let sit overnight or as long as possible.

Cook the polenta as directed in the recipe on page 219 and keep it warm in the top of a double boiler until needed. Stir in more water if it gets too thick. Mix in 4 tablespoons of the butter just before serving.

Melt 2 tablespoons of the butter in a sauté pan. Put the mushrooms in the pan and toss in the butter. Add the garlic and salt to taste. Cook 2 minutes; then stir in the stock. Cook over high heat another 5 minutes; stir in the remaining 2 tablespoons butter. Add pepper and more salt if necessary.

Put a spoonful of the herb cream in the center of each plate. Spoon the polenta and then the mushroom ragout over the cream. Sprinkle liberally with the chopped parsley and serve immediately.

Risotto with Prawns

This is a basic risotto recipe. Its potential garnishes are almost endless—peas or asparagus, parboiled and added at the last minute; radicchio chiffonade put in raw with the prawns or even thrown on top of the hot risotto to wilt; cooked artichokes or leeks; ancho chili butter; black bean sauce or flavored aioli drizzled on top. But never add cheese to a seafood pasta or risotto, as it tends to make the seafood taste old or spoiled.

2 tablespoons	olive oil
32	prawns, shelled, shells saved
8 cups	fish stock (page 218)
6 tablespoons	sweet butter
1 large	onion, peeled, finely chopped
2 cups	Arborio rice
1 tablespoon	finely chopped garlic
	salt and freshly ground pepper

Serves 4

Heat the oil in a sauté pan until hot. Add the shrimp shells and sauté, stirring constantly, for 5 minutes. Spoon off all the oil you can and add the fish stock. Simmer for 30 minutes. Strain, discard the shells, and skim any oil from the surface of the stock.

Melt 2 tablespoons of the butter in a heavy frying pan over low heat. Add the onion and sweat it covered until translucent, about 5 minutes. Do not let it brown. Add the rice and sauté over medium heat, stirring constantly until all the rice is coated with the butter, about 5 minutes.

Add the stock, a cup at a time, and cook the rice over medium heat, stirring constantly, and keep adding more stock a cup at a time as it is absorbed by the rice. When the rice is just tender, after about 15 minutes, add the prawns and garlic. Cook until the prawns are done, 5 to 7 minutes. Garnish as desired and season with salt and pepper. Add the remaining butter and stir until it is incorporated. Serve hot.

Truffled Sweetbread Ravioli

Any pasta shape that can be stuffed can be used here, especially if you are not up to making ravioli or tortelli. Truffles are not mandatory, for while they make this dish breathtaking, it is delicious without them. If you cannot stand the idea of brains, don't worry: They are superb here, and you can't see them. I invented this dish for Gerald Asher's birthday party at the Santa Fe Bar & Grill, and everyone approved, though knowing what was in the ravioli.

I like to make large shapes and serve two or three only. Buy sheets of fresh pasta dough if you do not have a pasta machine. Be ready: This is a lot of work—but worth it.

4	calf brains
2 cups	court bouillon (page 221)
4 pairs	veal sweetbreads
¼ cup	whipping cream
1 tablespoon	finely chopped tarragon leaves
1 ounce	fresh black truffle, finely chopped
	salt and freshly ground pepper
1 recipe	pasta dough (page 219) (or 2 pounds bought fresh pasta sheets)
2 large	eggs
6 tablespoons	butter
2 pounds	combined fresh wild and domestic mushrooms, sliced
	salt and freshly ground pepper
2 tablespoons	chopped garlic
1½ teaspoons	fresh thyme leaves, finely chopped
2 tablespoons	chopped fresh parsley

Serves 4

Soak the brains in salted cold water to cover for 1 hour. Peel off the membrane and poach in the court bouillon for 10 minutes. Drain, puree in a food processor, and press the puree through a sieve.

Braise the sweetbreads as directed in the recipe on page 222. Strain the sweetbread braising liquid and reduce to 2 cups. Pull the sweetbreads apart into almond-size nuggets. Discard any membrane; puree and sieve a quarter of the sweetbreads. Add the sweetbread puree, cream, tarragon, truffle, and salt and pepper to taste to the brain puree and mix well.

Divide the pasta dough in 4 equal portions and roll each out into a sheet approximately 4 inches by 16 inches long and as thin as it can be and still be handled. Cover the sheets with a towel as you roll them to prevent them from drying out.

Beat the eggs together and have a small brush on hand. Using 1 tablespoon of filling for each ravioli, make 1 row of mounds 2 inches apart along one side of the pasta sheet. Brush the other side lightly with the egg mixture and fold it over the mounds, pressing down with your fingers between and around the mounds to make sure the edges are tightly sealed; cut the ravioli with a pasta cutter or a knife, leaving a ½-inch border on all sides.

Bring a large flat pot of salted water to a boil.

Melt 2 tablespoons of the butter in a sauté pan. Put the mushrooms in the pan and toss them in the butter. Add the salt and pepper to taste, garlic, and thyme. Cook for 2 minutes and add the reduced braising liquid. Cook over high heat another 5 minutes. Add the sweetbreads and remaining butter and stir until the butter is incorporated.

Meanwhile, put the ravioli carefully into the boiling water and barely simmer until the pasta is tender, about 5 minutes. Lift the ravioli out of the water, drain a few seconds on a towel, and put them on plates. Spoon the mushroom–sweetbread sauce over the pasta and sprinkle with the parsley.

Pasta Salad with Baked Eggplant and Tomatoes

There are as many pasta salads as there are ingredients. But the method of cooking pasta to serve cold is always the same, and the secret is to prevent the pasta from sticking together by stirring the boiling water when you add the pasta. When draining the pasta, you can rinse it under cold water until it is cold and then toss it in oil. While this is the easiest method, it robs the pasta of maximum flavor. More trouble but more delicious is to toss the pasta in olive or herb oil while it is hot so that it absorbs the oil's flavors. You must toss the pasta until it is well coated but not swimming in oil, put it in the refrigerator, and take it out every minute or so and toss it again, until the pasta is cold and all the pieces are separate. The salads that follow are main courses.

½ pound	*dried spaghetti or linguine*
1 cup	*herb oil (page 222)*
	salt and freshly ground pepper
10	*Japanese eggplants*
1 teaspoon	*chopped garlic*
1 teaspoon	*balsamic or red wine vinegar*
½ cup	*cilantro leaves, coarsely chopped*
2 tablespoons	*fresh lemon juice*
⅓ cup	*olive oil*
½ cup	*tomato concasse (page 220)*
12 small	*yellow tomatoes*

Serves 4

Heat the oven to 350°F.

Bring a large pot of salted water to the boil, add the pasta, and stir for 1 minute. Cover the pot so that it comes back to the boil as soon as possible and then remove the cover. Cook until the pasta is *al dente,* about 10 minutes. Drain the pasta and immediately toss with ½ cup of the herb oil. Cool as described in the headnote. Season with salt and pepper to taste.

Cut the eggplants lengthwise into ¼-inch-thick slices and put the pieces on a sheet pan. Brush with the remaining herb oil and season. Cover the pan with foil. Bake until tender, about 20 minutes.

Set aside 24 of the best-looking middle slices of the eggplants. Chop the remaining eggplant and then mix with the garlic, vinegar, cilantro, and salt and pepper to taste.

Mix the lemon juice with salt and pepper and whisk in the olive oil.

Put the eggplant slices on plates. Divide the pasta into 4 portions and twist into nests. Put the nests in the center of each plate. Spoon the chopped eggplant over the pasta. Toss the tomato concasse in the lemon dressing and put on the plates. Cut the yellow tomatoes in half, dress them, and put them on the plates. Pour any remaining dressing over the eggplant and serve.

Warm Pasta Salad with Smoked Duck and Radicchio

This is a dish and method that I invented for fast lunches at Stars. It uses up odds and ends, and as with the cold pasta salad, there is no limit to the possible variations. Everything can be prepared beforehand, even the pasta, which you cook and treat as in the previous recipe, then reheat in boiling water. You can, of course, cook the pasta from the dry state just for this dish, and by the time it is done, all the other ingredients will be assembled and heated in a bowl over the pasta water. Use little bits of left-over sauces or roasting juices—in fact, use whatever is on hand. Many different shapes of pasta can be used, from bowties to little ears; here, penne is used. If you don't have radicchio, use Belgian endive, or cooked asparagus, leeks, eggplant, etc.

2 small	*hearts of radicchio*
½ pound	*combined dried green and white macaroni*
1 cup	*smoked or roasted duck meat, shredded*
1 teaspoon	*fresh rosemary, chopped*
1 tablespoon	*fresh thyme leaves, chopped*
2 tablespoons	*reduced meat juices or duck stock*
	salt and freshly ground pepper
16 slices	*Fontina, raclette, or Gruyère cheese, about 6 by 4 by ¹⁄₁₆ inch*
¼ cup	*walnut halves, toasted*
1 cup	*tomato vinaigrette (page 32), made without shallots*
¼ cup	*coarsely chopped duck cracklings (page 108), optional*

Serves 4

Heat the broiler or the oven to 450°F.

Cut the cores from the radicchio and pull the leaves off. Bring a large pot of salted water to the boil and add the pasta; stir for 1 minute. Cover the pot so that the water comes back to the boil as soon as possible and then remove the cover. Cook until the pasta is *al dente,* about 10 minutes.

While the pasta is cooking, combine the duck meat, half the herbs, the meat juices, and salt and pepper to taste in a large bowl. Just before the pasta is done, put the bowl over the pasta water to warm it, tossing the ingredients a couple of times. When the pasta is cooked, drain it, add it to the bowl, and mix well. Toss in the radicchio.

Divide the pasta mixture among 4 plates. Cover each portion with 4 slices of the cheese and broil until the cheese melts.

Mix the walnuts and tomato vinaigrette and spoon over the salads. Sprinkle the duck cracklings on top and serve.

Top: Pasta Salad with Baked Eggplant and Tomatoes; bottom: Warm Pasta Salad with Smoked Duck and Radicchio.

Cornmeal Blinis with Smoked Sturgeon and Caviar

As irresistible as food can get!

1 cup	yellow cornmeal
½ teaspoon	salt
1½ cups	boiling water
2	eggs
1 cup	milk
½ cup	sifted all-purpose flour
2 tablespoons	melted butter
¾ cup	warm clarified butter (page 216)
8 tablespoons	sour cream
8 tablespoons	salmon caviar
8 teaspoons	black caviar
24 thin slices	smoked sturgeon

Serves 8

Mix the cornmeal and salt and stir in the boiling water. Cover and let stand for 10 minutes. Beat in the eggs one at a time; then slowly stir in the milk. Mix in the flour and 2 tablespoons melted butter; beat until the mixture is smooth. The batter should be the consistency of heavy cream; if it is too thick, thin with a little more milk.

Brush a well-seasoned crêpe pan with clarified butter and heat. When the pan is hot, pour in about 3 tablespoons batter and tilt the pan to distribute the batter evenly. Cook until the underside is lightly browned, 2 to 3 minutes. Turn and cook the other side another 1 to 2 minutes.

Put each blini on a hot plate and pour 3 tablespoons clarified butter over the blini. Put 1 tablespoon sour cream in the center of each blini, then 1 tablespoon salmon caviar in the center of the sour cream, then 1 teaspoon (or more) black caviar in the center of that. Put 3 slices sturgeon around each blini and serve immediately.

Blue Cornmeal Pancakes

Blue cornmeal from New Mexico is hard to find but worth the search. The earthy, almost "smoky" flavor of blue corn is subtle and powerful at the same time. If you don't have smoked duck or chicken, use cooked smoked ham.

1 pound	butter
1 teaspoon	ancho chili powder
2	smoked duck breasts, halved
1 large	red bell pepper
1 large	yellow bell pepper
¼ teaspoon	fresh lemon juice
1 teaspoon	olive oil
	salt and freshly ground pepper
1½ cups	fine blue cornmeal
¼ cup	sifted all-purpose flour
½ teaspoon	baking soda
¼ cup	sweet butter
1	egg
2 cups	buttermilk
4 tablespoons	clarified butter (page 216)

Serves 8

Melt the butter with the chili powder in a double boiler or over very low heat. Strain through a fine-mesh wire strainer or several layers of cheesecloth. Discard the milky solids in the bottom of the pan. Keep the butter warm.

Bone the smoked duck breasts and remove the skins. Make the skins into cracklings (page 108) and set them and the duck meat aside.

Roast, peel, and seed the peppers (page 167). Cut them into ¼-inch dice and combine them with the lemon juice and olive oil. Season with salt and pepper.

Combine the cornmeal, flour, 1 teaspoon salt, and baking soda in a bowl. With your fingers or a pastry blender, work ¼ cup butter into the dry ingredients. Mix the egg and buttermilk and then stir it into the cornmeal mixture. Cook the pancakes in clarified butter following the directions for blinis (opposite), stirring the batter thoroughly before making each pancake.

Warm the duck breast in the oven and then cut each half into 4 or 5 slices, and place on top of each pancake, with a spoonful of the pepper relish. Pour 2 tablespoons of the chili-flavored butter around each pancake and garnish with the duck cracklings.

Top: Blue Cornmeal Pancakes; bottom: Cornmeal Blinis with Smoked Sturgeon and Caviar.

Pasta with Rabbit and Chanterelles

The saddle or loin midsection of the rabbit cooks in much less time than the legs, so the cook is faced with a problem similar to that presented by chicken or duck: If you cook the bird until the thighs are done, the breast is overcooked. The best way to handle rabbit is to separate the legs from the saddle and slowly braise the former but quickly roast the latter. In this pasta dish, you do not have to include both sections of the rabbit but could use just braised legs. It is difficult to overcook rabbit legs; they just get more tender as they cook and do not dry out. Pull the meat off the bones, strain the braising juices, reduce them a bit, add butter or cream, and you have a wonderful sauce.

1	rabbit
	salt and freshly ground pepper
1½ tablespoons	fresh thyme leaves, chopped
½ tablespoon	fresh rosemary leaves, chopped
¼ pound	butter
1 pound	fresh chanterelles
2 tablespoons	chopped garlic
½ pound	white fettuccine (page 219)
½ pound	green fettuccine (page 219)
½ cup	tomato concasse (page 220)
3 tablespoons	chopped fresh parsley

Serves 4

Cut the rabbit up, separating the saddle from the hind and front legs. Bone the saddle. Braise the legs with the bones (page 127). Season the inside of the boned saddle with salt and pepper and stuff with ½ tablespoon thyme and the rosemary. Roll up the saddle and tie it with string.

When the legs are braised, let them cool and then pull the meat off the bones in bite-size pieces. Strain and reserve 2 cups of the braising liquid.

Heat the oven to 400°F.

Brush the saddle with 1 tablespoon of the butter and season with salt and pepper. Bake for 15 minutes; then let sit in a warm place. Remove the strings.

Bring a large pot of salted water to the boil.

Heat 2 tablespoons of the butter in a sauté pan. Put in the chanterelles (sliced, if large) and toss in the butter. Add the garlic and the remaining 1 tablespoon thyme. Cook over medium heat for 5 minutes, stirring or tossing occasionally. When the mushrooms are tender, add the reserved stock.

Put the fettuccine in the boiling water and stir until the water comes back to the boil.

Increase the heat under the mushrooms to high and cook 1 minute. Add the braised rabbit meat, the tomato concasse, parsley, and remaining 5 tablespoons butter. Toss or stir together until the butter is incorporated. Drain the pasta and add it to the rabbit ragout. Toss together and serve on warm plates. Slice the saddle meat and put in the center of each serving of pasta.

Timbale of Macaroni and Sweetbreads *(pictured on next page)*

This nineteenth-century-sounding dish can in fact be found in one of the greatest books of that century, the *École des Cuisiniers* of Urbain Dubois, but I first saw it in the book that inspired me from its first pages and continues to do so, *The French Menu Cookbook* by Richard Olney. Use a whole chicken breast, with an equal quantity of ham. Smoked mushrooms, tongue, truffles, are all welcome additions, and the dish could be made with the braised meat from lamb or veal shanks as well. The purpose of the forcemeat, which firms as it cooks, is to hold the macaroni in place and give structure so that the timbale will stand up when unmolded. You will need a smooth metal or heatproof glass 2½ quart dome-shaped mold. This one is for a rainy day or when you can count on lots of help in the kitchen. It can be done in advance.

2 pounds	sweetbreads
½ pound	thin macaroni (like spaghetti but larger, with a hole in center)
11 tablespoons	butter
4 tablespoons	all-purpose flour
1 cup	whipping cream
2 cups	chicken and ham forcemeat (page 216)
1 pound	fresh shiitake, domestic, and/or wild mushrooms, sliced
½ tablespoon	chopped garlic
1 teaspoon	fresh thyme leaves, chopped
1 tablespoon	tarragon leaves
	salt and freshly ground pepper
2 cups	tomato sauce (page 220)

Serves 6 to 8

Braise the sweetbreads following the instructions on page 222. Let cool in the braising liquid until needed, then strain and reserve the braising liquid and break the sweetbreads into half-inch pieces.

Bring a large pot of salted water to the boil. Put in the macaroni, stir a few times until the water comes back to the boil, and cook the macaroni until just a little more *al dente* than you would normally eat it, about 10 minutes. Drain the pasta, rinse under cold water, and lay it out on towels separately so the pieces do not stick together.

Melt 2 tablespoons of the butter in a saucepan. Stir in the flour and cook for 5 minutes, stirring constantly. Gradually whisk in the braising liquid and continue to whisk until smooth. Simmer for 45 minutes, occasionally skimming off the scum or skin from the surface. Stir in ½ cup of the cream and simmer 10 minutes more.

While the sauce is cooking, spread about 4 tablespoons of the butter over the inside of the mold (see headnote). Twist a piece of macaroni into a tight circle and put it at the center of the bottom of the mold. The idea is to get the macaroni to stick to the butter as you line the mold. Put the mold in the refrigerator if the butter is too warm. Line the inside of the mold completely with the pasta. When finished, refrigerate the mold to set the butter.

When the butter is set, spread the macaroni with a ½-inch layer of the forcemeat, leaving some to finish off the timbale. Put the mold back in the refrigerator to set the forcemeat.

Melt 2 tablespoons of the butter in a sauté pan. Add the mushrooms and toss in the butter. Cook for 2 minutes. Add the garlic and thyme and cook another 2 minutes. Put the mixture in a bowl and combine with the sweetbreads, cream sauce, and half the tarragon; season with salt and pepper. Refrigerate until cool.

Heat the oven to 350°F.

Spoon the sweetbread mixture into the mold and spread the top with the remaining forcemeat. Spread a parchment paper circle with 1 tablespoon of the butter and place on the forcemeat. Put the mold in a large pot and pour boiling water into the pot to come three-quarters up the side of the mold. Bake for 45 minutes.

Remove the mold from the pot and let sit for 15 minutes to settle. Unmold onto a serving platter. Some juices will leak out and can be left on the platter or removed as you wish.

While the timbale is settling, heat the tomato sauce with the remaining ½ cup cream. Whisk in the remaining 2 tablespoons butter and serve with slices of the timbale.

Overleaf Timbale of Macaroni and Sweetbreads.

Fish and Shellfish

When I think of fish and shellfish, I think of the black risotto of baby cuttlefish at Harry's Bar in Venice; the tiny tidepool crabs deep-fried and mounted on a platter, eaten whole at an unpretentious dockside restaurant south of Genoa; of Brittany mussels steamed with shallots, white wine, and cream. These vie with other memories: sitting at table on Hog Island in Maine, the cold fog rolling in, a huge fire going, as I tear apart big lobsters and dunk the chunks of clawmeat in hot butter; pink swordfish right off the boats in Montauk, grilled over charcoal that night; a big bowl of Oregon razor clams in steaming, buttery broth; Long Island littleneck clams right out of the water, eaten by the dozens with a squeeze of lemon; the Acme oyster bar in New Orleans between hangovers, paced by understanding shuckers so the numbers of oysters eaten rise alarmingly; herrings from the Irish Sea, fat with roe, so fresh they look like silver jewelry, marinated, grilled, or fried in cornmeal; Manx kippers; soft-shelled crabs; squid; fish stews; bouillabaisse, and the great fish soups.

Back in the summers of the sixties, my family lived in an old gambling casino in Montauk, Long Island, and although I have never lived out of sight of an ocean except in England (where the water seems only an hour away from anywhere), I have never been so deluged with fish and shellfish as there. In the morning my father would get up and go fishing for "snapper blues," the young bluefish that lived in the saltwater lake in front of the casino, then for lunch there was whatever anyone had caught from the ocean beach, from the dock out front (usually "tinker mackerel"), from the commercial docks (things like pink swordfish, striped bass), and then in the evening we would gather around the dock while someone went clamming at low tide, or, if the water was high, two or three people went in after the bay scallops, catching them swimming along and throwing them up on the shore. Some were eaten then, the rest shucked, to go within minutes into cornmeal and then be fried in butter. Or we would just sit around the rocks having cocktails and opening oysters right out of the water. That experience never failed to revive even the most jaded of guests, their palates resurrected by freshness and brine.

We would give a clambake every summer and invite forty people, most of whom could stay over in that old casino with its eighteen rooms. The bake was done very traditionally, the way my grandfather had done it on Cape Cod, although they were never as grand as the nineteenth-century events I had read about in a book about the Cape, which featured the endless baking of pies and cakes, and huge breakfasts. The book mentioned another treat I have always wanted to duplicate, which involved picking cantaloupes the day before the bake in the late afternoon, when the sun has been shining on them all day and their perfume is at peak. One cut off the top of the melon, shook out its seeds, filled up the cavity with old Madeira, replaced the top, and suspended the melon in a well to keep it just cool. At the end of the clambake next day, when the air was still very hot, when one was full of lobster, butter, corn, clams, and all sorts of fish, all of it rich food, the melons were pulled out of the well, the tops removed, and one drank deeply of the cool melon-scented Madeira, finally scooping out the Madeira-flavored cantaloupe. That moment tells all about simple elegance in a rough setting.

I have used a lot of lobster in this book, not just because it is delicious and everyone likes it, but because I wanted to show how to make an expensive food go a long way. The lobster gazpacho could use as little as 1½ pounds lobster for four people, and the shells of both lobsters *and* crayfish should always be saved for making essence that can go into salad dressings, cream and butter sauces, or bisques. The lobster and rocket salad (page 79), however, is not meant to be economical, but one of those moments of total indulgence.

How to cook a lobster is always controversial. Actually, the best lobster I ever cooked turned out perfect by accident. I was to have dinner with some friends who had a goat farm on the cliffs of Big Sur. That night a huge winter storm came in, and, as we helped a nanny goat with a breech birth, I remember seeing the cliffs above and just to the north of the property collapse into the ocean, with pouring rain, lightning, thunder, and falling boulders all around. All the events occurred while we waited what seemed like hours for the major part of our dinner, a lobster, to be cooked. I had chosen a 2½-pounder, because I think they offer the best meat, despite the good reputation of the 1-pound lobster. I had found a pot large enough, filled it with water, salted it, and put in the lobster. There was only a single electric hot plate to use. It was not large enough, and the electricity came and went with the progress of the howling storm. After an hour the water had still not boiled. Ages later, it seemed, the lobster turned red. I thought, to hell with it, I have eaten warm seviche before, and pulled the lobster from the pot and cut it up. The flesh was superb, the best I have ever eaten. It had never tightened to that tennis ball texture lobster can achieve, and was cooked to perfection.

Lobster: Basic Preparation

The two ways I give to cook a lobster are for two different purposes. The first is for lobster meat that is to be cooked further, as for a risotto, or to be heated in bisque, or for a ragout. The second is for lobster to be eaten as is, hot or cold, whole or in pieces, as for salad.

The meat yield will depend on the time of year and the thickness of the shell, but generally, from a 1-pound lobster the yield is 6 to 8 ounces, from a 2-pound lobster, 18 to 20 ounces, and from a 3-pound lobster, 1½ pounds.

Method 1—Cooking Lobster to Be Reheated

Put the lobsters in a pot and pour cold water over to cover them by 6 inches. Turn the heat on full and cook until just before the water boils. Turn off the heat and let sit according to the times below. Remove the lobsters and cover with ice so they cool down and stop cooking.

    1-pound lobsters: 1 minute
    2-pound lobsters: 3 minutes
    3-pound lobsters: 4 minutes

Method 2—Cooking Lobster to Serve Hot or Cold

Put the lobsters in a pot and pour cold water over to cover them by 6 inches. Turn the heat on full and cook until just before the water boils. Turn off the heat and let sit according to the times below. Remove the lobsters. For cold lobster meat, cover with ice so they cool down and stop cooking.

    1-pound lobsters: 7 minutes
    2-pound lobsters: 12 minutes
    3-pound lobsters: 20 minutes

To Remove the Lobster Meat

Twist off the small legs and reserve. Cut off bits of gill sticking to the knuckle ends and discard.

Twist off the two claw arms, twist off the claws. Gently crack the claws and lift out the claw meat in one piece if possible.

Save all the juices in a bowl or on a plate with the meat.

Crack the arms and scoop out the meat.

Twist off the flaps at the end of the tail and reserve. Twist off the tail and cut through the soft shell on the underside of the tail with a knife or scissors. Do not cut through to the meat. Hold the tail in both hands and break it open. Lift out the meat. Make a ⅛-inch-deep cut down the center of the tail and pick out the intestinal tract.

Lift the main shell off the central body of the lobster and reserve for display. Scoop out any coral (red) or tomalley (green) and reserve for sauces. Clean off the feathery pieces and discard. Cut the body into 2 or 4 pieces and reserve.

Pickled Herring with New Potatoes

I should have included this recipe among my personal favorites and memories. In 1975, while in Germany for my brother's wedding, we went, after days of feasting, to a local restaurant to recover. They brought to the table an earthenware crock of herring in sour cream. It was nothing like the usual dried-out, astringent herring, but was simultaneously soft and firm. The cream was fresh and velvety. With the herring came a bowl of hot boiled Northern European potatoes, which are a dream, and draft Pilsner Urquell beer (the best beer I have ever tasted) and frozen (for a week, at least) schnapps. We drank shots of schnapps, then quickly ate some cold, creamy herring and hot potatoes covered in butter. With that same meal, a loaf of rye bread. Heaven on earth.

12	*fresh herrings*
1 pint	*white wine vinegar*
½ cup	*water*
1 tablespoon	*salt*
1	*onion, sliced*
1 stalk	*celery, chopped*
1	*carrot, peeled, sliced*
4	*bay leaves*
1 sprig	*fresh thyme*
1 tablespoon	*mustard seeds*
2	*allspice berries, crushed*
10	*peppercorns, crushed*
1 small	*lemon, sliced*
3 cups	*sour cream*
20	*new potatoes*
4 tablespoons	*butter*
	freshly ground pepper

Serves 6 to 8

Fillet the herrings. Make the marinade as follows: Bring the vinegar, water, and salt to a boil. Turn the heat off and add the onion, celery, carrot, herbs, spices, and lemon. Let cool. Put the herring in an earthenware crock or glass container and pour in the marinade. Refrigerate for 1 week.

Take the herring out of the marinade and drain on paper towels. Put a layer of sour cream in a bowl, then some herring fillets, then more cream, and so on until there are no more fillets.

Boil the potatoes in salted water until tender; drain. Toss with the butter and freshly ground pepper to taste. Serve the herring with the hot potatoes and lots of frozen schnapps or vodka and beer.

Fish Stew with Fennel Aioli

This hymn to garlic is really a white bouillabaisse, a stew of mixed whitefish, its broth thickened and enriched with the garlic mayonnaise called, in the south of France, aioli. Correctly, aioli is just garlic mayonnaise with no other flavorings but I have taken liberties throughout the book, flavoring it with whatever seems appropriate. The best fish to use for this dish would be sea bass, cod, monkfish, conger eel, halibut, pollack, haddock, and whiting.

5 pounds	*fish (see headnote)*
3½ quarts	*water*
3 tablespoons	*olive oil*
2 medium	*onions, chopped*
2	*leeks (white part only), rinsed and sliced*
2 stalks	*celery, chopped*
2	*bay leaves*
2 sprigs	*fresh thyme*
12 sprigs	*fennel*
1 tablespoon	*salt*
1 cup	*dry white wine*
2 cups	*aioli (page 36)*
2 cups	*mussels, bearded, scrubbed*
8	*langoustines or large prawns*

Serves 6 to 8

Fillet the fish and cut into 1½-inch cubes. Save the bones.

Put ½ cup water, the oil, onions, leeks, celery, bay leaves, thyme, and 3 sprigs of the fennel in a pot. Cook over low heat for 10 minutes. Do not let the vegetables brown. Add the fish bones, the remaining water, and the salt. Bring to a boil and skim the scum from the surface of the stock. Cook for 20 minutes and add the wine. Cook for another 15 minutes and strain.

Crush the remaining fennel in a mortar with a pestle and mix with the aioli. Put the fish in a pot. Taste the fish stock for salt and add more if necessary. Pour enough stock over the fish to cover by 1 inch. Add water if there is not enough. Bring to a boil over high heat and add the mussels and langoustines. Cook until the mussels open and the fish is just done. Lift the fish and shellfish into a warm soup tureen. Turn off the heat and whisk 1 cup of the fennel aioli into the broth. Pour the broth over the fish and serve with the rest of the aioli.

Seviche

One of the best seviches I ever had was eaten one morning when, with a massive hangover, I crept into the kitchen at Ventana in Big Sur. Pedro, one of the Mexican cooks, saw my condition and made me a shrimp, lettuce, lime juice, warm salsa, and shrimp stock mixture in a large wineglass. I recovered in half an hour. This seviche is the one I developed for the opening menu of the Santa Fe Bar & Grill.

2 pounds	skinned fish fillets, rock or ling cod, salmon, halibut, red snapper, haddock, bass, or grouper
1 cup	fresh lemon juice
1 cup	fresh lime juice
2	fresh serrano chilies, seeded, finely chopped
1	fresh red hot chili, seeded, finely chopped
7 tablespoons	olive oil
½ teaspoon	salt
½ teaspoon	freshly ground pepper
2 medium	red onions, peeled, thinly sliced
10	lettuce leaves, washed and dried
½ cup	salsa (page 28)
8	lime wedges
12	Niçoise olives

Serves 4–6

Cut the fish fillets into ⅜-inch cubes. Combine the fish, ½ cup of the lemon juice, the lime juice, chilies, 1 tablespoon of the olive oil, the salt, and pepper in a glass, enamel, or stainless-steel bowl and marinate for 3 to 6 hours.

Toss the red onion slices in the remaining ½ cup lemon juice and marinate for 3 hours, tossing 2 or 3 times during the marination.

Put ¼ cup of the seviche marinade into a bowl and whisk in the remaining olive oil.

Roll up the lettuce leaves and cut into very fine strips. Toss the lettuce in the marinade dressing and put some lettuce in the center of each cold plate. Put the seviche on top and the salsa on top of the seviche. Place the onions around the lettuce and garnish with the lime wedges and olives.

Lobster Gazpacho

This is a dish I designed and cooked for a group of food writers who were guests of the Campbell Soup Company at Stars in 1984. I had to come up with a soup, "something new," and I chose this over another favorite, a ragout of lobster with Belgian endive, sweet red chilies, and a cilantro hollandaise. The secret here is wonderful ripe tomatoes. You could serve this with fresh cooked prawns or crayfish tails.

1½-pound	lobster, cooked (method 2, page 72)
6 large	ripe tomatoes
1	red bell pepper
1	yellow bell pepper
1	English cucumber
	salt and freshly ground pepper
3 tablespoons	fresh lemon juice
1 tablespoon	sesame oil
8 tablespoons	olive oil
4 tablespoons each	gold, red, and black caviar for garnish
12 stems	chives

Serves 4

Shell the lobster and slice the meat (page 73).

Peel, seed, and puree the tomatoes through a food mill. Refrigerate the liquid.

Seed the bell peppers and cut into ⅛-inch dice. Peel and seed the cucumber and cut it into ⅛-inch dice. Combine the peppers and cucumber.

Mix salt and pepper to taste and 1 tablespoon of the lemon juice. Whisk in the sesame oil. Toss with the bell pepper mixture and refrigerate covered.

Mix together salt and pepper to taste, the remaining lemon juice, and 3 tablespoons of the olive oil. Pour over the lobster and toss together.

Mix the tomato puree with salt and pepper to taste and the remaining olive oil.

Pour the puree onto chilled large plates. Spoon the cucumber-pepper salad in the center. Put the lobster on the puree and garnish with the caviars and chives. Serve immediately.

Shrimp Salad with Three Mayonnaises

I have never been certain, on whatever coastline, of the difference between shrimp and prawns. My heritage is the eastern coast, so I think of shrimp as small and prawns as large—probably an unfounded assumption. In this case, use whatever fresh shrimp or prawns you can find.

32 large	*fresh shrimp in shells*
	salt and freshly ground pepper
3 tablespoons	*fresh lime or lemon juice*
6 tablespoons	*olive oil*
1½ cups	*mayonnaise (page 36)*
1 cup	*fresh basil leaves, blanched, squeezed dry, and finely chopped*
1 cup	*fresh cilantro leaves, chopped*
¼ cup	*red bell pepper puree (page 32)*
2	*ripe avocados*
12 sprigs	*fresh cilantro*

Serves 4

Put the shrimp in a pot and cover with 3 inches of water salted like seawater. Bring almost to a boil, and remove from the heat. Cover immediately and let sit for 2 minutes. Drain the shrimp and cover with ice to stop them from cooking.

Stir salt and pepper to taste into the lime juice and then whisk in the olive oil. Peel the shrimp and put them in the lime juice mixture. Save the shrimp shells, put them in a food processor, and grind them up. Sieve the shells, pressing out all the liquid. Add the reserved liquid to the marinade and discard the shell debris.

Divide the mayonnaise into thirds. Mix the basil into one part, the chopped cilantro into another, and the pepper puree into the remaining part.

Cut the avocados in half, remove the pits, and scoop out each half with a spoon. Cut each half crosswise into ⅛-inch slices. Push gently down and across on each avocado half to make a fan; then lift each half onto a plate. Put the shrimp in the inside curve of the avocado and pour the shrimp marinade over all. Garnish with the cilantro sprigs and serve with the 3 mayonnaises.

Belgian Endive Salad with Lobster

There is something irresistible about Belgian endive and lobster. Add hazelnut oil, tarragon, and a whisper of garlic, and you have an instant, outstanding Saturday lunch. The lobster essence pushes the dish way up the scale, but don't dismiss the salad if you do not have the essence. Cut the endive at the last minute so it will not brown.

1 tablespoon	*lobster essence (page 221)*
1 tablespoon	*fresh lemon juice*
½ teaspoon	*finely chopped garlic*
20 leaves	*fresh tarragon*
	salt and freshly ground pepper
1 tablespoon	*extra virgin olive oil*
3 tablespoons	*hazelnut oil*
4	*Belgian endives*
1 cup	*cooked Maine lobster meat (method 2, page 72)*
12 sprigs	*watercress for garnish*

Serves 4

Mix the lobster essence, lemon juice, garlic, tarragon, and salt and pepper to taste in a bowl. Whisk in the oils.

Cut the cores from the endives, trim away any brown spots, and then cut into julienne strips. Pour three-quarters of the sauce over the endive and toss gently. Arrange the endive on 4 chilled plates. Mix the remaining sauce with the lobster meat and put the lobster on top of the endive. Dress the watercress in the sauce remaining from the lobster, garnish the plates with the watercress, and pour over any remaining dressing.

Lobster and Rocket Salad

¼ cup	fresh lemon juice
	salt and freshly ground pepper
½ cup	hazelnut or walnut oil
1 cup	cooked Maine lobster meat (method 2, page 72)
½ cup	tomato concasse (page 220)
1 cup	mayonnaise (page 36)
2 cups	rocket (arugula) leaves
1	green bell pepper, roasted, seeded, peeled
1	red bell pepper, roasted, seeded, peeled

Serves 4

Mix the lemon juice with salt and pepper to taste in a bowl. Whisk in the oil. Add ¼ cup of the dressing to the lobster meat and marinate 30 minutes. Mix the tomato concasse into the mayonnaise and season.

Toss the rocket in some of the remaining dressing. Cut the peppers into shapes, dip in the remaining dressing, and put around the lobster. Arrange the lobster on the rocket. Serve the mayonnaise separately.

Warm Salad of Crayfish with Cucumbers and Dill

There is some controversy regarding the cooking of crayfish—whether to bring them up to the boil from cold liquid, or just to throw them in boiling liquid. I think the latter method produces the firmest flesh, and is easier to time. If you don't have crayfish, lobster would do, and substitute tarragon for the dill. If you use prawns and shrimp, substitute basil for dill. Do not hesitate with the butter. The recipe here is for a main luncheon dish. For a first course, halve the recipe.

2 quarts	court bouillon (page 221)
48	crayfish
1 cup	fish stock (page 218)
2	English cucumbers
1 tablespoon	chopped fresh dill
6 tablespoons	butter
½ cup	tomato concasse (page 220)
	salt and freshly ground pepper
32 sprigs	dill

Serves 4

Bring the court bouillon to a boil. Cook the crayfish in 2 batches for 5 minutes, or more if the liquid takes a long time to come back to a boil. Take the crayfish out and let them cool. Take the heads off and shell the tails. Save 16 of the best heads for garnish.

Put the tail shells in a food processor and grind them up. Put the debris in the fish stock and simmer for 15 minutes. Strain the stock and discard the shells.

Peel the cucumbers and cut them lengthwise in half. Scoop the seeds out with a spoon. Make "noodles" of them in the food processor, using the julienne disk, or with a mandoline.

Heat the fish stock in a sauté pan. Add the cucumber noodles and cook for 5 minutes. Add the chopped dill, butter, and tomato concasse; season with salt and pepper. Toss or stir together until the butter is incorporated. Add the crayfish tails and cook, tossing constantly, until the tails are heated through, about 2 minutes. Arrange on plates and garnish with the dill sprigs and crayfish heads.

Warm Salad of Lobster and Avocado

This is a main-course recipe. If you want to serve it as a first course, use only one lobster for four people. The avocado in the photograph is garnished with lobster sauce, to be used only if you have lobster essence (page 221)—don't ignore the recipe if you don't have any.

2	*ripe avocados*
½ cup	*lobster essence (page 221)*
¼ pound	*butter*
2 tablespoons	*chopped shallots*
½ cup	*fish stock (page 218)*
12 leaves	*tarragon*
½ cup	*tomato concasse (page 220)*
2 one-pound	*lobsters, partially cooked (method 1, page 72)*
	salt and freshly ground pepper

Serves 4

Cut the avocados in half, remove the pits, and scoop out each half with a spoon. Cut each half crosswise into ⅛-inch slices. Push gently down and across on each avocado half to make a fan. Lift the avocado fans onto 4 warm plates.

Heat the lobster essence in a saucepan and whisk in 4 tablespoons of the butter. Keep warm.

Heat 1 tablespoon of the butter in a sauté pan. Add the shallots and 2 tablespoons of the fish stock. Cover and sweat the shallots over very low heat for 10 minutes. Remove the cover, add the rest of the stock, the tarragon and tomato, and turn the heat to high. Cook for 2 minutes. Add the remaining butter and cook for 1 minute. Add the lobster and cook another minute *only*. Spoon the lobster mixture around the avocados; then pour the lobster essence sauce over the avocados.

Toasted Lobster Sandwich

This sandwich is very good as presented here, but can be varied by placing hot cooked bacon under the lobster, putting caviar on top of it, or changing the chervil mayonnaise to black bean mayonnaise (page 36).

½ tablespoon	fresh lemon juice
¼ teaspoon	salt
2 pinches	freshly ground pepper
1 tablespoon	olive oil
1½ pounds	cooked lobster meat (method 2, page 72)
½ cup	fresh chervil leaves, finely chopped
½ cup	mayonnaise (page 36)
8 slices	country-style bread
2 tablespoons	butter, melted
¼ cup	tomato concasse (page 220)
12 sprigs	chervil

Serves 4

Mix the lemon juice, salt, and pepper in a bowl. Whisk in the oil. Toss the lobster meat in the mixture.

Mix the chopped chervil into the mayonnaise and then fold in the lobster. Brush the bread with the butter. Toast the buttered sides of the bread. Put the lobster meat on one slice. Spoon the tomato concasse over the lobster and grind some pepper over it. Top with the chervil sprigs and cover with the other slice of bread.

Tartare of Salmon and Tuna

In another version of this very popular dish, it is eaten with very cold, fresh oysters.

1	English cucumber
	salt and freshly ground pepper
½ cup	fresh lemon juice
2 tablespoons	sesame oil
8 ounces	salmon fillet, boned and skinned
8 ounces	tuna fillet, skinned, all dark meat removed
2 tablespoons	olive oil
¼ cup	tomato concasse (page 220)
	rocket (arugula), mustard or lime flowers, and chopped chives

Serves 4

Peel the cucumber, score lengthwise with a fork, and cut into $\frac{1}{16}$-inch-thick slices. Whisk salt and pepper into ¼ cup of the lemon juice; then whisk in the sesame oil. Toss the cucumber slices in the sauce and let stand for 1 hour.

Finely chop the salmon and tuna separately. Into each of the chopped fish, stir half the remaining lemon juice, a tablespoon of olive oil, and salt and pepper to taste.

To serve, arrange the cucumber on each plate with the slices overlapping. Spoon the two tartares in separate mounds in the center of each plate. Dress the tomato concasse in the bowl in which the cucumber marinated, and put 1 tablespoon on each plate. Garnish with rocket, mustard or lime flowers, and chives.

Tartare of Salmon and Tuna.

My Favorite Fish Soup

This is the soup I cooked for Julia Child in the south of France and later made for Elizabeth David in London with success. So I call it "My Favorite Fish Soup." If you go all the way and use shellfish as well as fish carcasses, the ingredients are costly. A very good, though not sublime, version can be achieved using only the heads and backbones of non-oily white-fleshed fish: cod, bass, rockfish, conger eel, flatfish.

The soup is not clear because it has "body" from a pureeing of the carcasses after they are cooked.

You will need a food mill.

6 pounds	fish carcasses and heads
½ cup	olive oil
2 large	onions, peeled, thinly sliced
4 large	ripe tomatoes, chopped
10 cloves	garlic
3 sprigs	fennel tops
1 large	bouquet garni of thyme, bay leaves, leek tops, parsley
1 piece	orange zest, 3 by 1 inch
2 quarts	rich fish stock (page 218)
½ teaspoon	saffron threads
1 cup	dry white wine
½ pound	shiitake, domestic, or field mushrooms
1½ teaspoons	chopped fresh thyme
	salt and freshly ground pepper
½ pound	small pasta shapes
1 cup	rouille (page 36)
24	croutons

Serves 6 to 8

Remove all innards and gills from the fish heads and carcasses.

Put ¼ cup of the olive oil, the onions, tomatoes, garlic, fennel, bouquet garni, orange zest, and ½ cup of the fish stock in a pot. Cook over low heat for 5 minutes. Add the fish carcasses and heads and remaining stock. Bring to a boil and skim any scum from the surface of the stock. Simmer for 20 minutes. Warm the saffron in the white wine. Add the wine to the stock and simmer 25 minutes more.

Meanwhile, marinate the mushrooms in the remaining ¼ cup olive oil, the thyme, and salt and pepper to taste for 10 minutes; broil until tender.

Cook the pasta as directed for the pasta salad on page 60. Slice the mushrooms and hold.

Take the stock off the heat and put the fish and broth through a food mill fitted with a medium-hole disk or press through a sieve. Clean the pot and return the broth. Add the mushrooms and pasta and bring to a boil. Correct the seasoning if necessary and serve very hot in large soup plates. Spoon the rouille into the soup, or put the croutons in the soup and spoon the rouille on top of them.

If you want truly amazing fish soup, do it all over again, using this soup as the fish stock to pour over more fish bones.

Mark Franz's Calamari with Sweet and Hot Chilies

I have found that if you call calamari "squid," no one will eat it. An absolute mystery to me: I like the word "squid." In Australia when I was a child, they called rabbit "bush chicken" so that people would eat it, yet no one in America I have met has a problem with eating rabbit. Fortunately, squid is so wonderful and there are so many ways to prepare it and it is so inexpensive, I do not mind calling it calamari if that is what it takes for people to eat it. I love the version with tomatoes, garlic, basil, and lots of butter. It is great with Chinese black beans, ginger, and garlic; it is surprisingly good cooked for a long time in red wine with leeks; but it has a special affinity with chilies, dried or fresh. This recipe could very well have an ancho chili mayonnaise or butter sauce drizzled over (page 118), or sour cream with the terrifying but superb smoked chilies called chipotles.

4 pounds	fresh squid
2	Fresno chilies
2	Anaheim chilies
1	red bell pepper
2	pasilla chilies
¼ cup	olive oil
	salt
4 cloves	garlic, finely chopped
2-ounce piece	fresh ginger, peeled, finely chopped
½ cup	fish stock (page 218)
6 tablespoons	butter

Serves 4

Cut the tentacles away from the head of each squid just below the eyes; remove the "beak." Rinse, drain, and reserve the tentacles. Pull out all the innards and the translucent membrane in the body of each squid. Rinse under cold water and drain; cut crosswise into ½-inch-wide slices.

Cut the stems from the chilies and pepper, seed them, and cut into long thin slices.

Heat the oil in a sauté pan over high heat until the oil is very hot but not smoking, about 30 seconds. Season the squid slices and tentacles, put them in the pan, and toss them in the hot oil over high heat for 2 minutes. Lift all the squid out with a skimmer or slotted spoon and put it in a bowl. Turn down the heat to medium and put in the chilies, pepper, garlic, and ginger and cook for 5 minutes. Add the fish stock and any juices that have collected from the squid to the pan. Cook over high heat for 2 minutes. Add the butter and squid and toss together until the butter is incorporated. Check for seasoning and serve.

Grilled Calamari with Lobster Mayonnaise

In a sense, this dish is like a warm salad, with tomato and purple basil underneath the hot grilled calamari. There is a play of temperatures, as well as the different textures of smooth mayonnaise and tart vinaigrette. If you don't have lobster essence, use a basil, olive, anchovy-rosemary, or lemon–black pepper mayonnaise.

4 pounds	fresh squid
1 cup	olive oil
2 tablespoons	finely chopped fresh marjoram leaves
1 cup	mayonnaise (page 36)
⅓ cup	lobster essence (page 221)
	salt and freshly ground pepper
¼ cup	fresh lemon juice
2 cups	tomato concasse (page 220)
1 cup	whole purple or green basil leaves

Serves 4

Clean the squid as directed in the preceding recipe, but leave the bodies whole. Combine ½ cup of the oil and the marjoram in a bowl. Stir in the squid and marinate in the refrigerator for 1 hour.

Mix the mayonnaise and lobster essence; cover and refrigerate for 1 hour.

Start a charcoal fire or heat the broiler.

Thread the squid heads and bodies alternately on skewers, putting the skewers through the closed or tail end of the bodies.

Mix salt and pepper to taste into the lemon juice and whisk in the remaining olive oil. Mix in the tomato and all but a few of the basil leaves.

Grill or broil the squid for 2 minutes on each side. Put the tomato salad on warm plates, then the squid in the center of the salad. Spoon some of the mayonnaise over the squid. Serve the rest separately. Garnish the plates with the remaining basil leaves.

Overleaf Clockwise from top left: Grilled Salmon with Cucumbers and Black Bean Sauce (recipe on page 88); Grilled Calamari with Lobster Mayonnaise; Salmon Stew with Artichokes and Rose Peppercorns (recipe on page 88); Mark Franz's Calamari with Sweet and Hot Chilies.

Grilled Salmon with Cucumbers and Black Bean Sauce (pictured on page 86)

Of the hundreds of ways to serve grilled salmon, the following offers one of my favorite taste combinations. For a wonderful variation, put basil leaves, salt, pepper, and olive oil under rashers of bacon laid across a fillet, and then place under the broiler. The salmon comes out moist and perfumed with basil and the smoke from the bacon. A mint hollandaise on poached salmon is also very good, and Chinese black bean sauce made quite mild is haunting in taste and beautiful in color against the pale pink fish.

4 8-ounce fillets	salmon, about 2 inches thick
6 large sprigs	mint
¼ cup	olive oil
½ cup	black bean sauce (page 30)
2	cucumbers, preferably English
8 thick slices	bacon or pancetta
1½ cups	fish stock (page 218)
6 tablespoons	butter
¼ cup	tomato concasse (page 220)

Serves 4

Skin the salmon fillets.

Pull the leaves from the mint sprigs and set aside. Chop the stems coarsely and mix with the olive oil. Smear the mixture over the salmon fillets and marinate for 30 minutes.

Start a charcoal fire or heat the broiler or grill.

Heat the black bean sauce and keep warm.

Peel the cucumbers and cut lengthwise in half. Scoop out the seeds with a spoon and cut crosswise into ⅙-inch slices.

Lay the bacon on a rack and bake or broil until just crisp. Keep warm.

Wipe the marinade off the fish and put the fish, skin side up, on a hot grill at a 45° angle. Cook 2 minutes, turn 45°, and cook another 2 minutes. Flip the fillets onto the other side. Cook another 4 to 6 minutes for medium rare.

When you flip the fillets, put the fish stock in a sauté pan over high heat. Bring to a boil and put in the cucumbers. Turn the heat to medium and cook until tender, about 4 minutes. Add the mint leaves and stir in the butter until it is incorporated. Check the seasoning.

Spoon the cucumbers and sauce onto warm plates. Put the fish on top of the cucumbers and then the bacon on the salmon. Drizzle the black bean sauce over the fish and dot the plates with the tomato.

Salmon Stew with Artichokes and Rose Peppercorns

(pictured on page 87)

I can never keep track of whether rose peppercorns are legal or not. I know they are not peppercorns at all, and that they come and go in legality and fashion. I have always liked them, especially with salmon (but then any pepper is good with salmon), and still use them, if only for myself. I like artichokes with salmon as well, but another reason to put them in this dish is that it already has two or three strikes against it in terms of a fine wine—the salmon and all that liquid with onions—so one might as well go all the way, put the artichokes in as well, and enjoy the delights of a very hearty, powerful white wine or a cool light Gamay or Beaujolais.

1½ pounds	salmon fillets
2 tablespoons	olive oil
1 tablespoon	fresh thyme or savory leaves
4 large	artichokes
1	lemon, halved
24 small	white or pearl onions
3 cups	fish stock (page 218)
6 tablespoons	butter
2 tablespoons	rose peppercorns
	salt and freshly ground pepper
8 small sprigs	Italian parsley or chervil

Serves 4

Skin the salmon fillets and cut into 1-inch cubes. Combine the oil and thyme in a bowl and toss thoroughly with the salmon pieces.

Cut away the leaves of the artichokes and trim each one down to the base or bottom. Cut out the choke and rub the artichokes thoroughly with the lemon. Cook in salted boiling water with the lemon until tender, about 15 minutes. Drain and let cool; then cut crosswise into ⅛-inch slices.

Peel the onions and cook in the fish stock until tender. Drain and reserve the onions.

Put the salmon in a sauté pan and pour over the fish stock. Bring the stock to a simmer over high heat; immediately turn down the heat to low. Add the artichokes and onions and cook another minute. Spoon into warm soup plates, leaving the liquid in the pan. Turn the heat to very high. Add the butter and peppercorns to the liquid and boil until the butter is totally incorporated. Pour over the salmon in the plates, season to taste, and garnish with the parsley or chervil.

Mussels in Cataplana

If you don't have a cataplana (the cooking vessel in the photograph), which I don't expect anyone to have, just use a covered saucepan. The method of cooking used here is like the classic *moules à la marinière,* with white wine, shallots, herbs, and butter, still one of the best ways to cook mussels. Another way saw the light of invention and day recently at Stars, when a line cook, drawing on the *moules* tradition and on saffron with mussels, but wanting something new and reflecting current interest in Indian food, the Far East, and Mexico, made curried creamed mussels with a cilantro pesto drizzled over the top. It was fantastic. This recipe, however, is much less rich and complicated. The mussels cook quickly, so the onions and chilies must be sliced paper thin. Mussels vary in size, so I recommend twelve to fifteen per person.

4 pounds	mussels
1 large	red onion, peeled, very thinly sliced
3	Anaheim chilies, stemmed, seeded, very thinly sliced
2 cloves	garlic, finely chopped
1 cup	tomato concasse (page 220)
½ cup	olive oil
¼ cup	dry white wine
4 sprigs	fresh thyme
4 sprigs	parsley
2 sprigs	fresh tarragon
2	bay leaves

Serves 4

Beard and scrub the mussels.

If you are using a saucepan with a lid, combine all the ingredients except the mussels in the pan and cook covered over medium heat for 2 minutes. Add the mussels and cover the pot tightly. Cook over high heat, shaking the pot every 30 seconds, until all the mussels open, about 5 minutes. If 1 or 2 mussels are reluctant to open, don't overcook the others waiting for those 2 to cook—just pry them open with a knife. Check to see if the broth needs salt and serve.

If you are using a cataplana, put all the ingredients in and clamp down the lid. Cook over high heat for 5 minutes, shaking the cataplana every 30 seconds. Open carefully, check for seasoning, and serve.

Grilled Swordfish with Rosemary Mayonnaise

There are as many accompaniments to grilled swordfish as there are combinations of ingredients, but the most successful in my restaurants have involved some form of ratatouille: eggplant either pureed and made spicy with coriander or roasted with garlic and herb oil, or mixed summer squash ragouts with butter and powerful fresh herbs. Because of its richness, swordfish certainly needs and can handle strong herbs, and I especially like rosemary with it. It is great with tapenade (a puree of black olives and capers) and really cries out for the saltiness and mystery of good anchovies. Buy canned salted *whole* anchovies, fillet them yourself with thumb and forefinger under running cold water, and hold them in oil. Far less salty or brine-filled than the canned fillets, they have a velvety texture and far more interesting flavor. Since Richard Olney showed me this method, I have won over hordes of people who "hate" anchovies. If you can find the rare pink swordfish from the Gulf Stream, buy that.

4 8-ounce pieces	*swordfish, 1 inch thick (or one 2-pound steak, to be carved when cooked)*
2 tablespoons	*mixed fresh thyme and marjoram leaves, chopped*
¼ cup	*olive oil*
6 medium	*Japanese eggplants, sliced lengthwise (or 1 large regular eggplant, cut into ¼-inch slices)*
¼ cup	*herb oil (page 222)*
3	*salted anchovies, filleted, soaked 10 minutes and drained (or 6 anchovy fillets)*
2 tablespoons	*fresh rosemary leaves, blanched*
1 cup	*mayonnaise (page 36)*
1 cup	*tomato vinaigrette (page 32)*

Serves 4

Rub the swordfish with a mixture of the thyme, marjoram and oil and let marinate for 30 minutes. Paint the eggplant slices with the herb oil and marinate 30 minutes.

Puree or very finely chop the anchovies and rosemary. Mix into the mayonnaise and let sit 30 minutes.

Start a charcoal fire or heat the grill or broiler.

Season and grill the eggplant on the coolest part of the fire for about 5 minutes on each side. Push to the side of the grill to keep warm. Cook the fish on the hottest part of the grill, turning it twice on each side to get grill marks if you want to, for no more than 5 to 6 minutes on each side, because swordfish should be medium rare. Cook a little longer if you have just taken the fish out of the refrigerator, but ideally the fish has been at room temperature for 15 minutes before you cook it.

Put the fish and eggplant on warm plates. Spoon some of the tomato vinaigrette over the fish and some mayonnaise over that. Serve both sauces separately.

Grilled Dungeness Crab

Any large fresh crabs will do here, if you can't obtain Dungeness.

2	live Dungeness crabs, 2 to 3 pounds each
6	serrano chilies
8 to 10 cloves	garlic, peeled
½ cup	olive oil
½ teaspoon	salt
1 cup	salsa (page 28)
	crab butter (optional)

Serves 4

Divide the crabs in half by holding the claw and legs on 1 side of the crab in each hand and smashing the underside of the crab against the edge of a table or sink. Then twist the 2 sides in alternate directions, pulling the body away from the top shell. Clean out the body parts, removing the gills and other debris. Scoop out the coral from the shell and save for crab butter (recipe follows), if you wish. Discard the shell. Crack the claws and legs with a cracker or the flat of a heavy knife, being careful to keep the pieces intact.

Coarsely chop the chilies and garlic and combine them with the oil and salt in a large bowl. Toss the crabs in the oil mixture, making sure the cut sides are well coated. Marinate the crabs for at least 1 hour.

Meanwhile, heat the broiler or start a charcoal fire.

When the flames have died down, grill the crabs about 3 minutes on each side. Then turn them so that the cut sides are facing the grill and cook for another 2 to 3 minutes. The crabs are cooked when the meat is opaque and the shells red.

Serve with the salsa and crab butter.

Crab Butter

1 pound	butter
	coral from 2 crabs
1 teaspoon	fresh lemon juice
	salt and freshly ground pepper

Melt the butter over low heat. Skim the film from the top and pour off the clear butter, leaving the milky residue in the pan. Whisk the coral into the clarified butter over low heat; add the lemon juice and salt and pepper to taste. Keep warm.

Fish "Sausage" with Sorrel and Lobster Sauce

The technique for success here is to process the mousseline very cold and never let the poaching water boil. The water is maintained at 180 degrees and the internal temperature of the mousseline should not go over 150 degrees. This is a spectacular dish and very simple to put together, once you have mastered the more complicated basic techniques and preparations.

3 cups	mousseline of sole (page 218)
5 tablespoons	butter
¼ cup	water
3 cups	sorrel leaves, stemmed
1 one-pound	Maine lobster, partially cooked (method 1, page 72)
5 cups	fish velouté (page 221)
½ cup	heavy cream
pinch	cayenne pepper
	salt and freshly ground pepper

Serves 4

Prepare the mousseline of sole.

Put 1 tablespoon of the butter, ¼ cup water, and the sorrel leaves in a stainless-steel saucepan. Cover and stew gently, stirring occasionally, until the leaves are reduced to a puree. Uncover, increase the heat, and cook until most of the juices are evaporated and the sorrel is the consistency of thick mayonnaise. Cool and fold the sorrel puree into 1½ cups (half) of the mousseline. Keep chilled.

Prepare the lobster and reserve any juices. Cut the lobster meat into ⅛-inch pieces. Crush the shells in a food processor and add with the reserved lobster juices to the fish velouté. Simmer for 30 minutes. Strain, discard the shells, and chill the sauce.

Brush a piece of parchment with 2 tablespoons of the butter. With a pastry bag, pipe out a 1½-inch strip of the sole mousseline about 10 inches long and next to it a similar strip of the sorrel mousseline. Place the lobster meat down the center on top of the mousseline. Pipe 2 more strips of the white and green mousselines, but reverse them so that the green is on the white and vice versa. Cut the paper lengthwise 2 inches from one edge of the mousseline and fold over the remaining edge up over the mousseline. The colder the mousseline, the easier this will be. Roll up the whole sausage and twist the ends. Roll up in a piece of aluminum foil and twist those ends as well. Refrigerate the roll about 30 minutes to firm up the mousseline.

To cook, place the "sausage" in cold salted water. Bring the water to 180°F, or just below simmering, over high heat. Reduce the heat immediately and cook until the interior of the sausage is 150°F, about 20 minutes. Test the sausage by poking the thermometer directly through the foil and paper into the center of the roll. Remove from the liquid and keep warm.

Add the cream to the lobster sauce and bring to a boil. Add the cayenne and season with salt and pepper. Whisk in the remaining butter.

Unwrap the sausage, put on warm platter, and slice. Pour some sauce around the sausage and pass the rest.

Grilled Scallops with Tarragon Sauce

24	sea scallops
¼ cup	olive oil
4 branches	fresh tarragon, stemmed, stems and leaves saved
2 cups	fish stock (page 218)
½ cup	dry white wine
2 large	shallots, peeled, chopped
1 sprig	fresh thyme
1	bay leaf
½ bunch	watercress leaves
8 medium	spinach leaves
¼ cup packed	chervil leaves (if available); otherwise substitute watercress and spinach leaves
½ pound	butter
	salt and freshly ground pepper
¼ cup	red bell pepper puree (page 32)
4 tablespoons	salmon or steelhead roe

Serves 4

Toss the scallops in a mixture of the oil and chopped tarragon stems. Let marinate for 1 hour and discard the tarragon. Put 6 or 7 scallops on each of 4 skewers.

While the scallops are marinating, make the sauces. Put the fish stock, wine, shallots, thyme, and bay leaf in a saucepan and cook over medium heat for 20 minutes. Strain the liquid, discarding the herbs and shallots.

Heat the grill or broiler.

Blanch the tarragon leaves, watercress, spinach, and chervil in boiling water for 2 minutes. Drain and cool under cold water for 1 minute. Squeeze dry and chop fine. Add the herbs to the reduced fish stock and simmer 5 minutes. Cut up 10 tablespoons of the butter and whisk into the stock over low heat. Season and keep the sauce warm.

Heat the red bell pepper puree, reduce the heat, and whisk in the remaining 6 tablespoons butter. Season it.

Brush the scallops with the oil remaining from the marination. Season the scallops and grill or broil until the scallops are still a little translucent in the center, about 3 minutes each side. Spoon the tarragon sauce on warm plates and put the scallops in the center of each plate. Spoon some of the pepper sauce over the scallops and place some of the salmon roe on each plate.

Poached Turbot with Lobster

2 teaspoons	fresh lemon juice
¼ cup	lobster essence (page 221)
1 pound 4 ounces	butter, cut into 1-ounce pieces
	salt and freshly ground pepper
½ cup	mixed fresh green herb leaves: parsley, watercress, tarragon, chives, and chervil
2	egg yolks
8 small	rose fir or red new potatoes
4 ounces	small French green beans
1½ cups	fish stock (page 218)
1 tablespoon	finely chopped shallots
4 pieces (5–6 ounces each)	turbot, halibut, or other flat fish fillet, skinned

Serves 4

Add 1 teaspoon of lemon juice to the lobster essence and bring to a simmer in a small noncorrosive saucepan. Reduce the heat to low and whisk in 8 ounces of butter, 1 ounce at a time. Do not let the sauce boil. Season with salt and pepper. Hold over warm water or in a warm place.

Blanch the herb leaves in boiling water for 30 seconds. Drain, rinse under cold water, and squeeze dry. Chop the herbs very fine and combine them with the egg yolks and the remaining teaspoon of lemon juice in a stainless-steel bowl. Set the bowl over a pot of simmering water and whisk constantly until the mixture starts to thicken. Do not let the egg curdle. Whisk in 8 ounces of butter, 1 ounce at a time. If the sauce becomes too thick, thin it with a few drops of warm stock or water. Season with salt and pepper and transfer it to a clean bowl. Cover the surface of the sauce with plastic wrap or a thin film of butter to prevent it from forming a skin. Hold over warm water.

Cook the potatoes in salted water until done, about 10 minutes. Drain and peel if you wish. Keep warm.

Stem the beans and have ready boiling salted water.

Put the fish stock, shallots, and 2 ounces of butter in a large sauté pan. The pan should be large enough to hold the fish in one layer. Lightly salt and pepper the fish fillets and put them in the stock skin side down. Bring the liquid to a low simmer. Cover the pan and cook until the fish is done, about 2 minutes. Remove the fish from the stock and drain. Reserve the stock.

While the fish is poaching, cook the beans until done, 3 to 4 minutes. Drain them well and toss in a bowl with 1 ounce of butter. Season. Cut the potatoes in half, toss in the remaining 1 ounce of butter, and season.

Have ready 4 warm plates. Sauce the plates with the lobster sauce first. Place the fish on top and surround with the vegetables. Spoon the hollandaise on top of the fish and serve.

Catfish with Mark Franz's Black Bean Sauce

The first fish we cooked whole and served to the public at the Santa Fe Bar & Grill was viewed with great skepticism by myself (though I loved the idea) and the waiters (who were afraid the public would leave). Mark Franz, one of the chefs, prevailed and created this spectacular sauce, with the help of some favorite memories of Hong Kong, where we introduced the food of the Santa Fe Bar & Grill to the Mandarin Hotel in 1984. The first fish was a pike, and we later used catfish, French bream, and others. Only catfish needs skinning. The skin on the other fish becomes crisp and very tasty. The dish needs a good beer, and lots of it.

4 whole	catfish
1 gallon	peanut oil
½ cup	cornstarch
1 teaspoon	salt
2 cups	fish stock (page 218)
3 cloves	garlic, finely chopped
2-ounce piece	ginger, peeled, finely chopped
½ cup	Chinese fermented black beans, soaked in water 1 hour and drained
1 teaspoon	Chinese chili paste
½ cup	tomato concasse (page 220)
2 tablespoons	butter
2 tablespoons	sesame oil
2 tablespoons	chopped fresh parsley

Serves 4

Gut and skin the catfish.

Heat the oil in a heavy casserole or large wok to 375°F. Season the cornstarch with the salt. Roll the fish in the cornstarch, shake off the excess, and set aside.

Put the fish stock, garlic, and ginger in a sauté pan over high heat. Bring to a boil and cook for 3 minutes.

Put the fish in the hot oil, taking great care not to get burned in case the oil boils up and over. Cook for 8 minutes.

While the fish is cooking, add the black beans and chili paste to the stock mixture. Cook 1 minute, add the tomato, butter, and sesame oil. Stir to incorporate the butter and pour the sauce equally onto 4 warm plates.

Lift the fish out of the oil, drain for a second on paper towels, and put the fish on the sauce. Garnish each fish with parsley.

Tarpon Springs Soup

This is an adaptation of a recipe from a Florida cookbook I read in preparation for the first dinner I gave in the series of "Dinners from the Regions of America" at the Santa Fe Bar & Grill in 1982–83. It is delicious and has its Tarpon Springs and therefore Greek influence in the lemon–egg–garlic enriching and thickening treatment at the end. Sea bass, monkfish, lingcod, or halibut would do in place of the red snapper, but not as well.

2 pounds	red snapper fillets, skinned, cut into ½-inch cubes
1 large	red onion, peeled, finely chopped
2 stalks	celery, finely chopped
2	bay leaves
1 teaspoon	fresh oregano or marjoram leaves, chopped
3 sprigs	parsley, stemmed, chopped
1 teaspoon	fresh thyme leaves, chopped
¼ cup	olive oil
3 cups	fish stock (page 218)
1 teaspoon	salt
3	egg yolks
1	lemon, juiced
2 cloves	garlic, peeled, very finely chopped freshly ground pepper

Serves 4

Mix the fish, onion, celery, and herbs together and let marinate for 1 hour. Then separate the vegetables from the fish and put them in a pot. Add the oil, ¼ cup of the fish stock, bay leaves and other herbs from the marinade. Cover and sweat over low heat for 15 minutes.

Add the fish, remaining fish stock, and 1 teaspoon salt to the pot. Poach gently until the fish is opaque throughout and just cooked, about 7 minutes. Remove the fish, leaving the soup in the pot. Beat the egg yolks, lemon juice, and garlic together. Bring the soup to a boil, turn off the heat, and add the egg mixture. Stir until the soup thickens a bit. Check the seasoning and return the fish to the soup. Serve immediately.

Soft-Shell Crabs with Tomato and Basil

Soft-shell crabs can be sautéed or grilled, but deep frying, for me, gives the most even cooking and the crispest results. Crabs placed on top of a sauce, as they are in this recipe, do not become soggy, as they might if the sauce were poured over them.

8 small	soft-shell crabs, cleaned
1 cup	fresh Italian parsley leaves
1 cup	aioli (page 36)
½ gallon	peanut oil
1 cup	flour
¼ cup	fish stock (page 218)
4 cloves	garlic, peeled, finely chopped
1 cup	tomato concasse (page 220)
1 cup	fresh basil leaves salt and freshly ground pepper
6 tablespoons	sweet butter

Serves 4

Clean the crabs by lifting up the side flaps and pulling off the feathery gills. Remove the flap underneath. Rinse in cold water.

Puree the parsley in a mortar and pestle or in a food processor with the aioli. If using the mortar, mix the parsley puree into the aioli. Thin with a little water to a pouring consistency.

Heat the oil to 375°F. Very lightly dust the crabs with flour and immediately but carefully put in the hot oil. Fry the crabs for 3 minutes, then turn and cook 3 minutes more. Remove from the oil and drain on toweling or a rack.

While the crabs are frying, cook the fish stock and garlic over high heat for 1 minute. Add the tomato and the basil leaves, making sure all the basil is immediately submerged in the liquid so it doesn't turn black. Season the sauce and stir in the butter to make a liaison.

Pour the sauce on 4 warm plates and put the crabs on top. Drizzle the parsley sauce over the crabs.

Soft-Shell Crabs with Tomato and Basil.

Grilled Spiced Shrimp with Pearl Onions

24 large	prawns or shrimp
½ cup	olive oil
⅛ teaspoon	ground cinnamon
⅛ teaspoon	ground nutmeg
4 whole	cloves, crushed
1 pinch	cayenne pepper
1 tablespoon	dark rum
¼ pound	butter, softened
1 pound	pearl onions
2½ cups	fish stock (page 218)
2 tablespoons	flour
1 sprig	fresh thyme
1	bay leaf
½ cup	heavy cream
	salt and freshly ground pepper
½ cup	loosely packed fresh parsley leaves, finely chopped

Serves 4

Peel and devein the shrimp.

Combine the oil, spices, and rum. Marinate the shrimp in this mixture for 30 minutes. Drain the shrimp and mix the marinade into 4 tablespoons of the butter. Set aside.

Peel the onions and make a cross on the bottom of each. Place onions in a saucepan with ½ cup of the fish stock and 2 tablespoons of the butter. Cover and cook them very slowly over low heat until the onions are soft, about 15 minutes.

Make a velouté (page 221) with the remaining 2 tablespoons butter, the flour, and the remaining 2 cups fish stock. Add the thyme and bay leaf and any liquid from the onions. Bring to a simmer and cook for 20 minutes, skimming the surface as needed. Add the cream and simmer another 10 minutes. Strain through a fine strainer into another pan and add the onions.

Start a charcoal fire or heat the broiler.

Thread 6 shrimp on each of 4 skewers and lightly salt and pepper. Grill over a medium charcoal fire or broil for 1 to 2 minutes on each side.

Heat the onions and taste for seasoning. Remove the shrimp from the skewers and arrange them in the center of each plate. Arrange onions on the side. Place a spoonful of the reserved marinade butter on the shrimp and sprinkle the parsley all around.

Mixed Shellfish Plate

Although I have used prawns, crabs, and scallops in this recipe, you can easily substitute lobster, mussels (which you can cook in a deep-fry basket on top of the grill), razor clams, oysters, and any other shellfish. Cooking them in the shell preserves all the juices, and as they cook, the smoke from the wood or charcoal gives the shellfish a wonderful taste. Save the shrimp shells for making essence or soup.

2	Dungeness or similar crabs or 8 crab claws
16	fresh prawns or shrimp in the shell
8	sea scallops
1 clove	garlic, peeled, finely chopped
2 sprigs	fresh thyme, finely chopped
4 sprigs	fresh fennel tops, chopped
¼ teaspoon	saffron threads
1 cup	olive oil
	salt and freshly ground pepper
1 tablespoon	ground cumin
¾ cup	mayonnaise (page 36)
½ cup	tomatillo salsa (page 29)
16	lemon wedges

Serves 4

Divide the crabs in half by holding the claw and legs on each side of the crab in 1 hand and smashing the underside of the crab against the edge of a table or sink. Then twist the 2 sides in alternate directions, pulling the body away from the top shell. Clean out the body parts, removing the gills and other debris. Scoop the coral from the shell and save for crab butter (page 92), if you wish. Discard the shell. Crack the claws and legs with a cracker or the flat of a heavy knife, being careful to keep the pieces intact. If you are using claws only, crack them and the knuckles.

Thread 4 skewers with 4 shrimp each. Thread another 4 skewers with 2 scallops each.

Mix the garlic, thyme, fennel, saffron, oil, and salt and pepper together. Brush the marinade over all the shellfish and let marinate for 1 hour, turning the shellfish several times.

Mix the cumin and mayonnaise together and let sit 1 hour for the flavors to develop.

Heat the grill or broiler.

Put the crab on the grill and cook 3 minutes. Turn the crab over and put on the shrimp and scallops. Grill them just until cooked through, about 2 minutes on each side, and the crab 6 to 8 minutes total.

Spoon the cumin mayonnaise and the tomatillo salsa in little ramekins and put 1 of each on 4 warm plates. Put the shellfish on the plates and serve immediately. Pass lemon wedges and hot, damp napkins.

Grilled Spiced Shrimp with Pearl Onions.

Fish Paillard with Ginger, Garlic, and Tomatoes

What black bean cake did for the Santa Fe Bar & Grill in Berkeley, this paillard of fish did for Stars in San Francisco. I developed it with the same purpose: to have at the opening of a restaurant a fast, new, easily cooked, and easily understood dish. It was an instant hit, and can be with you at home. With a little advance chopping and slicing, you have a winner in five minutes. I call this dish a "paillard" because the piece of fish is cut like a paillard of veal—in a very thin slice and pounded even thinner, to use James Beard's words. It is so thin that you do not have to use a pan to cook the fish, and that is why you can't overcook it. The heat of the plate and the hot sauce poured over the paillard will do all the cooking. The original recipe had lobster butter drizzled over it, and since then it has also featured fresh chilies, Chinese black beans, and most of the other ingredients that recur throughout this book.

4 two-ounce slices	*salmon, tuna, halibut, grouper, red snapper, sturgeon, sea bass, or albacore, skinned, boneless; no thicker than ¼ inch*
6 tablespoons	*butter*
	salt and freshly ground pepper
1 cup	*fish stock (page 218)*
2-ounce piece	*fresh ginger, peeled, finely chopped*
3 cloves	*garlic, finely chopped*
⅔ cup	*tomato concasse (page 220)*
12 sprigs	*fresh cilantro*

Serves 4

Heat the broiler or oven.

Pound the fish slices until they are evenly ⅛ inch thick. Spread 4 heat-resistant plates with ½ teaspoon of the butter each.

Put the plates in the oven or under the broiler until hot. Season the paillards with salt and pepper and put 1 on each plate. Mix the fish stock, ginger, garlic, and tomato in a sauté pan. Bring to a boil and cook 2 minutes. Whisk the remaining butter into the sauté pan. Turn the pieces of fish over on the plates and pour the sauce over the fish. By the time you garnish the plates with the cilantro, the fish will be done.

Brioches with Marrow, Lobster, Poached Garlic, and Chervil

This is a dish I created for the opening of Stars. At first I wanted to use puree of salt cod, but I decided on lobster as safer.

4	*brioches*
1 1½-pound	*lobster, cooked (method 2, page 72) in salted water, cooled, meat removed, legs saved for garnish*
12 cloves	*garlic, peeled*
1½ cups	*fish stock (page 218)*
½ cup	*Italian parsley leaves*
1 cup	*fresh chervil leaves*
½ pound	*sweet butter*
	salt and freshly ground pepper
½ cup	*lobster essence (page 221)*
3 tablespoons	*dry white wine*
8	*beef marrow medallions*

Serves 4

Cut off the tops of the brioches and hollow out the interiors.

Slice the lobster tail into ¼-inch thick medallions. Cut the claws in half.

Poach the garlic cloves in ½ cup fish stock until soft (about 10 minutes). Add the garlic and 1 tablespoon of the poaching liquid to the lobster meat.

Bring the remaining fish stock to a boil and reduce by half over high heat. Stir in the parsley and chervil. Cook for 30 seconds, then process the liquid in a blender on medium speed for 1 to 2 minutes to coarsely puree the greens. Bring the puree to a boil in a saucepan, and whisk in half the butter. Season and hold in a warm place.

Heat the oven to 350°F.

Bring the lobster essence and wine to a boil. Cook until reduced to the consistency of a puree. Whisk in the remaining butter. Season and hold in a warm place.

Heat the brioches in the oven for 10 minutes to heat through. Remove the brioches and increase the heat to 400°F. Warm the lobster and garlic in a metal bowl or sauté pan over heat. Season and spoon the mixture into the brioches. Place the marrow on top of the lobster meat and put the tops on the brioches. Bake for 5 minutes. Place each brioche on a warm plate and pour the chervil sauce around it. Drizzle the lobster sauce over that and place the lobster legs around the brioche.

Brioche with Marrow, Lobster, Poached Garlic, and Chervil.

Poultry, Rabbit, and Game

Once when "my auntie Mame" came suddenly to visit, I was called upon to fix lunch and there was nothing in the house to eat. I ran down to the local Arab corner store to buy one of those ubiquitous paprika-colored spit-roasted chickens turning in the window. Remembering Alice B. Toklas's recipe for Giant Squab in Pyjamas, I split my fowl down the back, flattened it out and, just as she says, I threw a few nasturtium flowers around the dish. My guest was astounded and thrilled, the gesture earned me the reputation as a

quick-change artist, and for years after she constantly put me in situations that called for the loaves and fishes act. (With a great deal of effort, I managed to avoid having to search out again that particular type of chicken.)

Having spit-roasted chickens available everywhere *is* a good idea—if only they weren't always the cheapest kind, always overcooked, with that awful caramelized taste of chicken roasted until it falls off the bones. A good idea because this technique of cooking poultry on

a spit in front of a fire, originally called "roasting" (cooking in the oven being "baking"), easily ranks as the most delicious and satisfying way to cook a bird. Everyone will now immediately protest and bring up other most satisfying ways of cooking poultry—I will name a few myself—but the visual appeal and glorious tastes of a beautiful farm chicken (not the ones kept up all night to disco music in cages, eating each other as well as chemical foods) turned on a spit, basted with fresh herbs and olive oil, the bird picking up the aromas

of the smoke, are very difficult to top in anyone's cooking. The skin becomes quite crisp, yet the flesh stays very moist and the breast and leg meat cook evenly, especially if, in the last ten minutes of cooking, you stop the spit and turn the bird so that each of the legs faces the fire and gets additional cooking, while the breast meat does not.

That whole business of Brillat-Savarin and others saying, "*On devient cuisinier, mais on naît rôtisseur*"—one can become a cook, but one must be born a roast

[spit] cook—is very clever, pointing out correctly that the instinct involved in this kind of cooking is indeed very important. But it is important chiefly because the method exemplifies the dictum "It is so simple that it is hard." Balzac said that one has to be born a fruiterer or a roast cook, that the qualities needed for these two professions are the only ones that cannot be acquired through observation. The thousands of pages written on the theory and practice of spit roasting and the almost religious fervor with which the discussions are carried on (even to the point of Lucien Tendret's waxing eloquent about the warmth of the fire on limbs numbed with cold from the hunt, the eyes full of tenderness of the dog with his head on one's knees) should not discourage the enthusiast from unplugging the fireplace and buying or making a little motor-driven spit for cooking birds in front of the fire.

The wonderful thing about poultry is that it seems timeless, adapting itself to any number of moods, diets, nations, and cultures. In *Le Cuisinier François* of La Varenne, there is a recipe for *poulet d'Inde à la framboise farci,* which is a guinea fowl or turkey spit-roasted and braised, then presented with a sauce of raspberry vinegar, a handful of fresh raspberries thrown over it. That dish was popular in the seventeenth century; if presented today, it would be held as the latest in chic cooking. In one of the most ancient French cookbooks, *La Viandier* of Taillevent, some four hundred years old, there is a recipe for a hash of chicken with fresh ginger and unripe grape juice *verjus,* all of which ingredients are now on the cutting edge of American culinary fashion. The dish sounds, in fact, like a modernization of the "21" Club lunch menu.

I have yet to mention the sheer wonder of a beautiful farm chicken or capon stuffed under the skin and in the cavity with fresh black truffles, steamed in a tightly covered casserole with vegetables, brought to the table, and then uncovered with the huge, overwhelming wave of truffle aroma surging out of the pot, a simple enough dish to put together but a dish such as was served by Alexandre Dumaine in the thirties at Saulieu, and that inspired a decade of chefs, great palates, trenchermen, and gourmands. So I have included here a recipe for poached fowl. Very different in feeling, a great poultry-only pot-au-feu, or boiled dinner, when fitted out with interesting garnishes like marrow bones, little stuffed cabbage leaves, stuffed duck or goose neck sausage, or herb dumplings, can be very grand and simple at the same time. If there is any duck confit on hand (page 113), a leg or two added to the broth for the last ten minutes of cooking adds richness and mystery. For nothing is so mysterious as the pleasures that touch all nerves and all one's "buttons" through a confit of duck or goose. People tell me all the time that there is no time to cook, that coming home after work to face putting on a satisfying, let alone dramatic, dinner is almost more than is humanly possible. "Well," I say, "spend a Sunday making confit, which will last for months in the refrigerator, and all your last-minute problems are over, as long as you can get a good bottle of red wine and a nut-oil, mixed green—preferably endive—salad together with it. Short of candlelight, there is hardly anything else you need that night."

I shall use this chapter not so much to drum up all the most fascinating, esoteric, and fashionable recipes I have seen, cooked, and eaten, but rather to try and give a cooking lesson in the spirit of "the most one can do with the least amount of ingredients and finances."

Let us raise the curtain on someone faced with a weekend in the country with unanticipated guests, a last-minute need for something expensive like duck that one has to get the most out of. It could just as well be a turkey, capon, chicken, or any other fowl, but ducks and geese, with their fat and their fatty skin, offer the most possibilities. And one or two ducks, depending on the number of people being served, go a long way. The fat can be rendered in water to give a pale, golden, smooth, light, delicious elixir in which potatoes, eggs, and root vegetables can be cooked and taken to dizzying gastronomical heights. The skin is often a problem of fattiness for people, but treated the right way it becomes crisp cracklings, to be added to salads, eaten as snacks with drinks, or put into unctuous omelets; the neck skin can be stuffed with duck meat, Swiss chard, truffles, pistachios, pork and veal meat, and preserved in duck fat, or poached and served on polenta, or grilled and served the same way with fresh chilies. Meanwhile, the breast meat can become rather fancy dishes; the legs can become confit of duck or be grilled and served with turnips and mustard greens, cooked or in salad; the hearts and gizzards can go into stews or stocks, or finish sauces, or, height of blissfulness, be preserved in duck fat, warmed up, lifted out of the fat by the cook (there are never enough to go around for the guests), dipped into black pepper, and eaten right there as you slave over the stove. And did I mention the potatoes cooked in the fat from the duck? Or the wild mushrooms put in with them, or some fresh black truffles, to make the glorious potatoes Sarladaise, which are sort of hash browns with truffles? All that from a simple duck.

Duck

1 To truss a duck for roasting or braising whole, cut off the wings, leaving only the first bone. Tie string around the legs, then bring it around the thighs and between the breast, finally tying it under the front part of the breast.

2 Cutting up a raw duck will give you the two pieces of the breast for grilling or frying, the legs for braising or grilling, the fat for rendering, and the carcass and other pieces for making stock for soup or sauces. First remove the wishbone and slice down along the line of the breastbone to remove the two breast pieces. Then cut off the legs, including the piece called the oyster at the base of the thigh bone.

3 To make a stock for soup or sauces, prepare a mirepoix (page 127) or cut up equal quantities of carrots, onions, and celery. Make an herb bouquet. For a brown stock roast the carcass and pieces in a 400° oven for 30 minutes and follow the instructions on page 220. To make a white stock do not roast the bones and follow the same procedure.

4 For a quick grill or sauté, or for meat for salads, pastas, and fast ragouts, the duck can be preroasted in order to render some of the fat out from under the skin. Cut the duck in half, salt the two pieces, and rub them with dried thyme. Leave the duck to marinate for 3 hours, then roast in a 400° oven, the breast for 15 minutes and the legs for 25. Remove the pieces, let cool on a rack, and bone.

5 To bone pieces of a half-cooked duck (the next step in the above process), cut around the wing bone and remove the skin, and cut off the ball joint. Remove the thigh bone from the leg piece and any extra fat under the skin. The pieces are now ready for further marination in herbs and oil for grilling, or just salt and pepper if sautéing.

6 Remove the skin from the legs or breasts (as you would for salads, pasta garnishes, or fast ragouts), put it on a rack and bake in a 350° oven until the fat is rendered and the skin is crisp. Cut it up to sprinkle on salads, pasta, omelets, or sandwiches. Take raw or half-cooked fat and put in a pan with 5 times its volume of water. Simmer until the fat is dissolved. Strain and skim off the fat, or place the pan in the refrigerator until the fat is solid. Remove and discard the water. The fat can be kept covered in the refrigerator for 2 weeks. Do not discard the bits of skin and fat membrane from the straining, but bake or fry them and use the same way that you would crisp skin, or salt the pieces and use for snacks.

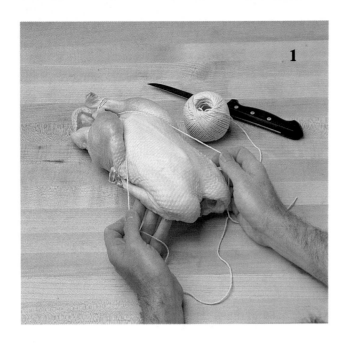

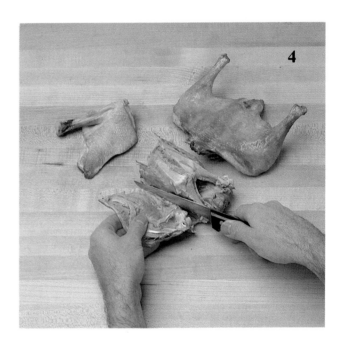

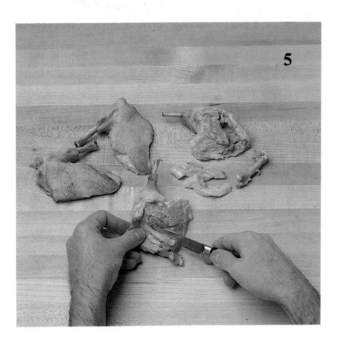

Warm Cabbage Salad with Duck Fat

I first prepared this salad at the Balboa Café in San Francisco in 1979. It was a popular success beyond my wildest dreams, especially because I thought at the time that cabbage and duck fat would be the last two things to capture the taste buds and imaginations of Californians. To this day, there are people who will not come to the restaurants without my promise that the cabbage salad will be available. Sometimes I do not use goat cheese but just bacon or pancetta, Italian bacon. Sometimes I add chopped shallots and use walnut oil instead of duck fat. But the procedure for a warm or "wilted" salad is the same: Mix the salad, seasonings, and acid beforehand, pour over the hot oil or fat, toss, and serve.

1	red cabbage
8 slices	bacon or pancetta
8 slices	white bread, preferably baguette or country bread
½ cup	walnut halves
1 clove	garlic, peeled, cut in half
2 tablespoons	red wine vinegar or fresh lemon juice
	salt and freshly ground pepper
¼ cup	rendered duck fat (page 113)
4 one-ounce rounds	fresh white goat cheese
1 tablespoon	chopped fresh parsley

Serves 4

Cut the cabbage in half through the root end. Cut out the core from each half. Turn the halves cut side down and slice crosswise into ⅛-inch pieces.

Lay the bacon out flat on a rack and bake or grill until crisp. When cool enough to handle, cut into 1-inch lengths. Keep warm.

Heat the oven to 350°F.

Bake the bread slices and walnuts on a sheet pan for 10 minutes. When the bread is cool enough to handle, rub the croutons with the garlic. Keep the croutons warm and let the walnuts cool.

Put the cabbage in a bowl. Add the vinegar or lemon juice and the salt and pepper and toss the cabbage thoroughly.

Heat the duck fat in a pan and put the cabbage in it. Toss quickly but thoroughly for 30 seconds. Add the bacon and walnuts and toss again for 1 minute.

Serve immediately on warm plates. Put the cheese in the center of the cabbage, sprinkle with the parsley, and put the croutons on the plates.

Duck Skin Omelet

	duck cracklings (page 108) from 1 breast or half a duck
3	eggs, room temperature
	salt and freshly ground pepper
1 tablespoon	butter or rendered duck fat (page 113)
2 sprigs	Italian parsley

Serves 1 or 2

Break or cut the cracklings into bite-size pieces.

Beat the eggs in a bowl with salt and a generous grinding of black pepper.

Heat an omelet pan over medium heat. Add the butter and tilt the pan so that the butter coats the entire bottom and side of the pan. When the pan is warm and the butter is just beginning to sizzle, pour in the eggs. When the bottom is just set, lift the edge with a spatula or fork to allow the unset eggs to flow underneath.

When most of the eggs are set, put the duck cracklings in the center and slide and roll the omelet to the edge of the pan. Invert the omelet onto a warm plate. Garnish with the parsley.

Clockwise from top left: Warm Cabbage Salad with Duck Fat; Duck Skin Omelet; Duck Soup (recipe on page 112); Warm Duck Salad with Turnip Pancake (recipe on page 112).

Warm Duck Salad with Turnip Pancake *(pictured on page 111)*

There are many versions of duck salad—the meat served with red cabbage, with curly or Belgian endive, with a vegetable ragout, with ham and tongue or other meats—but all of them, which I first started cooking in the early seventies at Chez Panisse, were inspired by the system at the Tour d'Argent in Paris, where they would serve the breast in a sauce first, followed (since they take longer to cook) by the grilled duck legs accompanied by a salad of curly endive (see page 115).

1 whole	duck breast, baked until barely pink
2	duck livers
	salt and freshly ground pepper
4 large	turnips, peeled ⅛ inch deep
6 tablespoons	rendered duck fat (page 113) or butter
2 tablespoons	fresh lemon juice
⅓ cup	walnut, hazelnut, or olive oil
½ pound	French green beans, ends trimmed
1 large	curly endive
¼ cup	tomato concasse (page 220)

Serves 4

Remove the skin from the cooked duck and save for another dish. Bone the breast and pull the meat apart with your hands into pieces 2 inches long and ¼ inch wide.

Cut the sinews out of the livers, season the livers, and set aside.

Grate or julienne the turnips in the food processor. Rinse the turnips under cold water and wring dry in a towel.

Put a pot of salted water on to boil. Heat the oven to 300°F.

Season the turnips and divide into 4 parts; flatten each part on waxed paper into a little pancake.

Heat 1 tablespoon of the duck fat in a crêpe pan over medium heat and slide in a turnip pancake. Cook until the bottom is golden and crisp, about 5 minutes. Flip the pancake over to cook another 3 minutes. Cook the remaining pancakes this way and keep hot in the oven. Heat the remaining 2 tablespoons duck fat in a pan over high heat. Add the livers and cook on each side for 1 minute.

Meanwhile, make a dressing by dissolving salt and pepper in the lemon juice and whisking in the oil.

Cook the beans in the boiling water for 5 minutes and drain.

Put the pancakes on warm plates. Toss the curly endive in a bowl with half the dressing and place on top of the pancakes. Add half the remaining dressing to the bowl and toss the hot beans in that. Put the beans around the pancakes and endive. Slice the livers and put them on the plate. Toss the duck in the remaining dressing and put the duck on the endive. Mix the tomato in the dressing left in the bowl and put in 3 mounds on each of the plates.

Duck Soup *(pictured on page 111)*

	heart and gizzard from 1 duck (more if you can obtain them)
	salt and freshly ground pepper
¼ cup	rendered duck fat (page 113)
4 cups	rich duck stock (page 220)
1 stalk	fresh lemongrass, very thinly sliced on the diagonal, or 1 teaspoon fresh lemon juice
1-inch piece	fresh ginger, peeled, cut into very fine julienne
12 sprigs	cilantro
16 leaves	purple or opal basil
8	chives, cut into 2-inch pieces
½ cup	tomato concasse (page 220)

Serves 4

Season the duck heart and gizzard with salt and pepper and cook them slowly in the duck fat over low heat until very tender, about 30 minutes. They should not brown. Remove them from the fat and cut into thin strips.

Heat the duck stock and add the lemongrass and ginger. Simmer for 5 minutes and then add the rest of the ingredients, including the heart and gizzard. Simmer for another 2 minutes, season to taste, and ladle into 4 warm bowls.

Duck Confit

One of the simplest grand meals in the world is confit of duck or goose, cooked in its rendered fat and then preserved in it. It is also one of the easiest, because once you spend a day making the confit, it takes only ten minutes to heat it in the oven or broiler or on a grill. Since it will last for weeks in the refrigerator, it is the ultimate fast food. This is a recipe for one duck, but it is better to cook about four, once you have decided to do the work. One never has enough duck fat with a single duck, so I save up the fat and freeze it until I have enough to make confit. You can supplement it with chicken fat.

1	duck, quartered
1 cup	kosher salt
¼ cup	mixed dried herbs (thyme, marjoram, and bay leaf), crumbled
1 tablespoon	peppercorns, crushed
½ tablespoon	allspice berries, crushed
½ tablespoon	juniper berries, crushed
8 cups	solid (unrendered) duck fat from the cavity and legs, etc.
2 sprigs	fresh thyme
2	bay leaves

Serves 4

Rinse the duck and pat dry. Mix the salt, dried herbs, and crushed spices in a bowl. Coat each piece of duck thoroughly with the salt mixture; put the duck in a dish, sprinkle with more of the salt mixture. Refrigerate for 24 hours, turning every 6 hours.

To render the duck fat, put the solid fat in a pot with 5 times the volume of water as duck fat. Bring to a boil and simmer for 2 hours. Do not let the water boil away. Strain, save the debris, and refrigerate the fat and water until the fat is hard. Lift off the fat and discard the water. (Fry and then chop the debris for use in omelets or salads.)

Wipe the duck pieces free of salt. Melt the rendered duck fat and put the pieces in it, fitting tightly so that the duck is covered with the fat. Simmer very gently until the duck is tender when pierced with a skewer, about 1 hour. (The breast pieces will be done first.) When they are cooked, take the pieces out and set aside. Strain the fat and let sit until the juices fall to the bottom. Carefully lift the fat off with a ladle so that you do not get any of the juices in the fat. Put the duck in a clean jar or crock and pour the fat over. Let cool in the refrigerator and then cover. The duck must be covered entirely with fat—it will then keep up to 2 months in the refrigerator. It has only to be heated in a tablespoon of its fat in a 400°F oven for 15 minutes before serving.

The illustration shows confit served with roasted peppers cut into squares (page 167) and potato pancakes (page 143) cooked in rendered duck fat, and garnished with basil and parsley leaves.

Duck Breast with Wild Rice and Mango-Chili Salsa

This dish could equally well use the fig-mint relish, the cherry chutney, the tomato chutney (pages 28–29), or the tomato vinaigrette made with shallots on page 32. The duck breast itself could be grilled, broiled, or sautéed. The point is to cook the breast so that it is still pink, the skin is crisp, and there is just a little bit of fat under the skin for flavor. And if you don't have wild rice, use the vegetable ragout on page 167, or the red cabbage salad on page 110.

2 whole	duck breasts
	salt and freshly ground pepper
2 cups	wild rice
4 tablespoons	butter
1 cup	mango-chili salsa (page 28)
16 sprigs	watercress

Serves 4

Heat the oven to 450°F or the broiler.

Season the duck breasts (ideally with a little of the salt mixture used in the preceding confit recipe). Place them skin side up on a rack on a sheet pan or roasting pan. Bake or broil for 10 minutes to render some of the fat from under the skin. Let the duck cool.

Meanwhile, boil a large pot of water, salt it, and put in the wild rice. Boil, stirring the rice a few times, until tender, about 30 minutes.

Heat the oven to 350°F.

Drain the rice, toss thoroughly with the butter, and put in an ovenproof casserole. Cover and bake for 15 minutes, stirring and fluffing the rice twice. Uncover the rice, stir again, and bake for another 15 minutes, stirring 2 more times to ensure that the rice grains are separate and firm.

While the rice is cooking, bone the duck breasts, leaving on the wing joints, so that you have 4 pieces. When the rice is done, heat a frying pan and put the duck pieces skin side down in the pan. Cook over high heat for 3 minutes; then turn down the heat and cook until the duck is medium rare, about 2 more minutes. Let the duck rest in a warm place for 5 minutes so that the juices are reabsorbed into the meat. Then slice off the wing joints and slice the breasts. Fan the slices on warm plates. Serve the wild rice alongside and spoon some mango-chili salsa on each plate. Garnish with the watercress.

Grilled Duck Leg with Endive Salad

Use whatever bitter greens you have on hand, mixing them, if you like. The richness of the duck is best balanced with the clean, biting taste of curly endive, Belgian endive, radicchio, escarole, watercress, rocket (arugula), and others. The combination of nut oils like hazelnut or walnut with the various forms of endive is very special and works well with duck.

4	duck legs
2	duck livers
	salt and freshly ground pepper
2 tablespoons	butter
2 tablespoons	Madeira or dry sherry
16 small slices	bread for croutons
3 tablespoons	tomato concasse (page 220)
1 tablespoon	chopped fresh parsley
2 tablespoons	fresh lemon juice
¼ cup	hazelnut or walnut oil
1 large	curly endive, picked, washed, spun-dried
½ cup	hazelnuts, toasted, skinned
4 tablespoons	duck cracklings (page 108)

Serves 4

Turn the legs skin side down. Cut along each thigh bone and remove it.

Heat the oven to 325°F.

Remove the sinews from the duck livers. Season and then sauté over high heat in the butter for 3 minutes. Pour in the Madeira or sherry and cook another minute. Puree the liver and juices in a food processor or through a food mill until smooth; then set aside.

Bake the bread for 10 minutes and then let cool.

Heat the grill or broiler. Season the duck legs and grill or broil for 5 minutes on the flesh side and 8 minutes on the skin side.

Spread the liver puree on the croutons, put ½ teaspoon of the tomato concasse on each crouton, and sprinkle with chopped parsley.

Dissolve salt and pepper in the lemon juice and whisk in the oil. Toss the endive and hazelnuts in the dressing. Put the salad on warm plates, a duck leg on top of each salad, the liver croutons around the salads, and the cracklings on top of the endive.

Squab Mousse with Field Salad

Although this is a deceptively easy recipe, great care must be taken each of the two times that the squabs are chopped up. The birds should not be pureed to baby-food consistency. The debris of bones (after the mixture is sieved) can be simmered with stock for a couple of hours to produce a beautiful sauce for some other dish, or, if clarified, a jelly to accompany this mousse. Serve the mousse with grilled brioche or toasts.

4	squabs, preferably with heads, feet, livers, gizzards
1/3 cup	fresh duck or chicken fat
2 sprigs	fresh thyme, chopped
1/4 cup	Cognac or Madeira
1 cup	rich duck, veal, or chicken stock (page 220)
	salt and freshly ground pepper
1/4 cup	rendered duck fat (page 113)
2 tablespoons	fresh lemon juice
1/4 cup	hazelnut or walnut oil
3 cups	mixed greens: rocket (arugula), dandelion, lamb's lettuce, curly endive, watercress, baby lettuces
1/4 cup	hazelnuts, toasted

Serves 6 to 8

Coarsely chop the squabs, livers, gizzards, and fresh fat. Put it in a bowl. Mix in the thyme and Cognac and marinate for 5 hours. Put the mixture in a food processor or pass through a meat grinder to the consistency of hamburger.

Heat the oven to 400°F.

Put the mixture in an ovenproof pot with the stock, salt, and pepper and bring to a simmer on top of the stove. Cover and bake for 15 minutes. Let cool slightly. Puree in batches in the food processor for 10 seconds. Put the puree through a food mill or sieve.

Let the puree cool to room temperature (if room is less than 75°F). Add salt and pepper and half the rendered duck fat and mix well. Check the seasoning. Spoon into little ramekins or a terrine. Melt the remaining rendered duck fat and pour 1/8 inch fat over the mousse. Refrigerate preferably 2 days so that the flavors develop.

Dissolve salt and pepper in the lemon juice and whisk in the oil. Put the greens in a bowl, add the hazelnuts, pour over the dressing, and mix together. Put a ramekin or a slice from the terrine on each plate and surround with the salad.

Grilled Duck Sausage with Polenta

If you are lucky enough to get ducks with their heads on, save the neck skin. If you buy one duck at a time, keep the neck skins, well wrapped up, in the freezer until you have four or six, and make sausages with them. You can grill, roast, broil, or make confit of the sausages, put them in soups with cabbage or shredded grilled tortillas, or serve them with a sorrel puree or with potatoes cooked in duck fat with wild mushrooms. If you do not have duck neck skin for casings, use chicken (or goose) neck skin or buy casings from a butcher.

1 pound	duck meat or combination duck and lean pork
6 ounces	pork fatback
1 teaspoon	chopped mixed fresh herbs, thyme, marjoram, sage
1/8 teaspoon	ground allspice
1 pinch each	ground cloves, coriander, and mace
1 teaspoon	salt
1/2 teaspoon	freshly ground pepper
6	duck neck skins, cleaned of excess fat, or 1 length medium sausage casing
6 triangles	cooked polenta (page 219)
1 cup	tomato chutney (page 29)
16 sprigs	cilantro

Makes 6 sausages

Trim the duck and pork meat of all excess fat and tendons and cut into 1-inch pieces. Cut the fat into 1-inch pieces. Grind the fat first through the coarse blade of a meat grinder; then feed it through again as you grind the meat. Make sure that the meat and fat stay cold during the grinding and mixing process. If you do not have a meat grinder, put the fat and the meat in a food processor and process, using on/off pulses, until the meat is coarsely ground.

Mix in the herbs, spices, salt, and pepper and work until it forms a cohesive mass. Cook a little bit of the mixture and taste for seasoning.

Tie one end of each duck neck with a string and stuff the necks, using a spoon or your fingers. The amount of stuffing for each one will depend on the size of the necks, but they should be stuffed somewhat loosely. Tie the ends with string.

Start a charcoal fire. Grill the sausages slowly until done, turning occasionally to brown all sides. At the same time, grill the polenta until the triangles are crisp on the outside but still creamy inside.

When the sausages are done, remove them from the grill and let them sit in a warm place for a few minutes before slicing them. Serve with the polenta and chutney and garnish with the cilantro.

Duck Livers with Andouille Sausage

If you do not have andouille sausage, use fresh Italian fennel or red pepper sausages, game or duck sausages, or whatever good fresh spicy sausages you can get. Chicken or rabbit livers can be substituted for duck.

6 whole	duck livers
1 pound	andouille sausage
2	shallots, peeled, finely chopped
6 tablespoons	butter
1 tablespoon	water
	salt and freshly ground pepper
½ cup	dry red wine
1 pound	pearl onions, peeled
24 cloves	garlic, peeled
1 cup	stock, chicken, duck, or mixed (page 220)
2 sprigs	fresh thyme, stemmed, leaves finely chopped
1 tablespoon	chopped fresh parsley

Serves 4

Cut any sinews from the livers and slice at an angle, ¼ inch thick, into scallops. Put the sausage in cold water, bring to a simmer, and parboil 10 minutes. Let cool and slice ⅛ inch thick.

Put the shallots, 1 tablespoon of the butter, and the water in a sauté pan. Cover and cook over low heat for 10 minutes. Turn up the heat, season the livers, and add them to the shallots. Sauté for 3 minutes on each side. Pour in the wine and cook for 30 seconds. Lift out the livers with a slotted spoon and set aside.

Add the onions, garlic, and stock to the juices in the pan. Cover and simmer until the onions and garlic are tender, about 15 minutes. Add the thyme and sausage. Simmer another 5 minutes. Add the remaining butter and stir until the butter is incorporated. Add the livers, heat them through for 30 seconds, and season. Serve immediately. Garnish with parsley.

Grilled Chicken Paillard with Ancho Chili Butter

Various garnishes are suitable with chicken paillard, but at the Santa Fe Bar & Grill it was usually served with grilled vegetables or French fries. The best vegetables to grill are fennel, red bell peppers, summer squashes, eggplant, and mushrooms. The vegetables are parboiled, drained, marinated in olive oil and herbs, then grilled over a moderate charcoal fire.

2 large	chicken breasts, skinned, boned
5 tablespoons	ancho chili powder
¼ cup	olive oil
6 ounces	unsalted butter
1 teaspoon	salt
8 wedges	lime or lemon

Serves 4

Put the chicken pieces between 2 pieces of heavy plastic and pound with the side of a cleaver until ⅜ to ¼ inch thick. Mix 2 tablespoons of the chili powder and the oil in a pan just large enough to hold the paillards in one layer. Add the paillards and marinate for 3 hours, turning occasionally.

Make the ancho butter by combining 3 tablespoons chili powder with the butter and salt. Let stand 2 hours to develop its flavors. If the butter is in the refrigerator, be sure to remove it to let it soften and whisk it to get the right serving texture.

Cook the paillards on a hot charcoal grill for 2 minutes on each side. Serve with the ancho butter on top and garnish with lime or lemon wedges.

Roast Quail with Pumpkinseed Sauce

This dish is inspired by the books of Diana Kennedy, as well as by her wonderful cooking. Her *mole verde de pepita* appears in *The Cuisines of Mexico*. This pumpkinseed sauce does not sound like much, but the flavors from the seeds are deep, complex, and very intriguing. Yet they do not overpower the delicate flavors of the quail.

8 small	quail
2 sprigs	fresh thyme, chopped
6 tablespoons	olive oil
½ cup	unsalted green pumpkinseeds
2 cloves	garlic, chopped
1 large	onion, chopped
4 medium	tomatillos, husks removed, pureed
1 cup	chicken stock (page 220)
	salt and freshly ground pepper
¼ cup	red bell pepper puree (page 32)
¼ pound	butter
16 sprigs	cilantro

Serves 4

Rub the quail all over with a mixture of the thyme and 4 tablespoons of the olive oil. Let marinate for 2 hours.

Heat the oven to 400°F.

Put the pumpkinseeds in a sauté pan and toast over medium heat, tossing them constantly, for 3 minutes. Do not let them burn. Set them aside on a plate to cool.

Put the remaining 2 tablespoons oil, the garlic, and onion in a pan. Cover and sweat over low heat for 5 minutes. Add the tomatillos and ½ cup of the stock. Simmer uncovered for 10 minutes.

Puree the pumpkinseeds with the remaining stock in a food processor or blender. Add the pumpkinseed puree to the onion mixture and cook over very low heat for 2 minutes, stirring all the time. Do not let boil. Hold while you cook the quail.

Rub the thyme off the quail, season them, and bake for 10 minutes. Remove and keep warm.

Heat the bell pepper puree in a saucepan and whisk in ¼ cup of the butter. Remove from the heat and keep warm.

Heat the pumpkinseed sauce very carefully, whisk in the remaining butter. Season and spoon the sauce equally on warm plates. Put 2 quail on each plate and drizzle with the bell pepper sauce. Garnish with the cilantro.

Smoke-Roasted Squab

Use a smoker that has the drip pan under the rack holding the birds. In this way, the liquid keeps a moist vapor around the squab. The sauce and the boning can be done in advance, since the squab halves can rest in the sauce. When reheating them, never let the sauce boil or they will become tough and overcooked. Plain watercress, or a mixed vegetable ragout, or a turnip and mixed root vegetable creamed gratin, would make a wonderful accompaniment.

4	fresh squabs, preferably with feet and heads
2 quarts	stock, veal, mixed veal and chicken, or duck (page 220)
2 sprigs	fresh thyme, stemmed, leaves chopped
	salt and freshly ground pepper
6 tablespoons	olive oil
1 cup	Cabernet or Zinfandel
2 tablespoons	sweet butter

Serves 4

Remove and chop the necks and feet of the squabs and add them to the stock.

Truss the squabs and marinate them in the thyme, salt, pepper, and 4 tablespoons of the olive oil at room temperature for at least 2 hours.

When the birds have marinated, brown them rapidly all over in the remaining olive oil in a sauté pan.

Put them in the smoker (see headnote) over a low fire that has been perfumed with vine cuttings or fruitwood. Smoke for about 1 hour, less if you like rare squab.

Remove the birds from the smoker and put them aside to cool. When the birds are cool, bone them into halves. Chop up the carcasses and add to the stock. Pour the stock and red wine into a pan and simmer for 30 minutes. Strain and degrease the sauce.

Put the meat in the warm (not hot) sauce and *slowly* heat it. Remove the meat to a serving plate. Whisk the butter into the sauce and pour over the squab.

Smoked Duck with Belgian Endive

In this recipe only the breasts are used, and the legs can go smoked or raw to be used in the grilled duck with endive salad on page 115, gumbo on page 124, or in the poached duck recipe on page 130. For smoking information see smoke-roasted squab, on this page.

2 whole	ducks
1 tablespoon	salt
	freshly ground pepper
1 tablespoon	dried thyme
½ cup whole	hazelnuts
4	Belgian endives
4 tablespoons	rendered duck fat (page 113)
½ pound	french green beans, trimmed
½ cup	tomato concasse (page 220)
¼ cup	reduced duck stock (page 220)
1 tablespoon	fresh tarragon leaves, coarsely chopped

Serves 4

Separate the breast from the legs of each duck by slicing the duck in half diagonally, leaving the breast whole and the two legs in one piece.

Mix the salt, pepper, and thyme and rub over the duck breasts. Marinate two hours.

Preheat the oven to 450°F.

Rub the salt and pepper off the breasts, place them in a shallow roasting pan, and put them in the oven for 15 minutes. Remove and let cool.

Smoke the breasts for about one hour, depending on the type and the heat of the smoker (about 275°), but do not let the breasts go more than rare to medium rare. Remove the breasts, let cool, bone them, and cut off the wings.

Toast the hazelnuts in a 350° oven for 10 minutes, let cool, and rub off the skins.

Pull the Belgian endive leaves apart into "spears."

Bring a pot of salted water to the boil.

Put one tablespoon of the duck fat in a sauté pan, put in the duck breast pieces skin-side down and cook over medium heat for 5 minutes.

Meanwhile cook the green beans 5 minutes and drain. Put in a bowl with the endive, hazelnuts, tomato, stock, tarragon, salt and pepper. Heat the remaining duck fat and pour over the endive. Warm the bowl over medium heat for 3 minutes and toss the endive with the other ingredients. Arrange the endive on hot plates, slice the duck breast, put in the center of the plates, and put the other ingredients on top of the endive.

Grilled Squab Marinated in Berry Puree

The purpose of the berry puree is to glaze the skin for crispness and give it color, without having to overcook the bird. With the berry marinade, the skin crisps up right away, and the acid in the berries counteracts and balances the richness of the squab and gives a richness of color variation over the surface of the bird. Instead of raspberries, blackberries or blueberries can be used. The recipe was inspired by the seventeenth-century cookbook *Le Cuisinier François,* in which a recipe for raspberry vinegar is also given.

4	*squabs, with livers and hearts*
2½ cups	*fresh raspberries*
½ pound	*butter*
	salt and freshly ground pepper
4 tablespoons	*olive oil*
½ pound	*salt pork, cut into 1- by ¼-inch pieces*
1 tablespoon	*chopped fresh thyme leaves*
16	*fresh mushrooms*
2 tablespoons	*fresh lemon juice*
½ cup	*walnut oil*
3 bunches	*watercress, picked, washed, dried*

Serves 4

Cut the backbones from the squabs. Flatten the birds and fold the wings under. Select 24 raspberries for garnish and puree the rest through a sieve. Divide the puree in half. Mix 1 half with the butter, salt, and pepper in a food processor and stir 2 tablespoons of the olive oil into the other half. Season the birds and cover with the raspberry-oil marinade. Let marinate for 1 hour.

Meanwhile, blanch the salt pork, rinse, and drain. Trim the squab livers. Mix the remaining olive oil and the thyme and marinate the salt pork, livers, hearts, and mushrooms in the oil for 45 minutes; then put them on skewers.

Start a charcoal fire or heat the broiler.

Grill the squabs breast side down for 5 minutes, moving them to a cooler part of the grill if they begin to brown too fast. Turn the squabs and grill cavity side down until the breast meat feels firm to the touch, about 8 minutes. Don't overcook them; they are best still a little pink. Put them aside to rest for 5 minutes, while you grill the skewers for 5 minutes, turning them often.

Mix salt and pepper with the lemon juice and whisk in the walnut oil. Dress the watercress and put it on warm plates. Put the squabs in the center of each plate and the skewers around. Dress the whole raspberries in the sauce remaining in the bowl and scatter them around the plate. Put some of the raspberry butter on top of each bird and serve.

Warm Squab Salad with Okra

This salad could be made with quail, fresh or smoked duck, smoked chicken, or wild birds like doves or partridge. The bird should be warm and the okra piping hot.

2 1-pound	*fresh squabs*
2 sprigs	*fresh thyme, finely chopped*
2 tablespoons	*olive oil*
4 ears	*fresh corn*
1 large	*red bell pepper, seeded, cut into fine julienne*
1 tablespoon	*fresh marjoram or oregano leaves, coarsely chopped*
½ cup	*chicken stock (page 220)*
½ cup	*cornmeal*
	salt and freshly ground pepper
1 pound	*fresh okra, cut crosswise into ½-inch pieces*
½ cup	*peanut oil*
4 tablespoons	*butter*

Serves 4

Rub the squabs all over with a mixture of the thyme and olive oil. Let marinate at least 4 hours, but preferably overnight, in refrigerator.

Cut the corn off the cobs and reserve the kernels.

Heat the oven to 400°F.

Let the squabs warm to room temperature. Put them in a roasting pan and roast until the breast meat is just firm to the touch, about 20 minutes. Remove them and let sit for 10 minutes in a warm place. Slice the squab halves off the carcass.

Put the corn, bell pepper, marjoram or oregano, and stock in a sauté pan. Bring to a boil and cook for 10 minutes.

While the corn is cooking, cut the wings and legs off the squab halves and slice the breast as shown.

Mix the cornmeal with salt and pepper. Toss the okra in the cornmeal. Heat the peanut oil in a sauté pan over medium heat and add the okra. Cook, tossing the okra constantly, for 5 minutes.

When the corn is cooked, stir in the butter until it is fully incorporated and season it. Put the corn in the center of warm plates, the squab on top of the corn, and the okra around the corn.

Toasted Chicken and Ancho Chili Sandwich

In any salad or sandwich using cooked chicken, the quality depends on not overcooking the chicken and on shredding it by hand rather than cutting it. Once you have made the ancho chili puree, the sandwich is very easy and satisfying beyond what the unprepossessing list of ingredients would suggest.

2 whole	chicken breasts
2 quarts	chicken stock (page 220)
½ teaspoon	salt
2 tablespoons	fresh lime juice
½ cup	mayonnaise (page 36)
¼ cup	ancho chili puree (page 30)
4	hamburger buns or pieces of baguette
2 tablespoons	unsalted butter
1 loose cup	cilantro sprigs
½ cup	salsa (page 28)

Serves 4

Put the chicken breasts in the chicken stock and bring to a boil. Turn the heat down and simmer just until the juices run white and not rose colored when the chicken is pierced with a thin skewer, about 20 minutes.

Take the chicken out and let it cool. Remove the skin and pull the meat off the bones. Pull the meat into pieces roughly 2 by ¼ inches. Add the salt and lime juice, and mix well.

Mix the mayonnaise with the chili puree. Taste for salt and then mix the chicken into the mayonnaise.

Cut the buns or *baguette* crosswise in half. Butter the cut sides lightly and toast under a broiler.

Put the chicken on the bottom piece of bread, the cilantro sprigs on top of the chicken, and top with the other pieces of bread. Serve the salsa on the side.

Warm Chicken, Sweetbread, and Pepper Coleslaw Salad

This salad is ideal if you have been braising sweetbreads for another dish and, after trimming them, you have bits and pieces left over. The warm chicken and sweetbread accompanied by the slightly chilled coleslaw is inspired by habit-forming Korean pickle *kim chee*, the best of which I tasted in Hawaii, at the house of the father of my assistant on this book, Noreen Lam. The coleslaw will last in the refrigerator for a couple of weeks.

1 large	white cabbage
4 cloves	garlic, finely chopped
2-ounce piece	fresh ginger, peeled, finely chopped
1 teaspoon	salt
½ cup	peanut oil
1 tablespoon	sesame oil
½ teaspoon	ancho chili powder
¼ teaspoon	cayenne pepper
¼ cup	fermented Chinese black beans
2 whole	chicken breasts, cooked, shredded (as in preceding recipe)
1 cup	braised sweetbreads (page 222), broken into bite-size pieces
2 tablespoons	fresh lemon juice
1 cup	sweetbread braising juices, reduced to ¼ cup
¼ cup	olive oil
1 cup	fresh cilantro sprigs, stemmed, coarsely chopped
	salt and freshly ground black pepper

Serves 4

Cut the cabbage in half through the root end and then cut out the core. Place the halves cut side down on a cutting board and cut crosswise into ⅛-inch shreds.

Mix the garlic, ginger, salt, peanut and sesame oils, chili powder, and cayenne in a bowl. Add the cabbage and toss together very well. Cover and let sit for 2 hours or longer to develop the flavors.

Soak the black beans for 1 hour, changing the water once. Drain and chop them coarsely.

Put the chicken, sweetbreads, and lemon juice in a bowl and mix well.

Heat the reduced braising juices in a pan and whisk in the olive oil. Add the black beans. Pour over the sweetbread and chicken mixture, add the cilantro, and toss together. Check for seasoning. Put the chicken and sweetbread mixture in the center of warm plates and serve with the coleslaw around.

Stars Gumbo

This version makes no pretense of being definitive gumbo or even using classic gumbo-making techniques. It does include the basic ingredients, the most important being the roux. I have not included okra—despite the fact that the word "gumbo" comes from an African word for okra—or filé, the powder made from dried sassafras leaves, because they can be difficult to find, and you can have a wonderful gumbo without them. I do, however, prefer the glutinous texture that okra or filé gives to a gumbo: If you use filé, add it at the very last second or sprinkle it over the gumbo in the plates. If you have duck livers, chop them up and add them in the last two minutes of cooking, stirring them in well. Serve the gumbo alone, with boiled rice, or with grilled polenta (page 219).

1	smoked duck
¾ cup	peanut oil
¾ cup	flour
2 large	onions, finely chopped
1	green bell pepper, stemmed, seeded, finely chopped
2 bunches	scallions, roots removed, finely chopped
2 stalks	celery, finely chopped
6	bay leaves
4 sprigs	fresh thyme
2 quarts	chicken stock (page 220)
1 pound	andouille sausage, sliced ¼ inch thick
	salt
10 cloves	garlic, peeled, finely chopped
1 cup	chopped fresh parsley
2 large	fresh mild chilies, seeded, finely chopped
4	medium-hot fresh red chilies, seeded, finely chopped
2 cups	tomato concasse (page 220)
12 large	prawns, peeled

Serves 8

Bone the duck so that you have 2 breasts and 2 legs (with thighs). Take the skin off the breast meat and chop the skin finely. Pull the breast meat into ½-inch pieces.

Heat the oil in a heavy pot or casserole over medium heat until very hot but not smoking. Being very careful not to splash any of the oil on your hands, gradually stir in the flour with a wooden spoon. Cook, being careful not to let the flour burn, until the flour is very dark brown, almost black.

Add the onions, green pepper, scallions, celery, bay leaves, and thyme. Mix well and cook for another 10 minutes. Pour in the chicken stock and stir well, making sure to include any roux stuck in the corners of the pot. Simmer 2 minutes. Add the duck legs, sausage, and salt to taste. Simmer 30 minutes, stirring occasionally.

Add the garlic, parsley, chilies, and tomato. Simmer until the duck is tender, another 20 to 30 minutes. Add the prawns and duck breast pieces and simmer for 3 minutes. Turn off the heat and let the gumbo sit for 10 minutes. Skim off the fat from the surface of the liquid, correct the seasoning if necessary, and serve.

Braised Rabbit with Leeks and Prunes

If you don't have young leeks, cut large ones in quarters lengthwise.

4	rabbit legs
	salt and freshly ground pepper
2 tablespoons	olive oil
¼ cup	Armagnac or good brandy
1 cup	mirepoix (see below)
2 sprigs	fresh tarragon, stemmed, stems and leaves saved
1	bouquet garni (see below)
1 cup	stock, chicken or mixed chicken and veal (page 220)
½ cup	dry white wine
½ cup	heavy cream
6	prunes, pitted
6 young	leeks, trimmed and washed
1 tablespoon	rose or pink peppercorns

Serves 2

Season the rabbit legs. Heat the olive oil in a sauté pan. Add the rabbit and lightly brown the legs on both sides. Pour in the Armagnac and flame it. Put the mirepoix around the rabbit legs; add the tarragon stems and bouquet garni. Cover the pan and cook over low heat for 15 minutes.

Add the stock and white wine. Cover and simmer very slowly until the legs are very tender, about another 45 minutes.

Take the legs out, cover, and keep warm. Strain the cooking juices; discard the vegetables and bouquet garni. Return the juices to the pan and reduce by half.

Add the cream, prunes, tarragon leaves, and leeks to the sauce. Cook uncovered over medium heat for 10 minutes. Add the pink peppercorns and rabbit legs with any juices that have collected.

Simmer for 5 minutes more, turning the rabbit legs a couple of times in the cream sauce. Check the sauce for seasoning and serve.

- *Mirepoix:* Equal quantities of peeled and chopped onion, carrot, and celery.

- *Bouquet garni:* A bundle of herbs that is either tied up with string or wrapped in cheesecloth if the herbs are dried. It is made into a packet so that it can be easily removed from a stew or stock without the herb leaves floating or getting mixed up in the other ingredients. For this recipe, use a sprig of parsley, thyme, tarragon, and a bay leaf wrapped in leek leaves with some celery tops.

Saddle of Rabbit with Black and Rose Peppercorns

Unless you make the old-fashioned type of country rabbit stew, cooking the rabbit for a couple of hours until all the meat turns very tender and falls off the bone, the same problem exists with rabbit as with poultry: namely, the breast meat—in this case the saddle—cooks faster than the legs and thighs. In order not to overcook the saddle, I have separated it from the rest of the rabbit, and in the next recipe use a longer, moist cooking for the legs.

4	rabbit loins or saddles
2	rabbit livers
4 tablespoons	olive oil
2 sprigs	fresh thyme, stemmed, chopped
1 sprig	fresh tarragon, stemmed, chopped
4 medium	carrots, peeled
2 stalks	celery
1 large	onion, peeled
2 tablespoons	black peppercorns
2 tablespoons	rose or pink peppercorns
6 tablespoons	butter
¼ cup	chicken stock (page 220)
8 large sprigs	fresh chervil

Serves 4

Rub the rabbit pieces and livers all over with a mixture of the oil, thyme, and tarragon. Let marinate for 2 hours.

Cut the carrots, celery, and onion into ⅛-inch dice. Heat the oven to 375°F.

Coarsely crush the black and pink peppercorns. Rub over the tops of the saddles.

Put the onion, celery, carrots, 2 tablespoons of the butter, and the chicken stock in a pot. Cover and sweat the vegetables for 15 minutes, taking the cover off for the last 5 minutes. Put the rabbit pieces on a sheet pan in the oven and bake for 15 minutes. Add the livers to the pan for the last 5 minutes. Let rest for 5 minutes in a warm place.

Stir the remaining butter into the vegetable mixture and spoon it onto warm plates. Put the rabbit saddles on the vegetables; slice the livers and put those around the rabbit. Garnish the plates with the chervil sprigs.

Overleaf Left: Poached Duck with Duck Sausage and Horseradish Sauce; right: Capon with Wild Mushrooms and Mint Béarnaise (recipes on page 130).

Top: Braised Rabbit with Leeks and Prunes; bottom: Saddle of Rabbit with Black and Rose Peppercorns.

Poached Duck with Duck Sausage and Horseradish Sauce

(pictured on page 128)

This recipe, like the following one, is inspired by the French pot-au-feu, but it is a faster-cooking dish than the chicken. Here you can use the legs only, breast and leg meat together, or just the breast meat—the fastest to prepare. The duck is first broiled or baked at high temperature to render some of the fat. The purpose of the astringent sauce is to balance the richness of the sausage and duck, so a mustard cream, for example, would work as well.

½-pound piece	fresh horseradish root
1 cup	sour cream
	salt and freshly ground pepper
1 whole	duck
1 small	cabbage, cored
½ recipe	duck sausage (page 116)
3 quarts	duck or chicken stock (page 220)
4 large	turnips, peeled, cut in oval shapes 2 inches by ¾ inch
1 large	celery root, peeled, cut in sticks 2 inches by ¼ inch
20	baby carrots, peeled
16	pearl onions, peeled
8 small	fresh shiitake mushrooms
8 small	fresh tree oyster mushrooms
4 sprigs	fresh tarragon
4 sprigs	fresh thyme

Serves 4

Peel the horseradish root, wash it, and grate or puree it in a food processor. Stir into the cream and season with salt and pepper. Let sit 1 hour to develop flavor.

Heat the broiler or the oven to 400°F.

Season the duck and bake for 15 minutes to brown it slightly and render some of the fat. Let the duck cool and bone it so that you have 4 pieces. Trim off any excess fat, cut off the ends of the wings, and scrape the bones clean.

Bring a pot of salted water to a boil. Turn off the heat and add the cabbage. Let it sit in the hot water for 5 minutes. Lift out the cabbage and let it cool.

Peel off the leaves one by one. Choose 8 of the best middle-size leaves and cut out the core 2 inches up into each of the leaves. Divide the duck sausage meat into 8 equal parts and place 1 part on each leaf. Roll up the leaves and tie each one with string.

Put the stock and duck pieces in a pot. Bring to a slow simmer and cook for 40 minutes. Add the vegetables, sausage packets, and herbs and cook until the vegetables are tender, about 20 more minutes. Serve with the horseradish cream sauce.

Capon with Wild Mushrooms and Mint Béarnaise *(pictured on page 129)*

If you cannot find a capon, any large chicken, even a roasting chicken, will do for this recipe. The main thing is not to use a little, 1½-pound chicken that will cook so quickly that the broth will get no flavor from the meat and the meat no flavor from the vegetable broth. The same recipe could be used for game birds, and the size and age of any of the birds will determine the cooking time. To get the best results, cook the chicken with carrots, onions, celery, and turnip peelings, remove them, and then add the vegetables that you want to accompany the chicken. Use stock in the first cooking instead of water, and you will get even richer results, ending up with the best soup or consommé you ever tasted.

1 five-pound	capon, boiling fowl, or roasting chicken
6 slices	bacon, cut into ½-inch pieces, parboiled 10 minutes
1 cup	coarsely chopped mirepoix (page 127)
1	bouquet garni (page 127)
2 large	turnips, peeled but peelings reserved, quartered
2 quarts	water or stock
	salt
24 small	carrots, peeled
24 small	white onions, peeled
6	fresh chanterelles or other wild mushrooms
8 small	new potatoes
6	leeks, trimmed, rinsed thoroughly
4 sprigs	fresh tarragon
2 sprigs	fresh thyme
6	fresh marrow bones, each 3 inches long
1 cup	mint béarnaise (page 40)

Serves 6 to 8

Put the chicken in a pot just large enough to hold it and the vegetables. Add the bacon, mirepoix, bouquet garni, and half the turnip peelings. Add water or stock to cover and add salt. Bring to a boil. Skim off any scum that rises to the surface. Turn down the heat and barely simmer for 1 hour or more, depending on the kind of chicken you are using. The way to test for doneness is to roll the chicken over on its side, pierce the thigh with a skewer, and check the color of the juices that come out. If they are rose-colored, cook some more until the juices from the thickest part of the thigh run clear.

When the chicken is almost done, add the vegetables. Cook for 15 minutes. Add the herb sprigs and marrow bones; cook another 8 minutes. Lift the chicken onto a warm platter and put all the vegetables and marrow bones around it. Pour some of the boiling broth over the chicken and carve. Serve 2 cups of the remaining broth and the mint béarnaise separately. Save the additional broth for another use.

Rabbit Chili

The chili in this recipe is not very hot, although you can make it hotter by adding more cayenne or putting a smoked chili (chipotle) in with the rabbit while it is cooking. I have made the accent sauce very hot.

2	rabbits, cut up
½ cup	ancho chili puree (page 30)
	salt
¼ cup	ham or bacon fat, finely chopped
2 large	onions, finely chopped
8 cloves	garlic, finely chopped
2	bay leaves
2 tablespoons	ground cumin
1 tablespoon	oregano leaves
1 teaspoon	fresh thyme leaves, chopped
1 teaspoon	cayenne pepper
1 cup	beer
5 cups	chicken stock (page 220)
2	smoked dried chilies, stemmed, seeded
½ cup	garlic puree (page 30)
1	lime, juiced
¼ cup	heavy cream
16 triangles	cooked polenta (page 219)
4 tablespoons	olive oil

Serves 8

Heat the oven to 375°F.

Rub the rabbit pieces with the ancho chili puree and sprinkle with salt. Put the bacon or ham fat in a 6-quart casserole just large enough to hold the rabbit and the liquid. Add the onions and garlic and put in the rabbit pieces. Put the pot in the oven and cook uncovered for 30 minutes.

Remove the casserole and put it on the stove. Add the bay leaves, cumin, oregano, thyme, cayenne, beer, and 4 cups of the chicken stock. Bring to a boil and then simmer until the rabbit is falling off the bones, about 1½ hours.

While the chili is cooking, heat the remaining 1 cup chicken stock with the dried chilis. Simmer for 30 minutes. Let cool and puree in a blender or food processor. Put the puree in a saucepan and heat it. Stir in the garlic puree, lime juice, cream, and salt to taste. Keep warm.

When the rabbit is cooked, remove all the bones and stir the chili vigorously to break up the pieces of meat. If the chili is still very liquid, cook over medium heat until there is more body to the liquid, being careful not to let it stick to the pot.

Paint the triangles of polenta with the olive oil and sprinkle with salt. Broil or grill the polenta over charcoal until the outside is crisp and brown. The insides should still be soft and creamy.

Put 2 triangles on each hot plate, spoon some chili over the polenta, and drizzle some of the sauce over the chili. Serve the rest of the sauce separately.

Meats and Offal

I have always wanted to go to a Texas barbecue where a whole steer has been cooking all day on a spit over a wood fire, to walk up with a long carving knife and slice a few choice morsels from the sirloin and the shoulder, a bit off the shin, and a slice from between the ribs. I'd take only small pieces of each, because when meats are roasted on a spit over a charcoal or wood fire, one does not need very much to be completely satisfied. And meats are never any better than when cooked whole or in large pieces, then allowed to rest so that the juices are reabsorbed. A whole pig or lamb cooked on a spit bastes itself so that the roasting juices are constantly being rolled around the animal as it turns. If the meat is additionally brushed with herb branches dipped in garlic oil, the flavors and textures have a quality that is very difficult to approximate in small cuts of meat.

But it is possible to follow the principles of cooking whole animals or large cuts when preparing smaller ones. Take pork chops as an example. The half-inch-thick pork chops that are offered in jumbo packs in supermarkets are unfortunate packaging because it is impossible to cook anything decent with them. They are so thin that even a fast grilling or sautéing leaves them tough and fairly tasteless. Not everyone wants or can afford a whole pork loin, but if you are reaching for that jumbo pack, designed to feed six to eight people, ask instead for a whole piece of the loin, still on the bone. Let it stand overnight in a sugar and salt brine solution, take it out and wipe it dry, and marinate it for a few hours in chopped fresh thyme and garlic with a bit of grated orange zest or chopped fennel, or, in the German, Pennsylvania Dutch, or Alsatian tradition, with kirsch or fruit alcohol and juniper berries. Then roast the pork whole in a 350-degree oven for forty minutes, let it rest, cut it off the bone, and slice it thin. If instead you want chops for grilling, roast the loin ten minutes less, let the loin cool completely, cut it into chops that are at least two inches thick, marinate them again, and put them on a medium charcoal fire until they are just barely pink inside. You can serve these with a variety of sauces: a mustard butter sauce; a butter made with pureed dried wild mushrooms; one made with anchovies, orange zest, and chopped fennel tops; the great Montpellier butter (page 34); or one with very reduced meat juices and a bit of Madeira. Chops prepared this way will have a texture and flavor like those that come off the whole roasted pig.

The same idea, of course, applies to lamb, beef, and game animals. The best steak I ever ate was at the Holman Ranch in Carmel Valley, California. It was in the fifties, when Holman was both a dude ranch and a restaurant. There was a central courtyard lined with a raised veranda, where the guests sat for dinner. The cooking was done in the center of the courtyard for everyone to see, with the massive steaks on the charcoal grills, so that while one was eating a perfect Caesar salad with garlic bread and cool red wine, one could smell the aroma of the steaks cooking, aromas that drove one into a frenzy of anticipation. They were porterhouse steaks, at least three inches thick, that had been brushed with herb oil, seared over high heat for a few minutes, and moved to a less hot part of the fire to finish the cooking. The steak was then brought to the table to be carved into slices that were charred on the outside and deep-red medium rare on the inside. Cooked that way, the meat was much better than

individual steaks the same size. I forget if there was a polite fight for the bone, but I know that I eyed it during the whole carving process, since the meat still clinging to the bone is, or seems, the most tender and flavorful.

Whereas great meat roasts and grills are confined, by necessity, to special occasions or locations, like the barbecue or the out-of-doors, one should never forget the possibilities offered by a fireplace. What is better than to sit in front of a fire with cocktails or champagne, to have some double-thick lamb chops marinating in rosemary and olive oil, to rake out some of the coals and to grill the chops right there in the fireplace?

The Marquis of Cussy, in his *Art Culinaire* (1820), says, "*Rôtir est à la fois rien et l'immensité*"—roasting is at the same time nothing and a very great thing. It would be difficult to find anything as satisfying, at the right moment, as those lamb chops perfumed with the smoke of the fire and the rosemary.

Because the cooking time is short for a rack of lamb or a fillet of beef, in a sense these cuts are the easiest to cook, and are looked upon as the most foolproof. The other side of the coin is that there is no forgiveness whatsoever in the cooking time. But if you look at a recipe for something "lower on the hog," as are lamb shanks (page 148), you will see that there is a good deal of flexibility in the cooking. If you misjudge the braising time by fifteen minutes, very little damage will be done. That kind of error with a rack of lamb would be disastrous, and very expensive. What could be easier than a braised-beef-shin dish like the French *daube* or English and American hot pot? All you have to do is layer two-inch sliced rounds of beef shin with chopped-up aromatic vegetables (carrot, celery, and onion), herbs, garlic, and a little red wine, place it in a 250-degree oven for three hours, let it cool slightly, take out the meat, strain the juices, puree the cooked vegetables to return to the sauce, lift off the fat from the juices, put it all back together with some new vegetables like turnips and parsnips, cook again for thirty minutes, and serve it right from the dish. Made one day and finished off the next with the new vegetables, it is even better.

Looking through *The Pleasures of the Table* by Édouard Nignon, a very grand writer of the early twentieth century who is undergoing a revival, I see that in the chapter on hot entrées he lists boiled salt beef served with fresh horseradish cream; beef hash, a favorite of the King of Milan when presented in a pastry shell topped by poached eggs; braised beef tongue served with a ragout of eggplant and tomatoes enriched with butter and veal stock; lamb kidneys cooked as on page 143 but offered with wild mushrooms and bacon; and braised tripe *à la mode de Caen,* a simple dish that may not be fashionable, but which, like the others above, Nignon instinctively realizes offers a basic deep satisfaction without which any cooking can become pretentious.

I used to cook tripe with a fanatical devotion. Recently we revived it at Stars, as a first course served in little polenta cups. Much to my amazement, it is a big hit. But the first time I ever cooked this grand favorite dish of mine was at Chez Panisse. As with all braising, the secret is long, very slow cooking. The question, in a restaurant open for both lunch and dinner, was when to cook this grand dish. I decided, since some ancient book had recommended leaving it

in the fireplace overnight, to cook it in the ovens overnight. After the evening service, everyone went home and I stayed to nurse along the fifteen pots of tripe that I had carefully sealed with flour-and-water paste to prevent any of the precious aromas from escaping. The point was never to let them boil over or allow any of the paste seals to break. This meant careful monitoring of the ovens, since they were not designed to go much below 275 degrees, and that was too high. When I was satisfied that the ovens were calm, I bedded down in the dining room, with the kitchen door propped open. The resident black cat was very surprised to see me and somewhat miffed to have his

nocturnal prowling grounds preempted. The rest of the night was a total nightmare. Every time a surge of gas augmented the heat, the juices would rise up and escape from the pots, to hit the oven floor with a loud hiss. Waking from a sleep made already fitful by the heavy atmosphere of braising veal feet, I would rush in and open the oven doors to bring the temperature down. The tripe casserole would calm down and I would go back to sleep, only to leap to my uncertain feet at the sound of more juices dripping down on the hot oven surfaces.

This went on all night, and upon the arrival of the morning crew, I was a basket case. But then I had to take the casseroles apart, put them back together in individual pots, reseal them, and return them to the ovens. By the time I had cooked lunch and prepared the rest of the dinner, smelling all day what in small doses is one of the greatest kitchen aromas but is overpowering in massive doses, I could not even taste what I had looked forward to for weeks. All I could do was drink soda water and faintly wave directions to whichever oven had to be served from next. As it turned out, barely anyone came to the tripe dinner anyway, so I closed the restaurant and invited the staff to sit down with the twenty or so stalwarts who had shown up. It was one of the best parties I have ever been to, even though I had to wait until the next day before I could indulge in a big plate of divine, cider-braised tripe myself.

The best thing about braised meats is that they can be made the day before (in fact, may be better for it)

and are wonderful for leftover cooking. Recently, at a friend's house, I had a dinner that could not—considering that I had dropped in unannounced from six thousand miles away—have been more perfect or satisfying. There was some braised lamb shoulder left over from two days before. There were a couple of tomatoes, some dried macaroni, an onion, a carrot, some herbs from the garden, and not much else. As it turned out, "not much" was enough. The onion was peeled and thinly sliced. The carrot was peeled and chopped up. They were put in a large sauté pan with an herb bouquet and sweated for ten minutes over a low

flame. Then the left-over lamb was cut up, the bones left attached to the meat, and that was put in the pan with the juices from the initial braising. A cup of red wine was poured over all that and the pan was covered, to simmer over low heat for thirty minutes. The cook asked if we should put some tomatoes in the stew. I looked at the amount of sauce building in the pan and said yes, knowing that he wanted to put them in anyway. The dish could use the color and flavor of those Mediterranean tomatoes, I thought, so they were chopped and added. The stew, again covered, simmered another ten minutes. Then quarter-inch macaroni in long hollow strands was cooked in salted water, drained, and put in with the lamb. The pan was covered again and the pasta steamed in the fragrances of lamb, wine, and vegetables. The whole thing was tossed together in the pan with some butter to enrich the sauce and pull it together, seasoned with salt and freshly ground pepper, and brought to the table in the copper sauté pan.

Two hours earlier, after a decent and long lunch, I had been anxious about an appetite for dinner. But when I tasted that tender, moist, herb-perfumed lamb, tasted the enriched meat juices clinging to the macaroni, a whole new area of appetite that had been hidden from me, but was just waiting for stimulation, awoke and I ate joyfully, a healthy share. We drank Vieux-Télégraphe from the Rhone, a young one with the lamb and an older one with the cheeses. I know that I could have suffered a rack of lamb that night, but somehow that "rough" but elegantly done dish, eaten on top of a mountain with a storm outside, was the perfect cooking for the place and time.

My Steak Tartare

When you are hungry but cannot think of anything appealing, or, for one of several reasons usually relating to excess, you do not want anything else, steak tartare is a good bet. Because I have never liked the texture, color, or violent tastes of the recipe as it is usually mixed in front of you by a waiter, I developed this lighter, more colorful and digestible version for my restaurants, where we make it to order, chopping the meat in the food processor. Find whatever chilies you can, the more color the better, or substitute bell peppers mixed with chilies.

¼ cup	ancho chili puree (page 30)
½ cup	mayonnaise (page 36)
1 pound	lean sirloin or top round beef
2	eggs, hard cooked
1 medium	red chili
1 medium	green chili
1 medium	yellow chili
2 tablespoons	fresh lemon juice
½ teaspoon	Tabasco or hot sauce
	salt and freshly ground pepper
¼ cup	chopped fresh parsley
¼ cup	capers, rinsed

Serves 4

Mix the ancho puree with the mayonnaise and let sit 1 hour to develop the flavors.

Trim any tendons and fat from the beef. Cut into 1-inch cubes and grind in a food processor or chop fine by hand. Make sure you do not overprocess the beef.

Separate the yolks from the whites of the eggs and push each separately through a sieve.

Stem and seed the chilies. Slice in very fine strips.

Mix the lemon juice, hot sauce, and salt and pepper to taste in a bowl. Add the beef and mix well. Put the beef in the center of a cold plate. Put the egg yolks, egg whites, and chopped parsley around the beef in concentric circles. Spoon some of the ancho mayonnaise over the beef and scatter the capers over the mayonnaise.

Chopped Lamb Steak au Poivre

This is the more elegant presentation of the J. T. Burger I developed for the Balboa Café in San Francisco, and is wildly good, beyond its modest title. The chopped lamb should have about 15 percent fat and be cooked medium rare.

2 pounds	ground or chopped lamb meat
¼ cup	black peppercorns
32 cloves	garlic, peeled
2 cups	water
1 sprig	fresh thyme
	salt
¼ cup	tomato concasse (page 220)
1 cup	fresh mint leaves, parboiled, finely chopped
3 tablespoons	butter

Serves 4

Salt the lamb and shape into 4-inch patties, 1½ inches thick, as loosely as possible but still neatly and firmly packed. Either crush the peppercorns with a mallet, grind them very coarsely, or break them up in a spice mill. Coat the lamb patties on both sides with the pepper and let stand 1 hour.

Meanwhile, poach the garlic with the water, thyme, and some salt in a saucepan until just tender when stuck with a fork, about 20 minutes. Remove the thyme and discard. Strain the liquid and reduce it to ½ cup. Reserve the garlic separately.

Heat a griddle or frying pan over high heat. Sear the lamb patties 2 minutes on each side. Turn the heat down to medium and cook another 2 minutes on each side. Remove the patties and keep warm. Pour off all the fat and deglaze the pan with the garlic poaching liquid. Add the tomato, mint, and butter, turn the heat to high, and shake the pan to incorporate the butter.

Put the lamb patties on warm plates and place the garlic cloves around them. Spoon 1 teaspoon sauce over each patty and the rest around.

My Steak Tartare.

Bündnerfleisch with Vegetable Salad

Bündnerfleisch is the Swiss version of the *bresaola* of Italy. It is beef that is cured by drying, either in the high, cool mountain air of Switzerland or in front of a fan in a walk-in refrigerator. It is a perfect first course with champagne, very light but with enough flavor and bite to awaken the most slumbering appetite. Its one drawback for the home is that, like prosciutto, it has to be sliced very, very thin, and requires a mechanical slicer. So order it already sliced and use it that day. Serve it with any vegetable salad that appeals to you. This one was inspired by the chef at the Remington Hotel in Houston.

24 slices	**bündnerfleisch**
32 small	**French green beans**
2 medium	**yellow or crookneck squash**
2 medium	**zucchini**
1 bunch	**watercress**
	salt and freshly ground pepper
3 tablespoons	**fresh lemon juice**
½ cup	**extra virgin olive oil**
1½ teaspoons	**finely chopped fresh tarragon or marjoram leaves**

Serves 4

Arrange the beef in a single layer on each of 4 plates and prepare the salad as follows.

Put a pot of salted water on to boil. Cut the ends off the green beans and cut the squashes into thin strips.

Separate the watercress into sprigs and rinse and spin them dry. Store in the refrigerator.

Put ice and water in a large bowl.

Put the beans in the boiling water, cook 2 minutes, and then add the squash. Cook 3 minutes and drain. Plunge them in the ice water for 30 seconds. Drain well and set aside.

Dissolve salt and pepper to taste in the lemon juice and whisk in the olive oil and tarragon. Toss the watercress very lightly with the dressing and arrange it in a circular pattern in the center of each plate of beef slices. Toss the vegetables with the remaining dressing and put them on top of the watercress.

Grilled Whole Lamb Kidneys with Potato Pancakes

I first saw lamb kidneys still entirely enveloped in their own fat in Solliès-Toucas, in the south of France, in a butcher shop run by the Mutton sisters. I asked Richard Olney how they were cooked. We had them for lunch that day. Though simple, they are quite remarkable and are having a revival in smart Parisian restaurants today.

2 whole	**lamb kidneys, very *fresh and still encased in fat***
1 tablespoon	*olive oil*
4 sprigs	*fresh thyme*
4 large	*russet potatoes*
	salt and freshly ground pepper
2 tablespoons	*butter*
1 tablespoon	*chopped fresh parsley*

Serves 2

Trim the fat evenly on the kidneys so that it is 1 inch thick all around each kidney. Rub them with the olive oil and press the fresh thyme into the fat. Let marinate for 1 hour.

Peel the potatoes and either grate them in a mill or julienne them in a food processor. Rinse the cut potatoes in cold water, wring them dry in a towel, and form them into 4 6-inch pancakes, ¼ inch thick, on waxed paper squares. Refrigerate.

Season the kidneys and cook them in a heavy frying pan or casserole over medium heat for 15 minutes, turning them often to brown the fat slightly. Turn the heat down to very low and continue to cook, turning often, until the kidneys are still just barely pink inside, about 30 minutes. You will have to cut into one to test for doneness. Let the kidneys rest while you cook the potatoes.

Use ½ tablespoon butter in each of 4 crêpe pans and heat over medium-low heat for 30 seconds. Put the potato pancakes in the pans and cook for 10 minutes, making sure that the pancakes slide around the pans from the first minute. Turn or flip the pancakes and cook on the other side for 5 minutes. If you don't have 4 pans to use at once, cook the pancakes one at a time and keep warm in the oven. Put the pancakes on hot plates and the kidneys in the center of the pancakes. Sprinkle with the chopped parsley and serve.

Grilled Sweetbreads with Chili Butter

Most everyone these days cooks sweetbreads for a finished dish from the raw state, a practice that shortchanges the sweetbreads and gives them a bad reputation. But if you braise them first, on a flavorful bed of aromatics like mirepoix and fresh herbs, the sweetbreads take on a more complex flavor as well as a smooth and unctuous texture. It is best to cook the sweetbreads the day before serving them. I developed this dish for the Santa Fe Bar & Grill. If you do not want to cook French fries, cooked new potatoes that have been rolled in olive oil and chili powder and then grilled would do well.

4 large	*braised sweetbreads (page 222)*
2 tablespoons	*olive oil*
1 tablespoon	*finely chopped fresh tarragon or thyme leaves*
4 large	*potatoes*
2 quarts	*peanut or vegetable oil*
¼ cup	*ancho chili puree (page 30)*
6 tablespoons	*butter*
	salt and freshly ground pepper
1 cup	*salsa (page 28)*

Serves 4

Cook the sweetbreads as directed on page 222. When they are cool, wipe them dry and put them in a bowl. Add the olive oil and chopped tarragon, toss together, and let marinate for 1 hour.

Peel the potatoes and cut them by hand or with a machine into ⅜-inch-diameter fries. Hold them in water.

Start a charcoal grill or heat the broiler. Heat the oil to 375°F. Heat the ancho puree and whisk in the butter. Keep in a warm place.

Season the sweetbreads and grill over a medium fire until the sweetbreads are heated through and golden brown on the outside, about 8 minutes on each side. When you put the sweetbreads on the grill, drain the potatoes and spin them dry. When they are thoroughly dry, fry them in a basket in the hot oil until crisp, about 5 minutes.

Serve the sweetbreads on a bed of the salsa surrounded with fries. Pour the chili butter sauce on the sweetbreads.

Grilled Sweetbreads with Mushroom Butter

There are many ways to serve grilled sweetbreads, but whatever the combination, they should not be sauced except with a butter, chutney, or salsa, or the wonderful crisp grilled exterior will become soggy and some of the nutty flavor will be lost.

4 whole	*braised sweetbreads (page 222)*
1 tablespoon	*fresh thyme leaves, finely chopped*
¼ cup	*olive oil*
1 ounce	*dried cèpes, morels, or Italian field mushrooms*
1 cup	*veal, beef, or chicken stock (page 220) or sweetbread cooking liquid*
½ pound	*butter*
	salt and freshly ground pepper
8 small	*artichokes*
2 tablespoons	*fresh lemon juice*
4 small	*new red potatoes*
½ cup	*red bell pepper puree (page 32)*
¼ cup	*yellow bell pepper puree (page 32)*
1 tablespoon	*chopped fresh parsley*

Serves 4

Cook the sweetbreads as directed on page 222. When they are cool, mix the thyme and olive oil and rub the sweetbreads with half the oil mixture. Let them marinate for 2 hours.

While the sweetbreads are marinating, simmer the mushrooms and stock for 15 minutes. Let stand for 30 minutes. Strain the mushrooms and set aside. Reduce the stock to about ¼ cup. Puree the stock and mushrooms in a food processor, add half the butter, and puree again until smooth. Season and let the mushroom butter sit at room temperature for 2 hours for the flavors to develop.

Start a charcoal fire or heat the broiler.

Trim the artichokes to the heart and cook with the lemon juice in salted water until tender, about 10 minutes. Drain and pour the remaining oil mixture over the hot artichokes. Season and set aside.

While the artichokes are cooking, put the potatoes in salted water to cover. Bring to a boil and cook until tender, about 10 minutes. Toss with the artichokes.

Just before you are ready to cook the sweetbreads, heat the red puree in a saucepan, whisk in 6 tablespoons of the butter, and keep warm. Do not let it get too hot. Do the same with the yellow puree, whisking in the remaining 2 tablespoons butter.

Grill the sweetbreads, turning once, over a medium fire until heated through and golden brown on the outside, about 20 minutes. Grill the artichokes and the potatoes over low heat on the side of the fire for the last 8 minutes.

Put the red butter sauce on warm plates. Put the sweetbreads in the center and drizzle the yellow sauce around them. Put the artichokes and potatoes on the yellow sauce and the mushroom butter on top of the sweetbreads. Sprinkle with the chopped parsley.

Top: Grilled Sweetbreads with Chili Butter; bottom: Grilled Sweetbreads with Mushroom Butter.

T-Bone Steak Cowboy Style

Either a T-bone or a porterhouse steak—the best choices, since chewing on the bone is the most satisfying part—can be used in this recipe. Have them cut no less than one inch thick, leaving enough fat for maximum flavor, and cook them over real charcoal. I developed this recipe for James Beard.

4 one-pound	T-bone steaks, 1½ inches thick
4 large	sweet red onions, peeled
½ cup	clarified butter (page 216)
1½ teaspoons	chopped fresh thyme leaves
	salt and freshly ground pepper
½ cup	barbecue sauce (page 222)
12 sprigs	cilantro

Serves 4

Start a charcoal fire or heat the broiler.

Let the steaks come to room temperature.

Slice the onions ¼ inch thick and place the slices on a baking sheet or broiler pan. Paint them with the clarified butter, sprinkle with thyme, season, and cook under the broiler very slowly. The heat should be low. Cook the onions for 20 minutes, basting them with more butter every 5 minutes. They are cooked when tender and golden brown.

Season the steaks and grill over the charcoal until rare or medium-rare, about 8 minutes each side. Serve on hot plates with the onions. Spoon a bit of barbecue sauce on each onion and garnish the plate with the cilantro. Serve the remaining sauce separately.

Grilled Spicy Lamb Sausage with Oysters

This dish comes from the coast of Bordeaux. The sausages are usually finger-size, and the idea is to eat a piece of the hot, grilled, spicy sausage and then to swallow a fresh, very cold, salty oyster. The contrast of the two kinds of heat with the cold oyster is tantalizing, and when washed down with cool white or young red wine, the effect is very stimulating.

1½ pounds	lean lamb meat, shoulder or leg
½ pound	lean veal meat
¾ pound	pork fatback, very cold or frozen
2	fresh serrano chilies, seeded, finely chopped
¼ teaspoon	cayenne pepper
½ tablespoon	fresh thyme leaves, finely chopped
¼ tablespoon	fresh marjoram leaves, finely chopped
½ teaspoon	salt
	freshly ground pepper
48 small	very fresh oysters
16 wedges	lemon

Serves 4

Grilled Ham Hocks with Rocket and Mustard Aioli

I love the way braised meats taste when they are grilled, and this rather esoteric-sounding dish is really very simple in its effect. The bite of the rocket and mustard is a perfect foil to the richness of the ham. If you do not have rocket (arugula) and radicchio, use any bitter greens from the endive-chicory family, and maybe some wilted red cabbage for color.

4	ham hocks
2 medium	carrots, peeled, coarsely chopped
1 medium	onion, coarsely chopped
1 stalk	celery, coarsely chopped
1	bouquet garni (page 127)
1 tablespoon	fresh thyme leaves, chopped
¼ cup	Dijon-style mustard
½ cup	aioli (page 36)
2 tablespoons	fresh lemon juice
¼ teaspoon	salt
2 pinches	freshly ground pepper
¼ cup	olive oil
2 heads	radicchio, leaves separated
4 cups loosely packed	rocket leaves, washed, spun-dried

Serves 4

Put the lamb, veal, and fat through the medium-fine blade of a meat grinder. The fat must be cold, so that it will not clog up the grinder and will make it easier to handle the sausage meat.

Mix the meat, chilies, cayenne, thyme, marjoram, ½ teaspoon salt, and pepper together by hand, being careful not to overmix the sausage so that it doesn't become pasty. Fry a small piece and check the seasoning. Refrigerate the sausage meat for 4 hours to develop the flavors.

Wash the oysters and keep cold.

Start a charcoal fire or heat the broiler.

Form the meat into 2-ounce patties and set aside. Open the oysters, put on ice, and garnish with lemon wedges. Grill the patties on both sides and serve on a hot platter.

Put the ham hocks, carrots, onion, celery, and bouquet garni in a pot. Add water to cover by 6 inches. Bring to a boil and simmer uncovered until the hocks are tender when pierced with a skewer, about 2 hours. Skim off any scum that forms on the surface. While the hocks are cooking, skim off ¼ cup of the fat that is on the surface and mix it with the thyme.

Mix the mustard and aioli. Cover and let stand 1 hour for the flavors to develop.

When the hocks are cooked, remove them and coat with the thyme mixture. Let marinate for 1 hour.

Start a charcoal fire or heat the broiler.

Grill the hocks, turning them often, over a medium fire until they are heated through and crisp on the outside, about 15 minutes.

Meanwhile, mix the lemon juice with salt and pepper. Whisk in the oil. Put the radicchio leaves in a bowl, pour over half the dressing, and toss. Grill or broil the leaves for 1 minute, turning them once.

Put the radicchio around the edges of hot plates. Toss the rocket in the remaining dressing and put in the center of the plates. Put the hocks in the center of the rocket. Spoon some of the mustard sauce over the hocks and serve the rest separately.

Braised Lamb Shanks

Perfectly cooked lamb shanks are a breeze if you braise them slowly enough and turn them three or four times while they are cooking. A heavy cooking pan just large enough to hold them one layer deep is essential. Letting them stand, covered, in a warm place for twenty minutes after they are cooked is important to achieve the melting texture that makes them so wonderful. Eat them merely braised, grill them after they have been braised, or take them off the bone to use in stews.

4	lamb shanks, cut from the foreleg
	salt and freshly ground pepper
12 cloves	garlic, unpeeled
6	bay leaves
6 sprigs	fresh thyme
1 cup	fresh mint leaves
½ tablespoon	fresh rosemary leaves
1 quart	chicken, lamb, veal, or beef stock (page 220)
1 cup	aioli (page 36)
24 cloves	garlic, peeled
1 each large	red and yellow bell pepper, stemmed, seeded, cut in fine julienne
1 tablespoon	fresh thyme or marjoram leaves
1 tablespoon	butter

Serves 4

Heat the oven to 300°F.

Season the lamb shanks heavily and put them in a casserole or heavy pot with the unpeeled garlic, bay leaves, and thyme sprigs. Brown over medium heat for 15 minutes, turning them every 3 minutes. Cover the pot and put it in the oven. Cook until the shanks are very tender, about 2 hours.

While the shanks are cooking, blanch the mint leaves in boiling water for 1 minute. Drain, squeeze dry, and puree with the rosemary and 2 tablespoons stock in a blender. There should be a slight texture of the leaves in the puree. Mix into the aioli and let sit to develop the flavors.

Remove the shanks when they are done and keep warm and covered.

Pour the remaining stock into the cooking pot and bring to a boil, scraping loose any meat juices that have stuck to the pot. The moment the stock boils, turn off the heat and skim off all the fat. Bring the stock back to a boil and reduce the liquid to 2 cups. Keep skimming off any fat and scum and do not let any fat boil into the stock.

Strain the stock. Put the peeled garlic cloves in the stock and simmer until tender, about 15 minutes. Strain and reserve the garlic and stock separately.

Put the shanks, garlic, peppers, stock, marjoram, and a pinch of salt in a sauté pan. Cook over medium heat, turning the shanks a couple of times, until the peppers are tender, about 10 minutes.

Put the shanks on warm plates. Stir the butter into the peppers and season. Spoon the peppers and garlic cloves around the shanks. Spoon some aioli over the shanks and serve the rest separately.

Lamb Stew with Artichokes

This is another use of the lamb shanks as cooked in the previous recipe. I use the shanks for braising and stewing because their gelatinous quality prevents them from drying out. Serve this stew over hot polenta (page 219).

4	lamb shanks, cut from the foreleg
12 cloves	garlic, unpeeled
6	bay leaves
6 sprigs	fresh thyme
1 quart	chicken, lamb, veal, or beef stock (page 220)
20 cloves	garlic, peeled
2 bulbs	fennel
20 very small	artichokes
1	lemon
½ pound	shiitake, wild, or domestic mushrooms, sliced
½ cup	tomato concasse (page 220)
12 leaves	fresh sage
2 tablespoons	butter
	salt and freshly ground pepper

Serves 4 to 6

Cook the lamb shanks as directed in the previous recipe. Strain the stock after it has reduced and cook the peeled garlic in it until tender. Strain and reserve the stock and the garlic separately.

While the lamb is cooking, remove any brown or damaged outer surface from the fennel bulbs. Cut each bulb lengthwise in half. Cut out the roots and divide each half into 4 pieces.

Trim the artichokes down to the hearts. Cook 10 minutes in salted boiling water into which you have squeezed the lemon. Drain the artichokes.

Put the artichokes and fennel in the reserved stock and cook for 10 minutes. While they are cooking, bone the shanks and cut the meat into bite-size pieces.

Add the lamb, mushrooms, tomato, and sage leaves to the artichokes and fennel. Simmer for 10 minutes. Stir in the butter until it is incorporated. Taste for seasoning and serve.

Top: Lamb Stew with Artichokes; bottom: Braised Lamb Shanks.

The Chili Recipe

I know my Texan friends will tell me that chili is made simply with water, chili pods, meat, and salt—they have a point; I hate beans in chili. This slightly more complex version was inspired by one of the best chili recipes I know, which is in James Villas' superb book, *American Taste.* It was developed by a longtime friend, Oksana Czuczman, and it worked very well at the Santa Fe Bar & Grill. The chili is best if cooked the day before.

6 pounds	beef round or chuck
6 pounds	pork shoulder
1 cup	oil
½ cup	chopped bacon or ham fat
3 medium	onions, chopped
10 cloves	garlic, chopped
1 cup	masa harina or corn flour
1 teaspoon	cayenne
1 tablespoon	paprika
6 tablespoons	mild chili powder (ancho or pasilla)
2 tablespoons	red pepper flakes
4	bay leaves
6 tablespoons	cumin powder
4 tablespoons	fresh oregano, chopped
2	lemons, seeded and chopped
1	lime, seeded and chopped
3 tablespoons	cider vinegar
2 cups	tomato concasse (page 220)
6 cans	beer
6 to 8 cups	beef or chicken stock (page 220)

Serves a lot

Grind the meats coarsely (unless they are purchased already ground); set aside.

Heat the oil and fat in a large pot and put in the onions and garlic. Cook over low heat either in the oven or on top of the stove for 10 minutes. Put the meat in and brown it, stirring all the time.

Add the flour and cook, stirring constantly, another 5 minutes. Add all the spices and the lemons and lime. Cook over low heat, stirring often, for another 15 minutes.

Add the vinegar, tomato, beer, and stock. Simmer uncovered for 4 hours, stirring every 30 minutes. Let sit another 30 minutes and lift off the fat that has risen to the surface. Taste for seasoning and serve with soda crackers and cold beer.

Ham with Black Beans, Oranges, and Lime Cream

This recipe from the Florida regional dinner at the Santa Fe Bar & Grill combines Southern and Caribbean elements.

4 slices	country ham, cut 1½ inches thick
2 tablespoons	Barbados rum (medium dark)
1 whole	clove
2 cloves	garlic, finely chopped
1 tablespoon	fresh thyme leaves, finely chopped
1 tablespoon	grated orange rind
1 teaspoon	brown sugar
1 quart	chicken stock (page 220)
4	oranges
¼ cup	fresh lime juice
	salt and freshly ground pepper
1 cup	sour cream
1 tablespoon	grated lime rind
4 cups	cooked black beans (page 175)
½ cup	salsa (page 28)

Serves 4

Put the ham slices in a non-aluminum pan just large enough to hold them side by side.

Mix the rum, clove, garlic, thyme, orange rind, and sugar and rub over both sides of each slice. Let marinate for 1 hour. Pour over the chicken stock and simmer covered *very* slowly until the ham is tender, about 1½ hours.

While the ham is cooking, peel the oranges, cut out the sections between the membranes, and marinate with the lime juice and salt and pepper to taste.

Mix the sour cream and lime rind and set aside. Lift the ham slices from the cooling liquid, cover, and keep hot. Strain the cooking liquid and mix with the beans in a pan. Heat thoroughly; then add the juices from the orange marinade. Season if necessary and put on warm plates. Put the ham slices on top of the beans and the orange sections around. Put the salsa in the center of the slices and drizzle the lime cream over the ham.

Ham with Black Beans, Oranges, and Lime Cream.

Fricassee of Veal with Crayfish

3 pounds	white veal breast or shoulder, cut into 2-inch pieces
6 cups	white veal stock or chicken-veal stock (page 220)
1 cup	coarse mirepoix (page 127)
1	bouquet garni (page 127)
24	button mushrooms, stemmed, stems reserved
	salt and freshly ground pepper
2 tablespoons	fresh lemon juice
24	pearl onions, peeled
¼ pound	butter
¼ cup	flour
16	baby artichokes, trimmed, parboiled 10 minutes
16 small	carrots, peeled
8 small	turnips, peeled
24 tiny	French green beans, parboiled 2 minutes
4 sprigs	fresh tarragon
¼ cup	crayfish essence (page 221)
½ cup	heavy cream
3	egg yolks
4 whole	crayfish, cooked in salted water 10 minutes and cooled

Serves 4 to 6

Put the veal in a heavy saucepan or casserole just large enough to hold the pieces side by side. Add the stock. If the liquid does not cover the meat, add water until the meat is covered by 2 inches of liquid. Bring to a simmer and skim the surface of the liquid. Add the mirepoix, bouquet garni, and mushroom stems. Salt lightly and simmer very slowly until the veal is tender, about 1½ hours.

Remove the meat and set aside covered. Strain the cooking liquid, discard the vegetables, rinse out the pot, and put the liquid back in it. Toss the mushroom caps with the lemon juice and put them and the onions in the pot. Simmer gently until onions are tender, about 15 minutes. Drain mushrooms and onions, reserving liquid, and put them with the meat. Cover and set aside.

Put 3 tablespoons of the butter in the pot and melt it. Whisk in the flour and cook over low heat for 5 minutes. Whisk in the reserved cooking liquid and simmer for 40 minutes, skimming any skin or scum that rises and forms on the surface. Add the artichokes, carrots, and turnips to the sauce and simmer until the carrots are just tender, about 10 minutes. Add the beans, tarragon, reserved veal, onions, and mushrooms. Simmer for 5 minutes.

In these last minutes, heat the crayfish essence and whisk in the remaining butter. Keep warm.

Whisk the cream and egg yolks together for 30 seconds and pour into the fricassee of veal. Add the 4 crayfish. Immediately remove the pot from the heat and stir thoroughly but gently. The sauce should thicken slightly. Taste for seasoning and serve on warm plates. Drizzle the crayfish essence over each serving and place a crayfish on top.

Poached Beef Fillet with Vegetables

This version of *boeuf à la ficelle* is garnished with little new vegetables, but you could easily use big vegetables cut up, and could include cabbage, mushrooms, leeks and other roots, as well as marrow bones, duck sausage, garlic sausage, and tongue. Other herbs, like rosemary, can be substituted, and why not dot the plate with tomatoes dressed in olive oil and fresh herbs? Whole-grain mustard is a very good accompaniment. Barbara Kafka in New York does a superb version of this recipe using lamb loin.

4 eight-ounce	*tournedos (pieces cut from the beef fillet)*
2 tablespoons	*olive oil*
	salt and freshly ground pepper
4 sprigs	*fresh thyme*
4 sprigs	*fresh tarragon*
1 cup	*tomato concasse (page 220)*
½ pound	*fresh horseradish, peeled, rinsed*
½ cup	*sour cream or crème fraîche*
2 quarts	*rich beef, veal, or chicken stock (page 220)*
10 medium	*carrots, peeled, halved*
20 very small	*turnips, peeled but tops left on*
20	*pearl onions, peeled*
4	*parsnips, peeled, quartered*
16 small	*new yellow potatoes*
20 small	*yellow summer squash*

Serves 4

Rub the tournedos with the olive oil. Season them and press 1 sprig thyme and tarragon into each of them. Marinate for 1 hour at room temperature.

Put the tomato in a saucepan and cook over medium heat until the juices have evaporated to leave a thick puree, about 20 minutes. Stir every few minutes to prevent sticking and burning. Put through a sieve and let cool.

Grate the horseradish in a food processor or by hand. Mix the horseradish and sour cream and stir it into the tomato puree. Add salt to taste and reserve.

Remove the herb sprigs from the beef and set aside.

Bring the stock to a boil. Add the carrots, turnips, onions, parsnips, and potatoes; simmer for 5 minutes. Add the squash, herb sprigs, and tournedos; cook for 8 minutes for medium-rare beef.

Take the beef out and put it on warm plates. Surround the beef with the herbs and vegetables. Pour some of the horseradish sauce over the beef and serve the rest separately.

Overleaf Coulibiac of Sweetbreads (recipe on page 156).

Coulibiac of Sweetbreads

(pictured on pages 154–155)

Coulibiac is a lot of work, but once done, it is a dream for dinner parties, even large ones, since timing is not terribly crucial and it will hold admirably for up to half an hour. The brioche, crêpes, and sweetbread preparation can be done the day before.

4 pounds	*braised sweetbreads (page 222)*
1 cup	*sweetbread braising juices*
½ cup	*dry Madeira*
	salt and freshly ground pepper
2 pounds	*mushrooms, finely chopped*
4 tablespoons	*butter*
1 recipe	*brioche (page 217)*
8 to 10	*crêpes (page 217)*
8 slices	*ham or prosciutto, very thinly cut*
4	*eggs, hard-cooked, peeled, halved*
1	*egg, beaten*
2	*carrots, peeled, finely diced*
1 large	*onion, peeled, finely diced*
3 stalks	*celery, finely diced*

Serves 8

Braise the sweetbreads according to the recipe on page 222.

Heat the oven to 325°F.

Reduce the juices by half in a sauté pan. Add the sweetbreads and the Madeira and cook over high heat, tossing the sweetbreads, until the liquid has just evaporated. Season and cover them off the heat and refrigerate until assembling the coulibiac.

Cook the chopped mushrooms over medium heat with 2 tablespoons butter, tossing constantly, for 10 minutes. Season and set aside in a sieve over a bowl.

Divide the brioche dough into two parts, one about 6 ounces heavier than the other. Roll out both pieces into rectangles, the larger one about 14 inches by 8 inches, and chill until you assemble the coulibiac.

Put the smaller rectangle of dough on a sheetpan. Down the center of the pastry, leaving about 1½ inches of border all around, place 4 or 5 crêpes. On top of the crêpes put half the ham slices, then half the mushrooms, then all the sweetbreads, then the eggs stacked against each other like fallen dominoes, then the remaining mushrooms, ham, and crêpes. Brush the egg wash around the edge of the pastry. Place the other piece of brioche pastry on top and press down around the edges. Fold the edges over and trim. Decorate the top as desired. Put the coulibiac aside to rise for 30 minutes.

Heat the oven to 350°F.

Mix the carrots, onion, and celery together and cook, covered, in the remaining butter for 10 minutes. Season and add any collected mushroom juices. Keep warm.

Brush the coulibiac with the remaining egg wash and bake for about 40 minutes. Let cool 10 minutes, slice and serve with the vegetable mixture.

Roast Pork Loin Stuffed with Ham and Rosemary

A long time ago, I learned from Jane Grigson's excellent book on charcuterie that if you brine pork for a day before cooking it you have a sure way to guarantee moist and very flavorful pork, as long as you do not overcook it. Remember that pork can be very slightly beige-pink and still be safe in terms of trichinosis, the trichinae being killed at a meat internal temperature of 137 degrees. This dish could be served with a warm vegetable stew (page 167), roasted peppers (page 167), black-eyed peas (page 180), or red cabbage salad (page 110).

3 pounds	*center-cut pork loin*
¼ cup	*salt*
¼ cup	*sugar*
2 quarts	*water*
2	*bay leaves*
1 tablespoon	*allspice berries*
1 tablespoon	*dried thyme*
2 cloves	*garlic, left whole*
2 large	*shallots, finely chopped*
3 tablespoons	*olive oil*
½ pound	*country ham or prosciutto, finely chopped*
2 tablespoons	*fresh rosemary leaves, finely chopped*
	salt and freshly ground pepper
1 cup	*chicken stock (page 220)*
2 tablespoons	*Dijon-style mustard*
4 tablespoons	*butter*

Serves 6

Trim the loin so that there is only ¼ inch fat on top. Mix the salt, sugar, water, bay leaves, allspice, and thyme in a pan and heat until the salt and sugar are dissolved; let cool. Put the loin in a pan just large enough to hold it and the liquid and pour the brine over the pork. Let marinate overnight or at least 6 hours in the refrigerator.

When the pork is fully brined, remove it and wipe it dry. With the handle of a wooden spoon or with a round knife-sharpening steel, poke a hole carefully through the very center of the loin.

Put the garlic, shallots, 1 tablespoon of the oil, and 1 tablespoon water in a small sauté pan. Cover and sweat over low heat for 10 minutes; do not let the mixture brown. Stir in the ham and half the rosemary. Set aside to cool. When it is cool, push the mixture into the center of the loin so that it is evenly distributed. Mix the remaining oil and rosemary and rub all over the loin. Season and let marinate at room temperature for 2 hours.

Heat the oven to 325°F.

Heat a sauté pan over high heat and sear the loin and

brown it on all sides, about 5 minutes. Put the loin in a roasting pan just large enough to hold it and cook for 30 minutes. Remove the loin and let sit for 20 minutes in a warm place, covered with a piece of foil.

Pour any fat out of the pan and wipe it gently to remove all the fat. Pour in the stock and reduce it to ½ cup, scraping the pan to dissolve any of the browned meat juices. Strain the stock into a saucepan. Whisk in the mustard and then the butter until it is incorporated. Keep the sauce warm.

Cut the pork into ⅛-inch-thick slices. Put the slices on hot plates and pour the sauce over them.

Braised Sweetbreads in a Sealed Casserole

Braised sweetbreads is a dish that has many variations, but the one I like and that always makes me think of New Year's Eve is this one when it has fresh truffles in it. But then almost anything with fresh truffles in it is wonderful, and if you do not have them, try wild mushrooms, and if you cannot get them fresh, reconstitute dried morels, cèpes, field mushrooms, etc., in stock and use them, reducing the stock and putting that in as well. It is a dish of kings that, once you have cooked the sweetbreads and paid for the mushrooms, is easy to set up, cook, and serve. You will need two-cup-capacity covered ovenproof dishes. Ideal are the metal charlotte dishes from France.

2 large	*braised sweetbreads (page 222)*
2 medium	*carrots, peeled*
1 large	*onion, peeled*
2 stalks	*celery*
¼ cup	*malmsey Madeira*
1 sprig	*fresh thyme*
2	*bay leaves*
1 sprig	*fresh tarragon*
2 sprigs	*parsley*
	salt and freshly ground pepper
½ pound	*fresh cèpes, chanterelles, morels, or field mushrooms*
½ cup	*flour*

Serves 4

Prepare the sweetbreads, reserving 3 cups of the cooking liquid.

Cut the carrots in ¹⁄₁₆-inch-thick julienne; then cut crosswise to make a precise dice of ¹⁄₁₆ inch in diameter. Cut the onion and celery into the same size dice. Mix together and set aside.

Add all but 1 tablespoon of the Madeira to the sweetbread cooking liquid and reduce to 1 cup.

Heat the oven to 350°F.

Put the carrot mixture and herbs in a pot. Cover and bake for 10 minutes. Let cool covered and remove the herbs. Spoon the mixture into four 2-cup ovenproof casseroles.

Pull the sweetbreads apart into ¼-inch pieces. Season the pieces and toss them in a bowl with the remaining 1 tablespoon Madeira. Add them to the casseroles.

Chop the fresh mushrooms and truffles if you have them and put on top of the sweetbreads. If you are using dried mushrooms that you have reconstituted in stock, chop them and add to the casseroles. Pour over the reduced cooking liquid.

Turn the oven up to 400°F.

Make a paste of flour and water so that it can be rolled out in your hands to form sticky ropes. Press the ropes around the outer rim of the covers and then press the covers down on the casseroles so that they are sealed. If the paste falls down, push it back up to seal the cover and the dish.

Bake for 20 minutes. Take the dishes to the table and break open the seals to serve.

Vegetables and Fruit

I cannot think of any subject in this book that is more complicated than vegetables, which is not to say that the best vegetable preparations are complicated to cook. It is just that the range of possibilities seems vast in comparison with any other category of raw materials— and there is the challenge to keep it simple. In fact, a good rule with vegetables is: The less done to them in the cooking, the better.

In my early days at Chez Panisse, I used to make a carrot soup that unfailingly provoked the question: "What *did* you do to that soup?" And I would have to reply, "Nothing." What I did do was to make sure that the carrots cooked in the shortest amount of time and were then cooled down as quickly as possible so that they would not continue cooking and lose their freshness.

I used chicken stock in all vegetable soups in those days, and it was not until a couple of years later that, in the south of France, I tasted one of the best vegetable dishes I had ever eaten, a leek and potato soup made with water. Part of the reason it tasted so good was the set of events that led to this simple late-night repast, events that were made up of eating and drinking far too much at the great wine estate of the Peyraud family, Domaine Tempier in Bandol, near Marseilles. Richard Olney and I had started with tasting from the barrels at ten that morning. We had gone in to lunch with the family, eating such wondrous things as sea bass grilled over vine cuttings and served with a sauce made from the livers of monkfish and the roe of the bass, followed by leg of lamb cooked in the kitchen fireplace on a spit, then a massive tray of cheese, and finally an almond cream dessert. With the lunch we drank the bottles that had been opened in the cellars after tasting from the barrels, as well as some older vintages of those same bottles. Then at the end of lunch we drank some marc, the alcohol distilled from the lees of the wine, and by six o'clock that evening, after a final bottle tasting on top of the hill at another cellar, we set off on the three-hour drive home over the mountains.

Curiously after that large lunch, we later felt a pang of interest in food. We certainly needed something to keep body and soul together until the morning. Richard said that there was only one thing that would save us. He went into the garden with a flashlight and pulled some leeks. He sliced them and some potatoes, put them in a pot with cold water and salt, simmered everything until the leeks were tender, ground fresh pepper into the soup, and served it with a pat of butter in the center. It awoke my palate and stimulated my appetite. The fresh, clean, simple flavors of the leeks and potato, uninterrupted by anything else except for a certain smoothing over the edges by the butter, perked up my very quickly fading interest in life at that moment. In no time at all, instead of falling into bed, we were searching out the cheeses and opening up a good red wine to go with them.

In the first part of this chapter I try to show what is possible with a basket of vegetables collected in the garden or gathered at a pass down the line of the fruit and vegetable counter at a good supermarket. And they do not have to be "baby" vegetables, either. The current restaurant fad is a continuation of the European tradition celebrating the first spring vegetables, called *primeurs* in France, and they are delicious and a welcome sight after months of winter root vegetables. But fashion has made its relentless demands, prices have soared, and the fad has led people almost to lose

sight of the pleasures of vegetables that have grown beyond the infant stage. People have almost forgotten also which vegetables are best when very small and which need to grow a bit more to develop their flavor. Certainly little green beans, the French *haricots verts,* when tiny and the texture of silk velvet, are infinitely better than in their maturity. But must artichokes always be the size of a large thimble, even though the little purple ones that size are delicious eaten raw with lemon juice, salt, and olive oil? Or pumpkins, when they get the size of a large beach ball—are they to be relegated to decoration? Peeled, seeded, and cut into quarter-inch cubes; tossed with a little flour, some salt, finely chopped garlic and parsley; put into an earthenware dish sprinkled with oil and baked in the oven for two hours at 225 degrees, they produce one of the most meltingly rich and superb vegetable dishes possible. As for asparagus, I love the big, fat New Jersey ones, carefully peeled so that none of the stem is wasted, cutting deeply at the stalk end and releasing the pressure on the knife as one pares up the stem to the tender green tip. Must we be sentenced to wispy, undernourished, whiplike asparagus because it looks younger? Do leeks have to look like emaciated scallions, or can we enjoy the big, healthy-looking ones, poached in chicken stock or water or red wine, served hot with beef marrow, or cold with a basil vinaigrette?

Most vegetables, in fact, lead a dual life: They are very good young as well as mature. The only family that is pretty much a dead loss in the cradle stage is squash. Zucchini, when they still have the flower on and are only two inches long and the thickness of a little finger, are ravishing to look at and intellectually stimulating to work with, but have no taste. Then again, when they are the size of a large club—a stage that, as every gardener knows, seems to arrive the moment one's back is turned—they are useless. The middle stage of zucchini—when they are six inches long, one inch thick, firm, dark green (or golden), and very fresh—is when they are at their peak.

When I think of vegetables now, I think of a vegetable stew or ragout, one version of which appears on page 167. I think of a summer afternoon, and sitting on a terrace or under a grape arbor, a checkered cloth on the table, a bucket of ice with white wine chilling, some platters of country sausage being passed around with the first glass of wine, and an empty spot in the middle of the table, the guests' glances at it anticipating the heavy copper sauté pan that will soon arrive, steaming with the aroma of fresh herbs, a wisp of garlic, and the all-enveloping bouquet of a mixture of vegetables cooked together, vegetables picked from the garden or bought at the market that morning.

The selection depends on whatever is available, but I always look forward to buying some little pearl onions, either red or white leeks, artichokes, red bell peppers, little green beans, fava beans, pieces of fennel, sugar snap peas, and squashes. These I cook with a little bundle of thyme, tarragon, and parsley, the only liquid being water, and the sauce that is produced from all the vegetable juices, enriched with olive oil or butter, is among the extraordinary tastes and culinary pleasures. Perhaps the effect is powerful because not very much is expected from a platter full of cooked vegetables, even though the colors and the aromas are startling. The aromas get most of their kick from whatever is added just before the vegetables are brought to the table. In that last moment, I throw in a mixture of freshly chopped mixed herbs, garlic, and sometimes lemon zest. I toss that with the hot vegetables, adding more butter or olive oil, grind over it a good deal of black pepper, toss everything together again, cover the ragout,

and bring it to the table for the assembled guests. As undramatically as possible, I remove the cover and let the explosion of herb, garlic, vegetable, and pepper rise up and turn on everyone's appetite.

Garden Salad with Salmon Caviar Croutons *(pictured on page 166)*

I have developed many variants of the garden salad over the years. This version, without the croutons, is the basic one, using whatever greens, flowers, and herbs you have in a garden or find in whatever market you use. You can do the same thing with just one green, as in a watercress and walnut oil salad with grilled bread, or a rocket salad with grilled herb brioche; or you can roll goat cheese rounds in bread crumbs, sauté them for a few seconds, put in a 375-degree oven for five minutes, and place them at the center of this salad, with olive puree on the croutons.

1 small head	curly endive
4 small	red leaf lettuces
4 small	green leaf lettuces
1 bunch	watercress
2 tablespoons	fresh lemon juice
¼ teaspoon	salt
2 pinches	freshly ground pepper
¼ cup	walnut or hazelnut oil
¼ cup	virgin olive oil
2 tablespoons	fresh chervil leaves
1 tablespoon	fresh tarragon leaves
16	fresh rose petals
16	nasturtium flowers
1 tablespoon	calendula petals
1 tablespoon	fresh sage flowers
½ cup	fresh salmon or steelhead roe
12	croutons

Serves 4

Pick over the greens, removing any stems and blackened leaves. Use only the inside tender leaves of the endive. Wash and spin dry the leaves. Keep cold in the refrigerator.

Mix the lemon juice with salt and pepper to taste in a bowl large enough to hold all the greens. Whisk in the oils.

Put the greens and herbs in the bowl. Toss together thoroughly but gently and put the salad on cold plates. Put the flower petals throughout the salads. Spread the roe on the croutons and put 3 on each plate. Pass the salt and pepper mill separately.

Grilled Vegetable Salad with Texas Ham *(pictured on page 166)*

There are as many versions of this vegetable dish as there are vegetables—or almost as many, since I would never grill members of the cabbage family, like broccoli or cauliflower. But pepper, squash, endive, onions, and root vegetables take on a new dimension when they are cooked, marinated in olive oil and herbs, and lightly grilled. They are best lukewarm or at room temperature, and should not be refrigerated after they are grilled or they lose the light smoky flavor. If you do not have Texas ham, use prosciutto or any country ham.

4 small	zucchini, cut lengthwise into quarters
4 small	summer squash, cut lengthwise into quarters
4 small	scallopini squash, halved
8	scallions, trimmed
4	Japanese eggplants
4	red bell peppers
4	yellow bell peppers
½ cup	olive oil
	salt and freshly ground pepper
2 tablespoons	fresh thyme or marjoram leaves, finely chopped
½ pound	Texas ham, very thinly sliced
1 cup	aioli (page 36)

Serves 4

Cook the squashes in salted boiling water for 5 minutes. Remove and plunge into ice water for 2 minutes to stop the cooking. Drain them well. Do the same with the scallions, cooking them for only 2 minutes.

Heat the oven to 350°F.

Rub the eggplants and peppers with a little olive oil. Season and put them in a roasting pan. Bake covered until tender, about 20 minutes. Remove from the oven and take out the eggplants, leaving the peppers covered in the pan to cool down. When the eggplants are cool, remove the stem ends and cut each one lengthwise in quarters. Uncover the peppers and peel, discarding all seeds and stems. Cut them into quarters. Mix the remaining olive oil and the thyme together. Put all the vegetables together and pour the mixture over. Toss very gently and marinate for 1 hour.

Start a charcoal fire.

Season the vegetables and grill them over a moderate fire for 5 to 10 minutes. Place the ham on plates and put the vegetables on the ham. Drizzle some of the aioli over the vegetables and serve the rest separately.

Roasted Bell Pepper Salad with Anchovies

One of the most perfect dishes to set down in front of people for lunch or dinner in the summer, together with plenty of crusty bread, cool white wine, a bottle of green virgin olive oil, and a crock of country butter, is a huge platter of roasted or grilled bell peppers, accented with herbs and salted anchovies filleted and revived in olive oil. The peppers can be grilled or baked, covered, in the oven. They must be peeled, and the secret to easy peeling is to cover them after they are cooked while they are cooling down. The skins should then slip off easily.

8	red bell peppers
6	yellow bell peppers
4	green bell peppers
8	salted anchovies
1 cup	extra virgin olive oil
¼ cup	white wine vinegar
½ teaspoon	salt
¼ teaspoon	freshly ground pepper
6	Niçoise or small black olives
24	sage or other herb flowers

Serves 6 to 8

Whether grilling or roasting the peppers, do it as slowly as possible, and turn them frequently so that the skin blisters and blackens but the flesh does not burn. It should take about 10 minutes. Put the peppers in a pan, cover with plastic wrap or foil, and let stand until they cool. When cool, cut the peppers open, remove the stems and seeds, and scrape off the skin.

Laying them out flat, trim the tops and bottoms of the peppers. Cut them into fifths or sixths, depending on their size. Lay them out on a platter.

Fillet the anchovies under cold running water and place the fillets carefully in a bowl. Pour some cold water over them and leave 10 minutes. Drain the fillets on paper towels and put in a dish. Pour ¼ cup of the olive oil over the fillets and leave 30 minutes.

Mix the vinegar with salt and pepper and whisk in the remaining olive oil. Pour the dressing over the peppers.

Arrange the anchovies, olives, and herb flowers on the peppers and serve. Serve the olive oil in which the anchovies have been marinating for those who wish to dip their bread in it.

Clockwise from top left: Garden Salad with Salmon Caviar Croutons (recipe on page 165); Grilled Vegetable Salad with Texas Ham (recipe on page 165); Warm Vegetable Stew; Roasted Bell Pepper Salad with Anchovies.

Warm Vegetable Stew

I first tasted this most glorious dish in the south of France with Richard Olney, who taught me the technique of the progression of vegetables as they go into the cooking pan. No better description of the dish and the philosophy behind it, no better appreciation of vegetables, can be found than in his book *Simple French Food*. The combination here is only one of many, though I never use more than seven vegetables, and never use tomatoes unless they are cherry tomatoes. The addition of chopped garlic and herbs just before you bring the stew to the table causes a burst of rich fragrance which perfects the dish. I prefer water to chicken stock for a cooking liquid—the resulting sauce has a much fresher and purer vegetable taste—and I use either butter or olive oil to finish the dish.

16 small	pearl onions, peeled
1 sprig	fresh thyme
1 sprig	fresh tarragon
24 baby	carrots, trimmed and peeled
½ small	cauliflower, cut into flowerettes
½ small	broccoli, cut into flowerettes
6	pattypan squash, halved crosswise
4 small	zucchini, halved lengthwise
4 small	yellow zucchini, halved lengthwise
8	fresh ears baby corn
24 small	French green beans
24	fresh squash blossoms
1 tablespoon	mixed fresh herbs, finely chopped
2 cloves	garlic, finely chopped
¼ pound	butter, cut into ½-ounce pieces
	salt and freshly ground pepper

Serves 6 to 8

Bring a pot of salted water to boiling and maintain it at a steady boil while adding the succession of vegetables.

Put the onions, thyme, and tarragon, 1 cup of water, and a pinch of salt in a sauté pan. Cover and simmer for 5 minutes.

Put the carrots into the boiling water for 1 minute, then lift them out and add to the onions. Simmer covered while you cook the cauliflower and broccoli in the boiling water for 5 minutes. Then lift these out and add them to the onions and carrots with another ½ cup water. Cover and continue cooking, tossing the vegetables together every few minutes.

Meanwhile, put the squash and zucchini into the boiling water for 3 minutes and then add them to the other vegetables. Toss together again. Cook the corn and beans in the boiling water for 1 minute and add to the other vegetables. Toss, cover, and cook 5 minutes. Make sure there is about 1 cup of liquid in the vegetable pan.

Uncover the pan. Add the squash blossoms, herbs, garlic, and butter. Turn the heat to high and toss together until the butter is melted and the sauce thickens a little. Season and serve immediately.

Fresh Fig and Mint Salad

As a variation on this recipe, you could serve thin slices of country ham or prosciutto topped with the figs and dabbled with mint whipped cream and raspberry puree. Or you could do a smaller version of the garden salad (page 165), with goat cheese and figs. Another fruit salad favorite of mine is white peaches with a basil vinaigrette and rose peppercorns. The quantities given here are for a main luncheon course.

20	ripe black figs
¼ cup	fresh raspberry puree (page 32)
½ cup	heavy cream
2 tablespoons	fresh lemon juice
1 large pinch each	salt and freshly ground pepper
¼ cup	olive oil
16	fresh mint leaves

Serves 4

Cut the stems off the figs and cut in half from top to bottom.

Mix the raspberry puree and cream together in a bowl and whip to soft peaks.

Mix the lemon juice with the salt and pepper and whisk in the oil. Put the figs in a bowl and toss gently with the dressing.

Cut 4 of the fig halves again from top to bottom. Put 2 fig quarters in the center of each plate and surround with the fig halves. Toss the mint leaves with the remaining dressing in the bowl and put them around the figs. Spoon the raspberry cream over the center figs.

Watermelon and Onion Salad

If you can eat raw onions and like watermelon, this is a knockout in the summer, and is perfect for a lunch salad. It was developed by one of my cooks, Julie Dierkheiging.

1 small	ripe watermelon
2 medium	sweet red onions, peeled
¼ cup	raspberry puree (page 32)
¼ cup	olive oil
	salt and freshly ground pepper
3 tablespoons	fresh lemon juice
¼ cup	walnut oil
3 bunches	watercress

Serves 6

Cut the melon into 1-inch-thick slices. Cut around the line between the white and red part of the melon and discard all but the red. Remove all the seeds and cut the melon into cubes.

Cut the onions crosswise into ⅛-inch-thick slices.

Mix the raspberry puree, olive oil, and salt and pepper. Put the melon and onions in a bowl and pour the raspberry sauce over them. Mix thoroughly but gently.

Mix the lemon juice with salt and pepper and whisk in the walnut oil. Pour the dressing over the watercress in a bowl and toss quickly. Arrange the watercress on cold plates and put the melon and onions on top. Spoon any remaining raspberry sauce over the top of the melon and watercress.

Avocado, Papaya, and Rocket Salad

Rocket (arugula, roquette) and avocado are a magical pair, creating a taste which is far more than the sum of their individual characteristics.

2	ripe avocados
1	ripe papaya
1 large	sweet red onion
¾ cup	fresh lemon juice
	salt and freshly ground pepper
¾ cup	hazelnut or walnut oil
2 cups loosely packed	rocket leaves, selected, washed, spun dry
12	Niçoise or small black olives

Serves 4

Cut the avocados in half vertically, lift out the pits, and, with a large spoon, scoop the flesh out in one piece.

Peel the papaya, cut it in half vertically, and scoop out the seeds.

Slice the onion very thin and put in a bowl with all but 3 tablespoons of the lemon juice. Add a pinch of salt, toss together, and let marinate.

Mix the remaining lemon juice with salt and pepper and whisk in the oil.

Slice the avocados and papaya lengthwise. Alternate the avocado and papaya slices on cold plates. Spoon half of the dressing over the slices.

Toss the rocket in the remaining dressing and put on the plates. Place the onion next to the rocket and put the olives around the onion.

Mango and Avocado Salad

2 small	fresh hot red chilies (cayenne)
1 small	fresh hot green chili (serrano)
2 tablespoons	fresh lime juice
	salt and freshly ground pepper
½ cup	walnut oil
1 cup	chervil leaves
½ cup	mayonnaise (page 36)
2	ripe mangoes
2	ripe avocados
½ cup	tomato concasse (page 220)
12 sprigs	fresh chervil

Serves 4

Stem the chilies, cut them lengthwise in half, scrape out all the seeds, and finely dice them.

Mix the lime juice with some salt and pepper and whisk in the nut oil. Add the chilies to half the dressing.

Chop the chervil very fine and add to the mayonnaise. Peel and slice the mangoes vertically into segments. Put them in a bowl and pour over the chili-dressing mixture. Let marinate at room temperature for 1 hour and refrigerate for 30 minutes.

When ready to serve the salads, cut the avocados in half lengthwise, remove the pits, and scoop out the flesh with a large spoon. Cut the avocados crosswise into ⅛-inch-thick slices. Fan each half on a chilled plate. Arrange the mango slices in fans on the plates and spoon over the chili marinade.

Pour 2 tablespoons of the remaining dressing over the tomato concasse and toss it together. Put the tomato on the plates. Pour the remaining dressing over the avocados; then drizzle the mayonnaise over the avocados. Garnish the plates with the chervil sprigs.

Borscht with Pickled Mushrooms and Cucumbers

Some of the greatest Russian dishes are the soups like *botvinia, okroshka,* and chilled beet soup, especially when served with hot little meat pastries called *piroshki.* The soups contain sour elements like pickles, sorrel, lemon, dill, and horseradish, all very cooling in the summer. The soup plates in the photograph are the ones in which my aunt used to serve this violently colored soup, each thin crystal plate filled with a chunk of ice, and as you ate it, the spoon and the ice would ring against the fine crystal, the sound they made almost as cooling and satisfying as the soup. Use whatever wild mushrooms you have or buy some Chinese black ones. Pickle the mushrooms up to a week in advance.

6 large	*red beets*
8	*shiitake, tree oyster, or any wild mushrooms, stemmed, stems reserved*
1 teaspoon	*gin*
½ cup	*white wine vinegar*
1 clove	*garlic, peeled, finely chopped*
1½ teaspoons	*salt*
1	*cucumber, peeled*
1 medium	*onion, peeled, finely chopped*
1 large	*carrot, peeled, finely chopped*
1 stalk	*celery, finely chopped*
1 sprig	*fresh thyme*
2	*bay leaves*
2 quarts	*chicken or chicken-duck stock (page 220)*
1 cup	*sour cream*
1 small	*red bell pepper, roasted, peeled, chopped (page 167)*
1 small	*yellow bell pepper, roasted, peeled, chopped (page 167)*

Serves 6 to 8

Heat the oven to 325°F.

Scrub the beets. Bake in a roasting pan, covered with foil, until tender when pierced with a fork, about 1 hour. Let cool.

While the beets are cooking, heat the mushrooms, gin, vinegar, garlic, and ½ teaspoon of the salt in a saucepan for 1 minute. Cover and let marinate.

Cut cucumber lengthwise in half, scoop out seeds with a spoon, and thinly slice crosswise. Put cucumber and 1 teaspoon of salt in a bowl, mix, and let marinate.

When the beets are cooled, peel them, chop fine, and put in a pot with the onion, carrot, celery, thyme, bay leaves, and stock. Bring to a boil and then simmer for 15 minutes. Strain. Whisk in the sour cream until completely smooth, and cool the soup in an ice-water bath or in the refrigerator.

Drain the mushrooms and slice them. Drain the cucumbers and put in a separate bowl.

Taste the soup for salt and pour into a chilled tureen. Put cold soup plates on the table with chunks or cubes of ice in them. Spoon the mushrooms, cucumbers, and peppers into each bowl and ladle the soup over them.

Cream of Corn Soup with Crayfish Butter

When I found this soup in *The Epicurean,* the cookbook of Delmonico's restaurant in turn-of-the-century New York, it triggered the idea to stop looking slavishly at France for inspiration and to find it around me in California. My interest in American regional cooking, and the California movement, began—story told on page 12. The original recipe calls for "green" or very young corn, but I find the best corn to use is the newer white corn, with small kernels that are just formed. If you don't have crayfish essence, use lobster or shrimp essence, or a fresh basil or ancho chili cream.

8 ears	*fresh young corn*
2 tablespoons	*butter*
½ tablespoon	*fresh marjoram leaves*
2 cups	*chicken stock (page 220)*
¼ cup	*crayfish or shellfish essence (page 221)*
1½ cups	*heavy cream salt and freshly ground pepper*

Serves 4

Shuck the corn, remove all the silk from the ears, and slice downward on the ears between the husk and the kernels to remove the kernels without getting any of the husk.

Melt the butter in a saucepan and add the corn, marjoram, and a few tablespoons of the stock. Cover and sweat over very low heat for 5 minutes. Boil the remaining stock and pour over the corn. Bring the corn back to the boil and remove from the heat. As soon as it is cool enough to handle, puree it through the fine-mesh disk of a food mill or in a food processor; then press it through a sieve to get a fine puree.

Whip the crayfish essence and ½ cup of the cream in a bowl to soft peaks.

When you are ready to serve, reheat the corn puree with the remaining cream. Check the seasoning and pour into soup plates. Spoon the shellfish cream on the center of the soup.

Borscht with Pickled Mushrooms and Cucumbers.

Chilled Sorrel and Herb Soup with Tomato Cream

This recipe is a version of the summer soups common to nineteenth-century Europe and America. Called green soup or garden soup, they used whatever greens and herbs were in the garden: lettuces, endives, sorrel, herbs (including parsley and lovage), vegetable tops, watercress, etc. Water as the base will give a purer, truer taste of the greens themselves, but a light chicken stock will make it richer. I prefer water.

1 large	potato, peeled, diced
4 cups	water or chicken stock (page 220)
1 teaspoon	salt
½ cup	tomato concasse (page 220)
2 cups	heavy cream
1 cup loosely packed	sorrel leaves, stemmed
½ cup loosely packed	watercress leaves
6 cups loosely packed	tender mixed lettuce leaves
½ tablespoon	fresh tarragon leaves
2 tablespoons	fresh basil leaves
1 tablespoon	fresh chervil leaves
	salt and freshly ground pepper

Serves 6 to 8

Put the potato and water or chicken stock in a saucepan. Add a teaspoon of salt and bring to a boil. Simmer until the potato is tender, about 10 minutes.

While the potato is cooking, make the tomato cream. Put the tomato in a sauté pan and cook over medium heat, stirring all the time, to reduce and evaporate all the liquid in the tomato. Do not let it turn brown or burn. Cook for about 10 minutes and put it through a sieve. Stir in ½ cup of the cream and chill it.

When the potato is cooked, add the sorrel, watercress, lettuce, tarragon, basil, and chervil. Bring to a boil over high heat, stirring to make sure the leaves cook evenly. Immediately put the pan in an ice-water bath or pour the soup into a bowl sitting in ice water to halt the cooking and retain the freshness of the greens. Stir while it cools. When it is cold, puree the soup, leaving some texture of the leaves. Pour the puree into a bowl. Stir in the remaining cream, season, and chill.

Add a pinch of salt to the tomato cream and whip it to soft peaks.

Ladle the soup into chilled bowls and spoon some of the tomato cream onto each serving.

Garlic Soup with Sage and Ham Butter

When I put garlic soup on the menu at Stars, nothing prepared me for its enormous success. I attribute its continued popularity to its mildness, the result of using cooked garlic. For a garnish I stuffed little profiteroles with a butter made from chopped fresh sage and country ham. In this recipe, I use the same butter, which melts out over the surface of the soup and provides tantalizing bits of flavor as you eat the soup.

15 cloves	fresh garlic, unpeeled
3 cups	chicken stock (page 220)
5	fresh sage leaves
¼ cup	diced country ham or prosciutto
3 tablespoons	butter
	salt and freshly ground pepper
½ cup	cream
3	egg yolks

Serves 6 to 8

Put the garlic cloves and stock in a saucepan and simmer until the cloves are soft, about 30 minutes. Let cool slightly and then puree, using the fine-mesh disk of a food mill or a food processor; then press through a sieve.

While the garlic is cooking, very finely chop the sage leaves and ham together. Mix into the butter, season, and leave at room temperature.

Mix the cream and egg yolks together well.

Heat the garlic soup to boiling. Remove from the heat and stir in the egg mixture. The soup should thicken slightly. If not, return it to the heat for a minute but do not let it boil. Ladle into warm soup plates and spoon the ham-sage butter on the center of each serving.

Cucumber Vichyssoise with Crayfish Cream

The word vichyssoise is used loosely here to mean a chilled cream vegetable soup that is thickened with potatoes and enriched with cream, along the lines of the original one of Louis Diat. The cucumber provides a nice change from leeks, and you could use summer squashes as well, or even eggplant. If you do not want a shellfish cream, use the tomato cream described on page 172.

1 small white	onion, peeled, finely chopped
1 sprig	fresh tarragon
2 cups	chicken stock (page 220)
2 large	cucumbers, peeled, seeded, finely chopped
¼ cup	crayfish essence (page 221)
1½ cups	whipping cream
	salt and freshly ground pepper
4 sprigs	chervil
4	crayfish heads, cooked

Serves 4

Put the onion, tarragon, and 2 tablespoons of the chicken stock in a saucepan. Cover and sweat over very low heat for 10 minutes.

Add the cucumbers and cook covered for 5 minutes. Add the remaining chicken stock. Bring to a boil over high heat and remove from the heat.

While the soup is cooling, stir the crayfish essence into ½ cup of the cream and let sit for 30 minutes.

Puree the cucumbers with their cooking liquid in a food mill or food processor and stir in the remaining cream. Refrigerate until cold.

Whip the crayfish cream until it takes on a little bit of body, about 1 minute. Season the soup and serve in chilled bowls with the crayfish cream swirled on top. Garnish each serving with a chervil sprig and a crayfish head.

My Black Bean Soup

I heard about the famous black bean soup of the Coach House in New York City from James Beard, who told me about Leon Lianides and his wonderful food. So when I opened the Santa Fe Bar & Grill I put The Coach House Black Bean Soup on the first menu. Jim Beard tried it on a visit to the restaurant and said, "Well, Jeremiah, it is delicious, but it is not the Coach House black bean soup." So I dropped the name and it became more and more its own self.

1 pound	black turtle beans
1	onion, peeled, chopped
1 medium	carrot, peeled, chopped
1 stalk	celery, chopped
6 cloves	garlic
1	bouquet garni (page 127)
1	ham bone or 1 cup ham skin and scraps
2 to 3 quarts	chicken stock (page 220)
1 tablespoon	ground cumin
1 tablespoon	ancho chili powder
½ cup	sour cream
2 tablespoons	milk
	salt
½ cup	salsa (page 28)

Serves 6 to 8

Rinse and sort the beans, discarding any stones or discolored beans. Soak overnight in cold water, adding more water if needed. Put the beans, onion, carrot, celery, garlic, bouquet garni, ham bone, and chicken stock to cover in a large heavy pot. Bring to a boil and skim off any scum that rises to the surface. Simmer slowly, loosely covered, until the beans are tender, about 2 hours. Add more stock if the level falls below the surface of the beans and stir often to prevent sticking and to ensure that the beans cook evenly.

When the beans are cooked, put them through a meat grinder or food mill fitted with a medium- or fine-mesh disk. Mix the bean puree with the cumin and chili powder.

Mix the sour cream and milk until smooth.

Heat the bean puree, adding more stock to get a consistency that will pour out of a ladle like thin hot cereal. Season and pour into warm soup plates. Drizzle the sour cream over each serving and put the salsa in the center.

The Black Bean Cake

I think that the columnist Liz Smith's farewell to Rock Hudson—"So long, big boy, have a good rest"—is what I would like on my tombstone, but it will probably be: "He invented black bean cake." Like red cabbage salad (page 110), it is one of those dishes that the public will not let me take off the menu. It is simple, beautiful, easy, and fast. But it has never been imitated with any success, despite many tries. Here is the recipe.

3 cups	cooked black beans (opposite)
1 tablespoon	ancho chili powder
1 tablespoon	ground cumin
1 small	fresh hot green chili, stemmed, seeded, finely chopped
½ cup	cilantro leaves, coarsely chopped
¾ teaspoon	salt
½ cup	sour cream
1 tablespoon	milk
¼ cup	rendered duck fat, lard, or olive oil
¼ cup	salsa (page 28)
24 sprigs	cilantro, washed, spun dry

Serves 4

Cook the beans as directed in the previous recipe but, before you grind them, let them drain for about 2 hours. Don't worry if they look terrible after sitting that long. Save the liquid for soup. Put the cooked beans through a meat grinder or food mill and then mix them with the chili powder, cumin, fresh chili, cilantro leaves, and salt into a paste. Roll the paste into 4 equal balls. Put each ball between 2 pieces of waxed paper and press them into rounds ⅛ inch thick with the palm of your hand. Set aside.

Whisk the sour cream and milk until smooth.

Heat the duck fat in a crêpe or nonstick pan or on a griddle. When the pan is hot, put in the cakes and cook 2 minutes on each side. Put the cakes on warm plates and spoon the sour cream on the center of each cake. Spoon the salsa on the sour cream. Garnish the plates with the cilantro sprigs.

My Black Bean Soup.

Warm Salad of Artichokes and Grilled Prawns

Prawns grilled in their shells pick up additional flavor from them and are juicier than if cooked without. I have not served a sauce to dip the prawns in, but a chervil, savory, rosemary, or rosemary-tomato mayonnaise or aioli would be a delicious accompaniment. I prefer olive oil to pour over the prawns once I have shelled them at table, especially if the oil has been soaking with little Niçoise olives and there is a bowl of coarse salt to dip the prawns in after they are dipped in the olive oil. Lobster, crab, or scallops would work as well.

20 large	*fresh prawns*
3 cloves	*garlic, peeled, finely chopped*
1 tablespoon	*fresh thyme leaves, finely chopped*
½ cup	*olive oil*
6 large	*artichokes*
4 tablespoons	*fresh lemon juice*
	salt and freshly ground pepper
¼ cup	*hazelnut or walnut oil*
¼ cup	*tomato concasse (page 220)*
½ cup	*cilantro leaves*

Serves 4

Toss the prawns in a mixture of the garlic, thyme, and olive oil, and marinate in the refrigerator for 1 hour.

Trim the artichokes to just the bottoms. Put 3 tablespoons of the lemon juice in a pot of salted water, bring to a boil, and add the artichoke bottoms. Simmer until they are tender when pierced with a fork, about 15 minutes.

While they are cooking, mix the remaining lemon juice with salt and pepper; whisk in the hazelnut oil.

When the artichokes are cooked, drain them and let cool just until they can be handled. Slice them ⅛ inch thick and toss gently with the dressing. Let marinate 30 minutes at room temperature.

Start a charcoal fire or heat the broiler.

Wipe the garlic and thyme from the prawns and skewer them. Grill them over a medium-high fire or under the broiler for 3 minutes on each side. While the prawns are cooking, check the seasoning on the artichokes and arrange them on warm plates. Toss the tomato in the dressing remaining in the bowl and spot the tomato around the plate. Dress the cilantro leaves also with the remaining dressing and put them around the artichokes. Put the grilled prawn skewers on top of the artichokes and serve.

Artichoke Bottoms Stuffed with Fava Bean Puree

Richard Olney told me of the natural marriage of savory and fava beans and, as he made the dish, described how it was de rigueur in the nineteenth century as a garnish with roasted meats. It is easy to see why it never appears in restaurants today: the prodigious amounts of fava beans required to make the puree in any quantity, and the labor it takes to peel them. But the dish can be appreciated in the home because to make it for four is not all that daunting and well worth the effort.

4 large	artichokes
1	lemon
4 pounds	fresh fava (broad bean) pods
2 sprigs	fresh savory or thyme
2 cups	chicken stock (page 220)
½ pound	butter
	salt and freshly ground pepper
½ cup	red bell pepper puree (page 32)
½ cup	yellow bell pepper puree (page 32)

Serves 4

Cut half the top off each artichoke. With a stainless-steel paring knife, continue to cut around the artichoke, rotating it in your hand as you cut, until only the very bases of the leaves remain on the bottom of each

artichoke. Cut out the chokes or center fibers. Trim the stem to ⅛ inch.

Squeeze the lemon into a pot of salted water and add the lemon halves. Bring to a boil. Add the artichoke bottoms and simmer for 10 minutes. Remove them and plunge into ice water for 5 minutes. Drain well and set aside.

Take all the beans out of the pods; remove the outer pale green skins from the beans. Put the beans and savory in a pot and cover with the chicken stock. Bring to a boil over high heat; then simmer for 8 minutes. Drain, reserving the cooking liquid and beans separately. Put the beans through the medium blade of a food mill or puree in a food processor, using up to half the cooking liquid to help the process. Press the puree through a fine sieve. Cover and set aside.

Put the artichoke bottoms in a sauté pan just large enough to hold them. Add the remaining bean-cooking stock and 1 tablespoon of the butter. Cover and simmer over low heat for 10 minutes. While they are cooking, put the bean puree in a double boiler and heat it. When it is hot, add ½ cup of the butter and stir it in. Season, remove from the heat, and keep warm.

Put the pepper purees in separate saucepans. Bring to a boil and turn off the heat. Divide the remaining butter in half and whisk one half into each puree.

Remove the cover from the artichoke pan. Spoon bean puree into the artichoke bottoms. Spoon some of the yellow puree onto the center of each warm plate, the red puree around the edges, and place the filled bottoms in the center. Heat the beans for 1 minute over boiling water and spoon them around the artichokes.

Grilled Radicchio and Smoked Eel Salad

This salad may seem esoteric, but it only follows the tradition of serving smoked meats (like duck) with the bitter greens of the endive family. Here, the bitter "edge" of the radicchio balances and complements the richness and smokiness of the eel. Smoked trout, sturgeon, or whitefish can be substituted, and if you don't have radicchio, use Belgian endive, or a combination of endives. I have used cucumber flowers as a garnish, but you can use any herb flowers.

4 heads	radicchio
½ cup	olive oil
	salt and freshly ground pepper
1 small	fresh horseradish root
½ cup	sour cream
2	smoked eels or 12 to 16 small fillets of smoked eel
1 bunch	Italian parsley
3 tablespoons	fresh lemon juice
½ cup	walnut or hazelnut oil
4 tablespoons	golden or whitefish caviar
8	cucumber flowers

Serves 6 to 8

Remove any blackened leaves from the outside of the radicchio. Cut the heads through the cores into sixths. Rub them with the olive oil, season with salt and pepper, and let marinate for 15 minutes.

Start a charcoal fire or heat the broiler.

Peel and grate the horseradish. Mix with the sour cream and set aside.

Skin the eels and cut 4-inch-long fillets from the bones. Pick over the parsley and trim off the stems. Rinse, spin dry, and set aside.

Mix the lemon juice with salt and pepper, and whisk in the nut oil. Grill or broil the radicchio for 2 minutes on each side and coat each piece very lightly with some of the dressing.

Put the radicchio pieces around the edge of a large platter. Crisscross the eel fillets on the center of the platter. Dress the parsley with the remaining dressing and put it around the eel. Spoon the horseradish sauce over the eel and place the caviar in teaspoon-size mounds on the cream. Put the cucumber flowers around the salad and serve.

Mushroom Caps with Bone Marrow

As far as I know, this recipe is an original of Stars, and comes of my love of grilled mushrooms and marrow on toast. The cheese could be Fontina or Gruyère, but I like the aged dry Jack as made by the Vella cheese company in Sonoma. The mushrooms could be shiitake, field, or large domestic mushrooms, or even fresh cèpes or porcini. This first course is very rich.

6 large	shiitake or field mushroom caps
½ tablespoon	fresh thyme, finely chopped
1 teaspoon	finely chopped garlic
¼ cup	olive oil
1 cup loosely packed	Italian parsley leaves
½ cup	mayonnaise (page 36)
2 large	center-cut marrow bones, cut 4 inches long
	salt and freshly ground pepper
7 slices	aged dry Jack cheese, as large as the mushrooms

Serves 6

Rub the mushroom caps all over with a mixture of the thyme, garlic, and olive oil, and let sit covered for 30 minutes.

Puree the parsley and stir into the mayonnaise.

Put the marrow bones in salted water to just cover and bring to a boil. Cook for 1 minute and then plunge into ice water.

When the bones are cool enough to handle, wipe them dry. Using a very thin-bladed knife, cut around the inside of the bone to remove the marrow in sausage-shaped pieces. Cut the marrow into ¼-inch-thick rounds and set separately on a plate. If the pieces are still warm, refrigerate until cool and then hold at room temperature.

Start a charcoal fire or heat the broiler.

Wipe the garlic and thyme off the mushrooms and season them on both sides. Put them, undersides down, on the grill. Cook over medium heat for 5 minutes and then turn them over. Put the marrow in the center of the caps and a slice of cheese over the marrow. Cook until the mushrooms are tender, the marrow is warm, and the cheese starts to melt, about 7 more minutes. Put the mushrooms on a platter and spoon the parsley sauce on the centers of the mushrooms.

Top: Grilled Radicchio and Smoked Eel Salad; bottom: Mushroom Caps with Bone Marrow.

Warm Salad of Black-Eyed Peas

I first saw fresh black-eyed peas in a supermarket in Cambridge, Massachusetts, about fifteen years ago, tried them hot with a vinaigrette as an accompaniment to baked ham, and fell in love. They came—and still come—in little plastic packets. This dish is meant as a lunch course or a substantial first course and is accompanied by corn muffins.

3 cups	fresh black-eyed peas
4 large slices	ripe tomato
1 tablespoon	white wine vinegar
	salt and freshly ground pepper
¼ cup	olive oil
4 rounds	fresh goat cheese
2 tablespoons	chopped parsley
	salt
16 slices	pancetta or lean bacon
½ tablespoon	fresh marjoram leaves, finely chopped
1½ cups	chicken stock (page 220)
6 tablespoons	butter
1 small	red bell pepper, roasted, peeled, finely chopped

Serves 4

Rinse the peas and set aside to drain.

Put the tomato slices in a dish. Mix the vinegar with salt and pepper and whisk in the olive oil. Pour this vinaigrette over the tomatoes and let marinate for 30 minutes.

Roll the edges of the goat cheese rounds in the parsley.

Bring a pot of salted water to a boil.

Heat the oven to 375°F.

Put the bacon on a rack and bake until just crisp, about 10 minutes.

While the bacon is cooking, cook the peas in the boiling water for 8 minutes. Drain and transfer them to a sauté pan. Add the marjoram and stock. Bring to a boil; then simmer for 5 minutes.

Remove the bacon from the oven, drain on paper towels, and keep hot.

Add the butter and bell pepper to the peas and stir until the butter is incorporated. Season and spoon onto warm plates. Put a tomato slice in the center of each plate, then the goat cheese in the center of the tomato, and the bacon over the peas.

Okra, Tomato, and Basil Warm Salad

I am very fond of salads that have slightly chilled and very hot elements in them. Here, the cool tomatoes, with the sharpness of the vinegar and richness of the olive oil, are in contrast to the heat of the sautéed okra. For a memorable meal this salad follows close on the heels of the "Baltimore" salad recommended to me by James Beard, which is basically a bacon, lettuce, and tomato sandwich without the bread, again combining hot and cold.

2 pounds	fresh okra
	salt and freshly ground pepper
2 tablespoons	white wine vinegar
½ cup	olive oil
3 large	ripe tomatoes
12 leaves	fresh purple or green basil
36 small	golden cherry tomatoes (optional)
½ cup	cornmeal
½ cup	lard, bacon fat, rendered duck fat, or olive oil

Serves 4

Cut the stems off the okra and slice the okra crosswise ¼ inch thick. Season the slices and set aside.

Mix salt and pepper into the vinegar and whisk in the olive oil.

Slice the tomatoes, put them in a dish, and pour over the dressing. Marinate for 15 minutes.

Put the tomato slices on room-temperature plates. Toss the basil leaves in the dressing in the bowl and put them on the tomato slices. Toss the cherry tomatoes in the remaining dressing and put them on the plates. Pour any dressing remaining in the bowl over the tomatoes.

Toss the okra with the cornmeal; then put it in a very coarse sieve and shake off the excess cornmeal. Heat the lard in a sauté pan over medium heat until hot but not smoking. Add the okra and fry, tossing it all the time, for 8 minutes, being careful not to let it burn.

As soon as the okra is cooked, spoon it onto the center of the tomatoes and serve immediately.

Top: Warm Salad of Black-Eyed Peas; bottom: Okra, Tomato, and Basil Warm Salad.

French-Fried Eggplant with Florida Guzpachy Sauce

This was among the most popular dishes served at one of the first American regional dinners I gave at the Santa Fe Bar & Grill. "Guzpachy" is obviously a step away from "gazpacho," the soup that has somewhat the same ingredients as this sauce, which is really a relish or salsa. Like all relishes, it needs to sit an hour for all the flavors to develop. The combination of the sharp, cold sauce with the rich, piping-hot, fried eggplant is very successful. You could serve a big platter of eggplant and pass a bowl of sauce, or serve individual portions as a first course.

1 large	cucumber
	salt
1 medium	sweet red onion, finely chopped
1	hard-cooked egg yolk, finely chopped
1 tablespoon	fresh mint leaves, finely chopped
2 tablespoons	olive oil
¼ cup	fresh lime or lemon juice
¼ cup	white wine vinegar
3 cloves	garlic, finely chopped
1 small	red bell pepper, stemmed, seeded, finely chopped
8 medium	Japanese eggplants
4	eggs
½ cup	seasoned flour
½ cup	fresh white bread crumbs
	vegetable oil for deep frying

Serves 4

Peel the cucumber and cut lengthwise in half. Scoop out and discard the seeds and then cut the cucumber into ⅛-inch dice. Sprinkle with 1 tablespoon salt and let drain in a colander for 15 minutes. Taste a piece of the cucumber. If it is too salty, rinse it and drain well. Combine the cucumber, onion, egg yolk, mint, olive oil, and lime juice in a bowl.

Put the vinegar and garlic in a non-aluminum saucepan and bring to a boil. Add the bell pepper, cook 30 seconds, and pour over the cucumber mixture. Mix together well and set aside.

Cut the stems off the eggplants and then cut them lengthwise into quarters. Put the eggplant in a colander, sprinkle with 1 tablespoon salt, and let drain for 30 minutes.

Wipe the salt off the eggplant. Whisk the eggs in a bowl, put the seasoned flour in another bowl, and put the bread crumbs on a plate. Heat the vegetable oil to 375°F. Dip the eggplant pieces first in the flour, then in the egg, and then roll them in the bread crumbs. Lower them into the hot oil and fry for 5 to 10 minutes, depending on the size of the pieces, until golden brown and tender. Be sure to maintain the temperature of the oil, especially if you put several pieces in at once.

Put the guzpachy in the center of each warm plate and place the hot eggplant pieces around the sauce like the spokes of a wheel. Serve immediately.

Minestrone with Artichokes, Sausage, and Pistachios

This soup was inspired by a seventeenth-century Italian recipe for minestrone containing black truffles and artichokes, an idea so appetizing that I decided to develop a simpler recipe, but one as different from the modern minestrones as the old Italian version was. The seventeenth-century soup called for roast partridge and orange as well, but no pasta. Basically, one should feel free to invent one's own version. Here's mine.

6 small	artichokes
½ pound	garlic sausage, mild andouille, or kielbasa
1	lemon, thinly sliced
1	red bell pepper
	salt and freshly ground pepper
3	Japanese eggplants or 1 small regular eggplant, quartered
3 cups	chicken stock (page 220)
2 small	zucchini, quartered
2 small	yellow zucchini, quartered
12 baby	green beans, ends trimmed
8	pattypan squash
24	pistachios, shelled, blanched, and peeled
12 leaves	marjoram
16 leaves	Italian parsley
12	thyme flowers
4 drops	truffle oil or 1 teaspoon chopped fresh truffle (optional)

Serves 4

Trim the artichokes and cook until tender in acidulated salted water. Poach the sausage until done, about 15 minutes. Grill or broil the lemon slices for 5 minutes. Roast or grill the red bell pepper; cover for 15 minutes; peel, and cut into thin strips. Season the eggplant pieces and grill or broil until tender, about 10 minutes.

Put the chicken stock in a pot and bring to a boil. Add the zucchini, green beans, and pattypan squash. Cook for 5 minutes; add the artichokes, sausage, pistachios, lemon, red bell pepper, eggplant, and all the other ingredients. Cook 1 minute, season, and serve.

Minestrone with Artichokes, Sausage, and Pistachios.

Eggplant and Zucchini Timbale Soufflé

This dish is considered a timbale because of its shape and the way it is constructed, and a soufflé because the eggs and cheese in the zucchini mixture rise like a soufflé and fall slightly when it cools. I think the flavors are best when the timbale is lukewarm, with just some olive oil drizzled over it. But served warm with the fresh tomato sauce accented by the Italian parsley and basil mayonnaise, it is pretty special. It is photographed here as a large timbale, which you would cut like a cake and serve in wedges.

3 pounds	*zucchini*
3 tablespoons	*kosher salt*
3 large	*eggplants*
½ cup	*herb oil (page 222)*
¼ cup	*olive oil*
3 tablespoons	*fresh marjoram, finely chopped*
	salt and freshly ground pepper
6	*eggs, 4 whole and 2 yolks*
1 cup	*ricotta*
¼ cup	*freshly grated Parmesan*
2 cups	*fresh tomato sauce (page 220)*

Serves 8

Hand grate or put the zucchini through the small julienne blade of a food processor. Put the zucchini in a bowl and sprinkle it with the kosher salt. Mix well and let stand for 30 minutes, tossing twice.

Heat the oven to 350°F.

Cut the eggplants lengthwise into ⅛-inch-thick slices. Brush the slices with the herb oil and put them on a sheet pan. Cover and bake for 10 minutes. Remove the eggplants from the pan and cool as quickly as possible.

Line a straight-sided large dish or several small ones with the eggplant slices, starting with a radial pattern on the bottom of the dish. Overlap the slices to completely cover the surface of the dish. The slices that have more of the skin showing will give a better pattern. Save any very small slices for the stuffing and save enough large slices to cover the top.

Wring out the zucchini until it is completely dry. Put the olive oil in a saucepan and heat it slightly. Add the zucchini and toss it over medium heat for 5 minutes. Add the marjoram and salt and pepper to taste; cook until the zucchini is dried out, about 5 minutes. Do not let it brown or color. Put the zucchini in a bowl and let cool. Add the eggs, ricotta, and Parmesan. Chop any of the eggplant slices you didn't use and add to the zucchini. Mix together very well and taste for seasoning.

Spoon the zucchini mixture into the lined dish to ½ inch from the top. Completely cover the zucchini mixture with the remaining eggplant slices.

Cover the dish with foil and put it in a larger baking pan. Put the pan in the oven and fill with boiling water ¾ up the smaller dish. Cook until a skewer inserted in the center comes out clean, about 1 hour. Take the timbale out of the pan and let it sit for 20 minutes in a warm place. Unmold the timbale onto a platter. Wipe up any juices that flow out and spoon the tomato sauce around.

Desserts

In restaurants in America, one problem I have always had with the dessert selection is the preponderance of cakes. Just as I believe that eggs are best eaten at one in the morning, I think cakes belong in the afternoon, with tea or coffee. After dinner, that big wedge of frosted fluffy cake tends to overwhelm what has come before, and to wipe out all memory of previous subtleties and flavors. So when I think of desserts, I can think of only two cakes I would like to try again: the Viennese chocolate torte, of the *reine de Saba* family, and the Lady Baltimore cake, which is the ultimate cake indulgence. I must mention one other cake, which evokes mixed emotions: the Frankfurterkranz, a masterpiece of *genoise* and buttercream that takes two dozen eggs, pounds of butter, and all day to make. My emotions are mixed because the first time I tried to make it, it took several attempts and I had to invite all the neighborhood kids in to keep running to the store for me, in exchange for which they got to eat about sixty eggs' worth of *genoise* and quarts of buttercream.

There is a family of cakes, like pound cake and poppyseed cake, that are always wonderful, and that I think of as accompaniments to beverages, ice cream, and fruit. Dinner at my aunt and Russian uncle's always ended in massive doses of ice cream—perhaps because my aunt's family fortune was partially derived from Abbott's Dairy in Philadelphia, which made superb ice cream. Ice cream is still, for me, one of the great wonders of the world, and I never grow tired of it. Waiting for the ice cream machine (or the person cranking away manually) to start complaining bitterly, which is the same time the ice cream is ready; impatiently pulling off the top of the canister; wiping away the salty and sometimes oily water around the edges; sticking a finger in the velvety cream, trying to lift out a piece of strawberry or peach, or fresh ginger or plum—the images are sharply nostalgic. A piece of warm pound cake or brioche, or ginger or butter cookies to go with the ice cream, and the ensuing sighs or silence tells everyone that heaven has descended for a moment.

Flavored creams are another passion of mine, and I have tried to revive the wonderful dessert *pots de crème.* The best *pot de crème* I know is an infusion of three flavors, the Peruvian Cream of Madame de St. Ange in her cookbook *La Bonne Cuisine.* The reason it is so good is that she calls for infusing the milk base with coffee beans, vanilla bean, and slab chocolate, rather than using coffee, vanilla extract, and cocoa powder. The secret to these egg-yolk-thickened creams is that they are cooked only until the cream is still fragile and trembling. Only with that texture can the flavors be sublime. The most transcendental of all the creams is the almond Bavarian, the great *blanc manger.* Translated as "eat white," this Bavarian cream does not sound especially impressive, but the flavor, especially when bitter almonds are used to supplement the dried, is ethereal. Try the recipe in *The French Menu Cookbook* by Richard Olney. If you are a Sauternes-lover, the combination of that wine and the *blanc manger* are right up in the category of if you have not tried it, you have not lived.

I have concentrated too much on dinner desserts. What about those for which you'd get up in the middle of the night or travel fifty miles at any time of the day and perhaps even have for breakfast if there were any left over? In this category has to be tarte Tatin, a dessert so simple it is almost impossible to find it really well prepared. Authenticity has much to do with the success of this dessert, starting with the quality of apples used. Cold-stored apples that have dried out may not work. The principle of the tarte Tatin is very simple: The apples must give out lots of juices that then blend with the sugar—white, *not* brown—and butter. You must then reduce and caramelize the juices in the oven and finish off on top of the stove to get just the right consistency and caramelization.

One morning, rushing through Normandy trying to get to the Hovercraft that crosses the Channel at Boulogne, I saw storm clouds gathering and told the other increasingly hungry people in the car that if the crossing was rough, I had to either stay in France or stop for lunch and drink enough so that I could pass out on the ferry. In a few seconds, agreement was reached and we stopped at Chez Georges, where we proceeded to eat our way through lobsters, Corton Charlemagne, Normandy veal, and other wonderful things, trying as always to get in as many tastes of France before leaving and going on to less civilized places. With a burst of inspiration someone said, "What about a tarte Tatin, since we are in Normandy?" The proprietor suavely agreed, and called also for an array of Calvados. Apple brandy carved a niche in my necessities-of-life file that day, as the very smooth gentleman proceeded to offer several bottles, each representing a different decade.

In the time it took him to clear the main course, lecture us on the merits of the apple, fail to mention the price of the Calvados, and generally distract us with huge snifters and stories of his cellar, the tarte Tatin arrived. It was just as I had always tried to make it. Golden brown (the color of an old refectory table), faintly steaming, just barely oozing apple and caramelized sugar juices, its crust dry but moist, and its heady perfume of orchards and apple cellars invading the room, the tart was cut and placed on plates mounded with crème fraîche, which immediately melted to form a circular puddle of warm cream within the surrounding cold and still mounded cream, and mingled with the juices of the apples. One taste of the warm cream, the chilled cream, and the tart, followed by a quaff of forty-year-old apple brandy, blew just about every circuit in my brain. I can remember the taste of the brandy to this day. Two years later, in a much-anticipated return visit to Chez Georges to repeat the experience, it turned out that the proprietor had forgotten how to make tarte Tatin. So it goes. My recipe is on page 204.

Almonds in almost any form seem to possess universal appeal: almond torte with raspberry sauce and chantilly; little marzipan fruits; all the Arab and Muslim desserts and dishes cooked with almonds; the whole family of almond creams that has developed through the ages, starting often as savory creams with purees of chicken breast; and all the pastries. Not so well known, however, are the pleasures of fresh almonds. They are beautiful in their French-drawing-room-green velvety shells, and very subtle in taste. At the restaurant Taillevent in Paris, at a dinner for the late Odette Kahn of the publication *Cuisine et Vins de France,* we ended the dinner with crêpes stuffed with a soufflé mixture made with pureed fresh almonds. Such a dish is perfect with dessert wines because of the delicacy of the flavors.

I think there was a raspberry sauce with those crêpes. The king of berries, raspberries, or any berries in the height of summer are an unfailing and never-changing pleasure. The sight of a plate or a basket of berries brings instant relief: All decisions have been made; there is no need to wonder what one is going to eat. How many times in a restaurant have you seen someone waver over the choice of a dessert, only to have the waiter say, "Won't you have a plate of strawberries?" and hear an immediate yes in reply. What is simpler, cleaner, more satisfying, easier, and more perfect than a plate of ripe berries, perhaps mixed berries, heavily doused with rich cream? I never grow tired of raspberry puree when made by hand with fresh berries. Early on at Chez Panisse, I introduced an old favorite of mine taken from old favorites of Auguste Escoffier, a dessert called Peaches Rose-Chéri, involving that culmination of all fruit, white peaches, poached in sugar syrup and served in a dish with fresh pineapple sherbet, champagne sabayon, raspberry puree, and pale rose petals. A stroke of genius.

But you do not have to be Escoffier to produce desserts on the satisfaction level of a genius. Apples cooked in butter and sugar, and eaten with a glass of dessert wine, as suggested by Elizabeth David in her *French Provincial Cooking,* are truly as close to one's heart as any simple dessert can get. Or I remember an afternoon in Cambridge, Massachusetts, when Cathy Simon (then in the School of Design with me at Harvard) cooked a black-bottom pie. I have been passionate about it ever since and think it is one of the great American desserts. I remember my mother's pineapple upside-down cake, and scooping out with my fingers, no matter how hot it was or how bad the burns, the brown sugar–butter mixture that had stuck to the black cast-iron skillet. Covered with whipped cream, that cake is sublime. I remember Indian pudding at Durgin-Park in Boston, with the crusty old waitresses, refusing to take no for an answer, setting the pudding down in front of you, about a gallon of it, and insisting that you have vanilla ice cream as well. Even after the pound of roast beef they had just served you it tasted wonderful, mollifying the pains of a stomach extended beyond its biological limits.

Very often, dessert can be simply a glass of Sauternes, of sweet Riesling, of port, of Madeira, of Eiswein, of Tokay or muscat, or of Angelica—the pride of the country of origin. During one luncheon with the Marquis de Lur Saluces at Château d'Yquem, we drank sweet wines throughout the meal. Even though Sauternes with crayfish sauce is very special indeed, the wine is best drunk with something sweet. The one rule to remember is that food eaten with a dessert wine must be less sweet than the wine. If it is more sweet, the wine will taste sour and flat. So when you are cooking, and are finishing a sauce—for example, for a warm fruit compote (page 193)—always taste the wine before serving and if needed correct the sauce with some acid such as lemon juice, to restore the balance between the wine and the dessert. If all that seems intimidating, take a bottle of muscat or Sauternes on a warm summer evening, sit outside with large napkins, and eat mangoes right off the pit, as you drink deeply of the cool, sweet wine. That tropical pleasure will seem so good it should be forbidden.

Warm Berry Compote

One of my favorite modernizations of a classic dish, this wonderful summer dessert can be cooked with any ripened fruit: mangoes, papayas, figs, peaches, plums, cherries—and of course berries. If you use raspberries, throw them in only for the last minute of cooking.

¼ cup	water
½ cup	sugar
2 teaspoons	fresh lemon juice
1 cup	strawberries, rinsed, cut in half
1 cup	blueberries, rinsed
1 cup	blackberries
4 tablespoons	sweet butter, cut into cubes or softened
1 pint	vanilla ice cream

Serves 4

Make a light sugar syrup by heating the water and sugar together in an 8-inch sauté pan, stirring until the sugar is dissolved. Add the lemon juice and berries to the syrup and cook over medium heat 2 to 3 minutes, shaking the pan gently to coat berries with syrup. Add the butter and continue to cook, swirling the berries and butter around in the pan, until the butter is melted.

Spoon the fruit compote onto 4 plates and place scoops of ice cream in the center of each serving.

Pears in Red Wine with Basil

I discovered this recipe when I was doing the desserts volume of the Time-Life series *The Good Cook.* Cooking pears in red wine while making lunch for the crew, I licked some reduced red wine syrup off my fingers, which had been handling basil. The combination stunned me. The best pears to use are Boscs or Bartletts, because the Anjou and Comice are too soft to cook. The pears should simmer slowly to pick up as much of the wine flavor as possible, and they are best if poached in advance and allowed to sit in the wine for two days. Garnish with basil flowers if you have them.

4	pears, of similar size, slightly underripe
1 bottle (750 ml)	red wine, preferably young and very red
¾ cup	sugar
1 piece	lemon rind, 2 inches long and ½ inch wide
2 tablespoons	sweet butter
16 large leaves	fresh basil

Serves 4

Peel the pears, cut in half lengthwise and core.

Heat the wine, sugar, and lemon rind in a saucepan large enough to hold both the wine and the pears, stirring constantly, until the sugar dissolves.

Add the pears to the wine and simmer until tender, about 30 minutes. To test, poke a skewer or toothpick in the thickest part of the pear; if the skewer goes in easily and the pear seems soft yet still firm, it is done. Remove the pears from the liquid, cover them with a damp towel, and let cool. Boil the wine until reduced by half, about 20 to 30 minutes. It should be thick and syrupy.

Strain the syrup into a sauté pan large enough to hold the pears. Heat the pears and syrup over medium heat; add the butter and basil leaves. Submerge the leaves in the liquid to keep them from turning black. Swirl all the ingredients together until the butter melts. Arrange the pears on a plate, slice them if you wish, and pour over the sauce.

Warm Berry Compote.

White Peaches with Raspberry and Blackberry Sauces

One of the few desserts left that refuse to give up their seasonality is white peaches. I look forward eagerly every year to that perfect perfumed white peach and, every year, I remember Escoffier's dessert Peaches Rose-Chéri, with pineapple ice and champagne sabayon, all covered with pink rose petals (see page 190).

2	*ripe white peaches*
½ teaspoon	*fresh lemon juice*
pinch	*salt*
3 cups	*medium sugar syrup (page 216)*
1 cup	*raspberry sauce (page 32)*
½ cup	*blackberry sauce (page 32)*
1 cup	*custard (page 213)*

Serves 4

Add the peaches, lemon juice, and salt to the sugar syrup and simmer until the peaches are tender, about 10 minutes. Remove from the heat, drain, and cool. Peel the peaches, cut in half, and remove the pits. Pour the raspberry sauce onto chilled plates and place a peach half in the center of each plate. Drizzle the blackberry sauce around and pour the custard over and around the peaches.

Russian Raspberry Gratin

This is one of those simple desserts that have far more impact than their few ingredients would seem to indicate. It is fast, easy, sinfully comforting and delicious.

1 pint	*raspberries*
2 cups	*sour cream or crème fraîche*
1 cup	*dark brown sugar, sieved*

Serves 6

Heat the broiler.

Pick over the raspberries and remove any mildewed ones, husks, or leaves. Place the berries in a shallow baking dish. Stir the sour cream until smooth and spread over the berries. Sprinkle with the brown sugar. Broil until the sugar begins to bubble and lightly caramelize. Be careful not to burn the sugar. Serve immediately.

Figs in Red Wine with Walnut Cream

A coffee cream or a Chartreuse cream would also go very well with this dessert, whose flavors of Provence make it one of my favorites. Prepared in advance, the figs will hold very well for a few days.

1 cup	*walnut pieces*
1 recipe	*custard (page 213)*
16 whole	*dried figs*
2 bottles (750 ml)	*red wine, fruity Zinfandel type*
3 to 4 sprigs	*fresh thyme*
½ cup	*sugar*
¼ cup	*wild thyme honey or other good honey*
½ cup	*heavy cream*

Serves 4

Heat the oven to 350°F.

Toast the walnuts on a cookie sheet for 10 minutes. Remove and let cool. Process or chop them fine and combine with the custard. Let stand at least 3 hours.

Put the figs and red wine in a bowl and soak 1 hour. Transfer to a non-aluminum pot and add the thyme, sugar, and honey. Simmer over medium-low heat until the figs are tender, about 1 hour. Strain, reserving the figs. Boil the cooking liquid until reduced to a thick syrup. Return the figs to the syrup and let cool.

Whip the cream and fold into the walnut custard. Put the figs on plates. Pour the wine syrup over the figs and then spoon some walnut cream on top.

Turtle Cay Bananas with Passion Fruit Sauce

This was a dessert I did for the Florida regional dinner at the Santa Fe Bar & Grill, and although perhaps it never saw Turtle Cay, it is new Florida cooking.

4	bananas
¼ cup	dark brown sugar
¼ cup	dark rum
1 teaspoon	finely chopped fresh ginger
2 pinches	salt
6	passion fruit
⅓ cup	light sugar syrup (page 216)
4 tablespoons	butter

Serves 4

Peel and cut the bananas lengthwise in half. Put the sugar, 2 ounces of the rum, the ginger, and 1 pinch salt in a dish. Stir to dissolve the sugar and then add the banana halves. Marinate 1 hour, turning them occasionally.

Cut the passion fruit in half and scrape the pulp into a bowl. Stir in the sugar syrup and a very small pinch salt.

Melt 2 tablespoons butter in a sauté pan, add the bananas, cut sides down, and all the marinade. Cook over low heat for 5 minutes. Add the remaining rum and raise the heat, igniting the rum. Shake the pan and when the flames have died, swirl in the remaining butter. Serve the bananas and juices on warm plates and pour the passion fruit sauce over them.

Summer Pudding

I am always surprised that this dessert never became an American mainstay, as it has in England, for it is a natural, given any occasion where you have lots of summer berries. It is very easy to prepare and since it has to be done beforehand, it's perfect for dinner parties. Can there be anyone who doesn't like it? Use whatever mixed berries you can find.

1½ cups	strawberries, hulled
1½ cups	raspberries
1 cup	red currants, stemmed
1 cup	blueberries, loganberries, or ollalieberries
1 cup	sugar
pinch	salt
½ cup	medium sugar syrup (page 216)
2 cups	raspberry puree (page 32)
10 to 15 slices	dense white bread, crust removed
2 cups	custard (page 213)

Serves 6 to 8

Coarsely chop the strawberries and put them and the other berries in a saucepan. Add the sugar and salt and cook over high heat until the berries are heated and just beginning to bleed their colors, about 5 minutes. Remove from the heat and cool.

Mix the syrup and the raspberry puree.

Line a 2-quart pudding mold or other deep bowl with cheesecloth. Dip both sides of some of the bread slices in the berry puree and arrange around the sides and bottom of the mold. Soak the remaining slices in the berry puree and layer with the berries, ending with bread to completely cover the top.

Using a plate that fits just inside the top of the mold, place it on top of the pudding. Put the mold in a pan and weight the plate. Refrigerate the pudding overnight.

To serve, unmold the pudding onto a serving platter, slice, and serve with the custard.

Raspberry Soufflés with Sabayon

I make fruit soufflés with the whites of eggs only, in order to preserve the fresh taste of the fruit. And for the same reason, the soufflés should cook as fast as possible, so I use metal charlotte molds. The most memorable of this kind of soufflé is one made with a puree of wild strawberries.

1 cup	raspberry puree (page 32)
2 tablespoons	butter, softened
1½ cups	sugar
4	egg whites
pinch	salt
1 to 2 cups	sabayon mousseline sauce (page 214)

Serves 4

Prepare the raspberry puree. Heat the oven to 400°F.

Butter four 4-inch charlotte molds. Using ½ cup of the sugar, coat the entire surface of each mold; discard any sugar that does not adhere to the butter.

Whip the egg whites in a clean bowl to soft peaks. Gradually beat in the remaining sugar and continue to beat until they are glossy and stand in stiff peaks, about 5 minutes. Quickly but gently fold in the raspberry puree and spoon the mixture into the prepared soufflé molds, filling each mold no more than three-quarters full.

Bake in the middle of the oven until risen 3 to 4 inches and lightly browned, 15 to 20 minutes. Serve immediately with the sabayon.

Apricot and Lemon Mousse

The mousses can be combined to make a multilayered, multicolored form, or they can be put in individual ramekins and presented together. Either way, serve with elderberry or blackberry sauce made the same way as raspberry sauce (page 32), or with chantilly cream flavored with espresso.

3	eggs
5	eggs, separated
¾ cup	fresh lemon juice
2 tablespoons	finely chopped lemon rind
1½ cups	sugar
¼ pound	butter
½ pound	dried apricots
1½ cups	water
1-inch piece	vanilla bean
¼ cup	fresh orange juice, strained
1½ teaspoons	grated orange rind
2 tablespoons	Grand Marnier
1½ cups	heavy cream

Serves 6 to 8

Mix the whole eggs, all the egg yolks, and lemon juice and strain into an enamel saucepan. Add the lemon rind, 1 cup sugar, and the butter and cook slowly over medium heat, stirring constantly, until the mixture thickens enough to coat a spoon heavily. Transfer the mixture to a bowl. Cover with plastic wrap to prevent a skin from forming on the top and chill.

Simmer the apricots, water, vanilla bean, orange juice and rind, ½ cup sugar, and the Grand Marnier in a saucepan until the apricots are soft and falling apart, 20 to 25 minutes. Stir occasionally to prevent scorching. Remove the vanilla bean and process the apricot mixture in a food processor or food mill until smooth. Push the apricot paste through a fine sieve until smooth. Chill.

Whip the egg whites until firm but not overbeaten and grainy. Fold half into each of the purees. Whip the cream and fold half of it into each of the purees.

Spoon the purees in alternate layers in a loaf pan or individual ramekins. Refrigerate until set, about 1 hour. To unmold, dip the pan in hot water for 20 seconds, wipe dry, and invert immediately onto a platter. Slice and serve with the berry sauce or chantilly cream.

Mango Mousse with Coconut Sauce

3	ripe mangoes
2 tablespoons	fresh lime juice
pinch	salt
4	egg yolks
⅓ cup	sugar
1 tablespoon (1 envelope)	unflavored gelatin
⅓ cup	white rum
3	egg whites
1 cup	heavy cream
1 batch	coconut custard (page 213)

Serves 6

Peel the mangoes and cut the flesh or pulp away from the pit. Puree the pulp through a sieve or food processor. Stir in the lime juice and salt. There should be about 1 cup puree.

Whip the egg yolks and sugar in a bowl until they are thick and pale yellow. Warm the gelatin in the rum until the liquid is clear and the gelatin is dissolved. Mix into the egg yolks and sugar and then mix in the mango puree.

Whip the whites to stiff peaks (but do not overwhip) and fold them into the yolk mixture. Whip the cream to soft peaks and fold that into the mixture. Pour into a large mold or several small ones. Freeze 2 to 3 hours, depending on the size of the mold.

To serve, dip the molds in hot water for a minute, run a knife around the edges, and slide them out onto plates. Pour the custard sauce over.

Fresh Plum Ice Cream

This ice cream keeps a perfect texture longer than any ice cream I know, and is exceptional when served with your favorite ginger or molasses cookies.

6	plums, Simka or Santa Rosa
½ teaspoon	pure vanilla extract
3 cups	half-and-half
5	egg yolks
1 cup	sugar
pinch	salt

Serves 4 to 6

Cut the plums in half, pit them, and set aside.

Heat the vanilla and cream in a saucepan until hot. Whisk the egg yolks, ¾ cup sugar, and the salt together. Then whisk the hot cream into the yolks. Return the mixture to the saucepan and cook over medium heat, stirring constantly, until thickened enough to coat a spoon. Do not let it boil. Remove the custard from the heat, pour it into a bowl, and put the bowl in another bowl, half full of ice and water. Stir the custard until cold. Strain through a sieve.

Put the plum halves in a saucepan. Add remaining sugar and cook over low heat, stirring occasionally, until the plums are soft and falling apart. Taste and add more sugar if necessary. The puree should be tart but not so much as to make your mouth pucker. Strain the plums through a sieve or fine food mill. Refrigerate until cold.

Stir the puree into the custard base. Freeze in an ice cream maker, following manufacturer's directions.

Tropical Fruit Compote

This compote is delicious by itself or with a dollop of vanilla ice cream or a spoonful of clotted cream, mascarpone, or crème fraîche, and always goes very well with dessert wines. But if you have a sweet tooth, try this version with the compote served in a meringue. Make the meringue the day before, remembering that the secret to wonderful meringues is that they cook, or rather dry out, very slowly and do not color at all in the oven.

6	*egg whites*
1 cup	*sugar*
1	*fresh coconut*
	salt
2 cups	*custard (page 213)*
1	*ripe mango*
1	*ripe papaya*
2	*ripe passion fruit*
1 cup	*medium sugar syrup (page 216)*
1 tablespoon	*fresh lime or lemon juice*
4 tablespoons	*unsalted butter*

Serves 6

Heat the oven to 225°F.

Whip the whites to soft peaks and, while continuing to whip, sprinkle in the sugar. Whip until glossy and stiff, about 5 minutes.

Line a cookie sheet with parchment paper. Put the meringue in a pastry bag and make four 4-inch round bases and 2 layers of wall on the outer edge to form round baskets.

Place the sheet in the oven, turn off the heat, and leave overnight.

The next morning, the meringues should be firm. Remove them from the sheet and store in an airtight container.

Hit the coconut with a hammer to break it in pieces. Gouge out the white part of the coconut from the shell, discard the shell, and cut the brown skin off the white meat. Grate or grind the coconut meat in a food processor and stir the coconut and a pinch of salt into the custard. Warm slightly and let steep for 2 hours. Refrigerate until cold. Freeze in an ice cream maker, following the manufacturer's directions.

Peel the mango and slice in pieces lengthwise. Peel the papaya, cut in half lengthwise, scoop out the seeds, and slice it crosswise. Cut the passion fruit in half and scrape the pulp into a small bowl.

Simmer the sugar syrup in a sauté pan and add the papaya, mango, and lemon juice. When the syrup begins to boil again, add the passion fruit, butter, and a pinch of salt. Stir quickly but gently until the butter is melted.

Put the meringues on warm plates, spoon the compote into them, put a scoop of ice cream in the center, and spoon a little compote over the ice cream.

Shortbread with Apples and Apricot Sauce

1 pound plus 4 tablespoons	*butter*
1 cup	*granulated sugar*
4 cups	*all-purpose flour*
½ teaspoon	*salt*
½ cup	*dried apricots*
½ cup	*light sugar syrup (page 216)*
6	*apples, Pippin or Granny Smith*
¼ cup	*superfine sugar*
1 recipe	*chantilly cream (page 214)*

Serves 6

Mix 1 pound butter and the sugar together until the sugar is incorporated, being careful to just barely mix it. Add the flour and salt and mix. The dough will become crumbly and then pull together when it's mixed.

Form the dough into a ball and roll out ½ inch thick on a lightly floured board. Cut into 4-inch circles and place on a parchment-lined cookie sheet. Chill for 1 hour.

Heat the oven to 250°F.

Bake cookies until firm, about 45 minutes to 1 hour. They should be white, not golden, in color.

Meanwhile, put the apricots and syrup in a saucepan and simmer, covered, until the apricots are soft, about 20 minutes. Puree and put through a sieve. Keep warm.

Peel, core, and slice the apples. Melt 2 tablespoons butter in a sauté pan, add the apples and sauté over low heat until they are soft but still hold their shape, about 8 minutes. Add the superfine sugar, remaining butter, and a pinch of salt; cook another 8 minutes, swirling to pull the sauce together.

Divide the apples over the shortbread and top with the chantilly cream and apricot sauce.

Cross Creek Tangerine Ice

This recipe is from Cross Creek, of Marjorie Rawlings fame, as presented in her book *Cross Creek Cookery*. I adapted it for the Florida regional dinner at the Santa Fe Bar & Grill, and served it with passion fruit sauce (page 196).

1 cup	*sugar*
1 cup	*water*
¼ cup	*grated tangerine rind*
3 cups	*tangerine juice, strained*
pinch	*salt*

Serves 6

Boil the sugar and water together for 10 minutes. Add the tangerine rind, cook another minute, and refrigerate. When the syrup is cold, stir in the tangerine juice and salt. Strain and freeze in an ice cream maker, following the manufacturer's directions.

Plum Napoleon with Sabayon

The best plums to use are ripe Simka, Santa Rosa, and
Queen Anne, but any other combination of cultivated
or wild plums will do, as long as they are ripe. The
Napoleon has to be assembled at the very last moment
so that the pastry does not become soggy. It takes only
a few minutes to assemble and is an ideal, very easy,
showstopper.

2 rectangles	*puff pastry (page 217), 12 by 5 by ¼ inches*
12	*ripe plums of 3 different varieties, pitted*
¼ cup	*granulated sugar*
pinch	*salt*
¼ cup	*water*
2 cups	*sabayon mousseline sauce (page 214)*
2 tablespoons	*confectioner's sugar*

Serves 6 to 8

Heat the oven to 350°F.

Put the cold puff pastry pieces on a wet baking sheet
and put them in the oven. Cook for 20 minutes. Let
cool. When the pastry is cool, slice the pieces
horizontally in half, so that you have 4 layers. Scoop
any uncooked pastry from the center. Put the pieces on
a tray and reserve.

Slice the plums and put them in a sauté pan. Add the
granulated sugar, salt, and water and cook over
medium heat until the plums are tender and beginning
to fall apart. Put in a bowl and cool.

When you are ready to serve, put a bottom pastry
layer on a platter, spoon some of the plums over the
pastry, and then spoon some of the sabayon over that.
Put another layer of pastry over the sabayon and
continue building the layers, saving the last piece of
pastry for the top. Put the top piece on and sprinkle
that with the confectioner's sugar.

Caramelized Apple Tart

This is it—the famous tarte Tatin from France, the secret of which is the apples' giving up their juices in the cooking process, combining with the sugar and butter, and caramelizing, so that the full range of flavors is in the caramel (quite different from making caramel and pouring it in the pan to start with).

8 large	*green apples, Newtown Pippins or Granny Smiths*
1 cup	*sugar*
pinch	*salt*
4 tablespoons	*butter*
1 9-inch circle	*tart pastry (page 217), rolled ¼ inch thick, chilled*
1 cup	*chantilly cream (page 214)*

Serves 8

Heat the oven to 375°F.

Peel and core the apples and cut them in sixths. Toss them in a bowl with the sugar and salt.

Spread 2 tablespoons butter in a heavy nonstick 10-inch skillet. Place the apples side by side in the skillet and dot with the remaining butter. Place the pastry over the apples, leaving a ½-inch gap all around between the pastry and the edge of the pan.

Bake until the apples are tender and the crust golden and cooked through, about 45 minutes. Look along the sides of the tart to see if the juices have started to caramelize. If they are deep golden brown, the tart can be left to cool for 5 minutes and then turned over onto a plate. If they are not, put the pan over medium heat and cook, moving the pan slowly around the burner, for 5 to 10 minutes to let the juices caramelize. Then let cool for 5 minutes and turn it out onto a platter. Serve warm with the chantilly cream.

Trifle

I suppose trifle comes under the heading of childhood memory food, a dish that resonates with nostalgia and good times. It was never part of my family traditions, but I remember one or two great trifles in restaurants, served covered with rich Jersey cream. One could write pages about trifle, and they would constitute almost a history of the nineteenth-century English household, since trifle is one of those dishes that are for using up leftovers, but leftovers in a kitchen for a large family, a kitchen that was going full tilt every day. Now one has to make the leftovers and probably buy all the jams, rather than using ends of jars and fruit purees. It cannot be made well in small batches, so plan on having ten people to serve it to.

6	*eggs, separated*
1 teaspoon	*vanilla extract*
1 tablespoon	*butter*
½ cup	*sugar*
1 cup	*cake flour*
5 cups	*custard (page 213)*
1½ cups	*raspberry puree (page 32)*
½ cup	*apricot jam*
½ cup	*strawberry jam*
1 cup	*cream sherry*
1 cup	*toasted almonds, finely chopped*

Serves 10 to 12

Heat the oven to 350°F.

Beat the egg yolks, vanilla, and butter together in a bowl.

Whip the egg whites to soft peaks, then, while adding the sugar, whisk until the whites are stiff and shiny. The whole process should take 7 minutes.

Fold the egg whites into the egg yolks while at the same time sifting the flour over the mixture. Continue to mix and fold until the yolks and flour are incorporated into the whites.

Butter and dust with flour a 16-by-12-inch jelly-roll pan. Pour the mixture into the pan and bake until the cake is golden brown and firm to the touch in the center, about 15 minutes. Let cool.

Cut the cake into rounds that will just fit in the large bowl you are planning to use for the trifle. Pour ½ cup custard in the bottom of the bowl, then pour in ¼ cup berry puree. Spread the first round of cake with some of each of the jams. Put the cake round in the bowl and pour ¼ cup of the sherry over it. Sprinkle with some of the almonds, then pour over it more custard and berry puree. Repeat the layers, until the bowl is full, ending with custard and puree. Cover and refrigerate for several hours or overnight.

Scoop out sections of the trifle so that everyone gets some of each layer and serve with thick cream, more custard, and whatever berry puree you have.

Pecan Puff Pastry with Chocolate Sauce and Sabayon

I invented this dish for a 1982 dinner at San Francisco's Clift Hotel done by a group of chefs. It was such a success that I used it again at the now legendary inaugural dinner, at the Stanford Court, of the American Institute of Wine and Food, the dinner being prepared by chefs from all over the United States. It is a superb combination of flavors and is very easy once you master puff pastry, a discipline that I have always thought was best left to other people. Lacking the willing other person, you may use the very good easy version of puff pastry on page 216.

4 rectangles	*puff pastry (page 217), 4 by 2 by ¼ inches*
1 cup	*pecan pieces*
½ cup	*light sugar syrup (page 216)*
pinch	*salt*
5 tablespoons	*Dutch-process cocoa*
¾ cup	*water*
½ cup	*sugar*
3 tablespoons	*butter*
1 tablespoon	*whipping cream*
1½ cups	*sabayon mousseline sauce (page 214)*

Serves 4

Heat the oven to 350°F.

Put the cold puff pastry pieces on a wet baking sheet and bake for 20 minutes. Let cool. Slice the pieces horizontally in half. Scoop any uncooked pastry from the centers. Put the pieces on a tray and reserve.

Toast the pecans on a tray in the oven for 10 minutes. Let cool. Then put them in a food processor and grind them. Add the syrup and salt and puree until smooth.

To make the chocolate sauce, mix 4 tablespoons cocoa with just enough of the water to make a smooth paste. Bring the sugar and remaining water to a boil and stir into the cocoa. Whisk until smooth and return to the saucepan. Simmer for 15 minutes, stirring constantly. Let cool a bit. When the mixture is still warm, stir in the butter and then the cream. Keep warm.

Warm the pecan puree in a double boiler.

Spoon the chocolate sauce on warm plates. Put the bottom pieces of the pastry in the center and spoon the pecan puree onto the pastry. Put the tops on, spoon some sabayon over, and sprinkle with the remaining cocoa.

Pumpkin Gingerbread with Rum Cream

2 cups	all-purpose flour, sifted
¼ teaspoon	salt
1 teaspoon	baking soda
1 large	egg
½ cup plus 1 tablespoon	sugar
½ cup	pumpkin puree
½ cup	vegetable oil
½ cup	molasses
2 teaspoons	ground ginger
½ teaspoon each	ground cinnamon, cloves, and allspice
½ cup	boiling water
1 cup	heavy cream
2 tablespoons	dark rum

Serves 6 to 8

Heat the oven to 350°F. Butter an 8- or 9-inch cake pan and dust with flour.

Sift together the flour, salt, and baking soda.

Beat the egg and ½ cup of sugar together in a bowl and mix in the pumpkin, oil, molasses, and spices. Mix in the boiling water.

Mix in the dry ingredients. Pour the batter into the pan and bake for 35 to 40 minutes or until a skewer inserted in the center comes out clean.

Mix the cream, rum, and 1 tablespoon sugar together and whip to soft peaks. Serve on the warm gingerbread.

Polenta Pound Cake with Madeira Cream

½ pound	sweet butter, softened
1 teaspoon	lemon zest, finely chopped
2 cups	sugar
6 large	eggs, separated
¼ teaspoon	almond extract
1 teaspoon	vanilla extract
½ teaspoon	baking soda
1 cup	sour cream
1¼ cups	fine cornmeal
2 cups	all-purpose flour
½ teaspoon	salt
1 cup	heavy cream
2 tablespoons	Madeira

Serves 6 to 8

Heat the oven to 325°F. Butter a 9-inch loaf pan and dust with cornmeal.

Beat the butter, lemon zest, and all but 1 tablespoon of the sugar in a bowl until light and fluffy, about 10 minutes. Beat in the egg yolks one at time. Add the almond and vanilla extracts, soda, and sour cream and mix. Mix in 1 cup of the cornmeal, the flour and salt.

Whip the whites until stiff but not dry and fold into the batter.

Bake until a thin skewer stuck in the center comes out clean, about 1½ hours. Cool on a rack for 15 minutes and then unmold the cake.

Whip the cream, remaining 1 tablespoon sugar, and Madeira together until soft peaks form. Serve with slices of the warm pound cake.

Saffron Brioche with Pear Glaze

This is a recipe I developed years ago because I love Russian *kulitch*, and the way Russians eat the cake with ice cream or a glass of Madeira in the afternoon.

1 teaspoon	saffron threads
1 cup	warm milk
1 cup	sugar
2 packets	active dry yeast
6	eggs
1½ teaspoons	salt
4¼ cups	all-purpose flour
¾ pound	sweet butter, cut into ½-inch cubes
1 cup	pistachios, skinned and toasted
2 cups	water
1 cup	dried pears
¼ cup	green Chartreuse
1 cup	chantilly cream (page 214)

Serves 8 to 10

Mix the saffron and milk together in a large bowl and let stand for 20 minutes. Then mix in ½ cup sugar and the yeast. Let it stand in a warm place until the yeast bubbles. Mix in the eggs, salt, and flour. Knead in the butter a few cubes at a time until all the butter is incorporated. This is best done with an electric mixer that has a dough hook, because it is important that the dough not get too warm. Add the pistachios with the last of the butter.

Cover the dough with plastic wrap and refrigerate until it is completely chilled, about 2 hours.

Butter and dust with flour a coffee or large juice tin. With lightly floured hands, shape the dough and place it in the tin, which should be no more than two-thirds full. Let the dough rise until it reaches the top of the tin.

Heat the oven to 350°F. Bake the brioche until it is dark golden and sounds hollow when thumped, about 1 hour. Let it cool and then remove from the tin.

While the brioche is rising, put the remaining ½ cup sugar and the water in a saucepan and bring to a boil. Add the pears and add more water if necessary to cover them. Simmer until the pears are soft and begin to break apart, about 1 hour. Add more water if necessary because the pears will absorb it. Let the pears cool, then push them through a sieve or fine food mill. Strain as often as necessary to get a fine sauce. Mix in the Chartreuse and then brush the glaze over the brioche. Serve each slice of brioche with chantilly cream.

Bourbon Pecan Tart

This is the standby tart of Stars, and is a hybrid of French almond tart and American pecan pie.

1	tart pastry shell (page 217)
2	eggs
¾ cup	dark brown sugar
1 cup	dark corn syrup
½ teaspoon	salt
2 tablespoons	bourbon
2 tablespoons	butter
1 teaspoon	vanilla extract
2 cups	pecan pieces
1½ cups	chantilly cream (page 214)

Serves 6 to 8

Heat the oven to 350°F.

Bake the tart shell for 10 minutes. Press any bubbles in the pastry down with a spoon and push up the sides if necessary. Cook until golden, about 5 more minutes. Let cool completely.

Mix the eggs and brown sugar together in a bowl. Add the corn syrup, salt, bourbon, butter, and vanilla extract and mix together. Stir in the pecan pieces. Pour the mixture into the baked shell (do not overfill the tart shell). Bake until the pecan filling rises and sets, 20 to 25 minutes. Serve warm with the chantilly cream.

Saffron Brioche with Pear Glaze.

Bittersweet Chocolate Torte

9 ounces	bittersweet chocolate
6 ounces	butter
6	eggs, separated
1 cup	granulated sugar
¼ cup	flour
¼ teaspoon	salt
2 tablespoons	confectioner's sugar
1 cup	coffee custard (page 213)
1 cup	chantilly cream (page 214)

Serves 8

Heat the oven to 325°F. Butter a 9-inch round cake pan and dust with flour.

Chop the chocolate into bits and melt with the butter in a bowl over simmering water.

Whip the yolks and ¾ cup of the granulated sugar together. Mix in the flour gradually. Add the melted chocolate and butter and mix well.

Whip the egg whites, salt, and remaining granulated sugar until it peaks and then fold into the chocolate mixture.

Pour the batter into the cake pan. Bake until center of the cake is moist but not runny, 30 to 40 minutes.

Let the cake cool and turn out onto a platter. Put the confectioner's sugar in a sieve and dust the top of the cake. Serve the slices of cake with the coffee custard underneath and the chantilly cream over.

Chocolate Paradise

When Carolyn Weil and I developed this dessert, the final version elicited my comment, in the back of the kitchen at the Santa Fe Bar & Grill, "Now, that is close to paradise." Hence its name. You will need a loaf pan 12 by 4 inches and 5 to 6 inches deep, a sheet or jelly roll pan, and parchment or greaseproof paper.

1 tablespoon	butter
1½ pounds	bittersweet chocolate
2 tablespoons	rich espresso coffee
½ tablespoon	vanilla extract
6 large	eggs, separated
pinch	salt
½ cup	sugar
2 cups	heavy cream
	sabayon mousseline (page 214)
	chocolate sauce (page 206)

Serves 10

Heat the oven to 350°F. Cut parchment paper to fit a sheet pan, butter it, and put the paper in the pan.

Boil a pot of water and lower to a simmer. Put 8 ounces of the chocolate in a metal bowl over the simmering water until it melts. Remove from the water and stir in the espresso and vanilla. Let the mixture cool slightly and then mix in the egg yolks.

Whip the egg whites and salt together until soft peaks are formed. While continuing to whip, sprinkle in the sugar gradually and then whip the egg whites to stiff peaks and until the sugar is dissolved, about 5 more minutes. Be careful not to overwhip. Fold the egg white mixture quickly but thoroughly into the chocolate mixture. Spread the mixture in the sheet pan.

Bake until the pastry is firm and has risen evenly, about 20 minutes. Let cool (it will fall as it does so).

While the cake is cooling, make the chocolate cream. Heat the cream in a large saucepan and remove from the heat just before it boils. Chop the remaining chocolate into small bits, add to the hot cream, and stir until the chocolate melts. Strain and set aside to cool until it is just warm.

To assemble the chocolate paradise, remove the chocolate pastry from the sheet pan and remove the paper. Cut into 3 even rectangles just smaller than the loaf pan. Line the bottom and sides of the loaf pan with parchment paper. Pour in a quarter of the chocolate cream, then place a layer of the chocolate pastry on top. Repeat the layers, ending with cream. Refrigerate until the chocolate is set, about 3 hours.

To unmold, dip the loaf pan in hot water for a few seconds to release the edges and then turn over onto a plate.

To serve, cut the chocolate paradise into ½-inch-thick slices. Serve on the mousseline and drizzle with warmed chocolate sauce.

Three Custards

The texture of a baked custard should be tremblingly
fragile and as smooth as kid gloves. There should be the
least amount of texture to interfere with the perfumes
and flavors, which in this recipe are pistachio, orange,
and caramel. Other flavors to use for infusing the milk
are pecans, walnuts, almonds, fresh ginger, cinnamon,
star anise, fennel seeds, coconut, and espresso.

¾ cup	*sugar*
¼ cup	*water*
2 cups	*whipping cream*
1 cup	*milk*
pinch	*salt*
2 tablespoons	*grated orange rind*
¼ cup	*Grand Marnier*
½ cup	*shelled pistachios, blanched,*
	peeled
6	*egg yolks*

Serves 4

Heat the oven to 300°F.

Put ¼ cup sugar and the water in a saucepan and boil
over medium heat until the sugar becomes golden
brown and caramelized, about 15 minutes.

While the sugar is cooking, mix the cream, milk, and
salt and heat almost to boiling. Divide into thirds. Stir
the orange zest and Grand Marnier into one part.

Grind the pistachios in a food processor or spice mill
and stir into another part.

When the sugar is caramelized, let it cool 5 minutes
and pour the last third of the milk and cream mixture
into the caramel. Stir until the caramel is dissolved. Let
the mixtures steep for 1 hour.

Put 2 egg yolks and ¼ cup sugar in each of 2 bowls
and beat until light yellow and smooth, about 5
minutes. Put 2 egg yolks in another bowl and beat until
smooth.

Heat each of the milk infusions and strain each flavor
separately into the bowls, putting the caramel milk into
the bowl with yolks only. Stir until each egg mixture is
dissolved in the flavored milks.

Pour each mixture into 4 ramekins and put them in
a baking dish. Put the dish in the oven and pour boiling
water around the ramekins until the water comes three-
quarters of the way up the sides of the ramekins. Cover
the dish with foil and bake until the custards are set,
about 20 minutes.

Take the dish out of the oven carefully. Take the
ramekins out of the water and let them cool. Serve at
room temperature.

Nougat Ice Cream

I usually do not like ice cream with pieces of anything in it, let alone soggy nuts, but this ice cream from *The Alice B. Toklas Cook Book* reminds me of Morocco, hashish, the early days at Chez Panisse, and all other things exotic—and the almonds stay crisp. If you like orange-flower water, you will love the ice cream.

¼ cup	pistachios
½ cup	blanched almonds, split in half
½ cup	fine orange honey
4 cups	custard (opposite)
pinch	salt
1 tablespoon	orange-flower water

Serves 6 to 8

Heat the oven to 250°F.

Blanch and peel the pistachios, then dry them in the oven for 10 minutes. Let cool. Put the pistachios and almonds in an ice cream maker. Dissolve the honey in the custard. Stir in the salt and orange-flower water. Add the custard to the nuts and freeze, following the manufacturer's directions.

Custard

To make flavored custards, infuse nuts, fresh ginger, cinnamon sticks, star anise, fennel seeds, orange or lemon rind into milk and follow directions for infusion in coconut custard (below).

½ cup	granulated sugar
6	egg yolks
¼ teaspoon	salt
2 cups	milk
1-inch piece	vanilla bean
	ice

Serves 4 to 6

Mix the sugar, yolks, and salt in a bowl and whisk until pale yellow (about 5 minutes).

Heat the milk and vanilla bean together until almost boiling, and pour slowly into the yolk mixture while whisking. Cook over simmering water in a double boiler, stirring constantly, until the custard begins to thicken and coats the spoon.

Remove from heat and place over an ice bath, see sabayon mousseline sauce (page 214) to cool, stirring constantly with a spoon—this prevents the custard from overcooking (curdling) and forming a skin when it cools. Strain and serve.

- *Coffee custard:* Heat 2 cups of milk with ¼ cup ground espresso coffee until almost boiling; let sit for 30 minutes. Strain and proceed as in above.

- *Coconut custard:* Crack the shell of a fresh coconut and remove the meat from the hard outer shell. Chop the coconut meat fine with a knife or in a food processor. Steep it in 2 cups warmed milk for at least an hour, or until the milk takes on the coconut's flavor. Then strain the milk, discarding the coconut, and use in the recipe above. Some of the milk may be absorbed by the coconut, so correct the quantity before beginning the recipe.

Chantilly Cream

1 cup	heavy cream, chilled
1½ teaspoons	superfine sugar
½ teaspoon	pure vanilla extract
pinch	salt

Yield: 1½ cups

Mix all ingredients together and whip to soft peaks. Serve chilled.

Sabayon Mousseline Sauce

The secret to holding sabayon (zabaglione) is to keep whisking it over ice without stopping until it is quite cold.

6	egg yolks
½ cup	sugar
pinch	salt
1 cup	champagne or white wine
1 cup	heavy cream

Yield: 2 to 3 cups

Put two trays of ice in a container large enough to just hold a wide, rather shallow, stainless-steel mixing bowl. Half fill the container with water and keep this ice bath by the stove. Boil a pot of water that is large enough to hold the cooking bowl so that it sits half down into the pot.

Combine the yolks, sugar, and salt in a stainless-steel mixing bowl. Mix well and add the champagne or wine.

Over barely simmering water, whisk the mixture vigorously until it is thick and pale yellow, about 10 minutes. Put the cooking bowl immediately into the ice bath and whisk vigorously again until the sabayon is cold. Keep chilled. When you want to use the sauce, whip the cream and fold it into the sabayon.

Standard Preparations

Clarified Butter

The main benefit of clarified butter is that it does not burn as easily as does whole butter when heated for sautéeing or frying. One pound of whole butter will yield ¾ cup of clarified butter.

Melt 1 pound of butter in the top of a double boiler or over very low heat. When it is completely melted, set aside in a warm place for 15 minutes. Skim off all the foam from the top. Then spoon off the clear yellow liquid (the clarified butter) and reserve it. Discard the milky liquid in the bottom.

Chicken and Ham Forcemeat

12 ounces	*chicken breast, boneless*
4 ounces	*cooked ham*
2 large	*egg whites*
¼ teaspoon	*salt*
2 pinches	*freshly ground pepper*
2 to 2¼ cups	*whipping cream*

Yield: 5 cups

Put the chicken and ham in a food processor and puree, gradually adding the egg whites, until smooth, about 3 minutes. Add the salt and pepper and briefly mix in. Put the puree in a bowl inside a bowl of ice and refrigerate for 1 hour.

Beat in 1 cup of the cream. Whip a second cup of cream to soft peaks and fold into the puree. Cook a piece of the forcemeat in salted, simmering water to check for seasoning and texture. If it is too dense, add another ¼ cup of cream. Keep chilled until needed.

Sugar Syrup

Light sugar syrup is used for poaching fruit or adding to fruit compotes, hot or cold. Medium syrup is for sweetening fruit purees to be frozen as ices, and heavy syrup is for sweetening fruit purees to be used for sauces.

Light syrup

½ cup	*sugar*
1 cup	*water*

Yield: 1¼ cups

Medium syrup

⅔ cup	*sugar*
1 cup	*water*

Yield: 1½ cups

Heavy syrup

1 cup	*sugar*
1 cup	*water*

Yield: 1¾ cups

In each case, put the sugar and water in a pan. Bring the water to a boil, stirring constantly, until all the sugar is dissolved. Simmer 5 minutes and let it cool until needed.

Quick Puff Pastry

<table>
<tr><td>¾ pound</td><td>all-purpose flour</td></tr>
<tr><td>¼ pound</td><td>cake flour</td></tr>
<tr><td>½ teaspoon</td><td>salt</td></tr>
<tr><td>1¾ cups</td><td>heavy cream</td></tr>
<tr><td>1 pound</td><td>sweet butter, cut in 1-inch cubes, chilled</td></tr>
</table>

Yield: 7- by 4-inch rectangle

Sift the two flours and salt together in a bowl. Quickly cut in the butter by hand. Pour in the cream and stir briefly. The dough should be coarse, and neither wet nor dry.

On a lightly floured surface, pat the dough into a 6-inch square. Roll the dough out into a 12-inch square and fold it over by thirds, using a scraper to help you, forming a 12- by 4-inch rectangle. Remove it from the board and chill for 30 minutes. Roll out and fold again, and chill for 15 minutes, doing this step three more times until the dough is smooth.

Now you'll need to make a double or "book" turn: Roll the dough out to 14 by 8 inches; fold each 8-inch edge so they meet in the middle, then fold in half. Roll and fold the dough in this way two more times.

Wrap and refrigerate dough for 2 to 3 hours before using.

Tart Pastry

<table>
<tr><td>2 cups</td><td>all-purpose flour plus additional as needed</td></tr>
<tr><td>¼ cup</td><td>sugar</td></tr>
<tr><td>½ teaspoon</td><td>salt</td></tr>
<tr><td>½ pound</td><td>unsalted butter, cut in pieces</td></tr>
<tr><td>¼ cup</td><td>cold water</td></tr>
<tr><td></td><td>flour for dusting</td></tr>
</table>

Yield: One 9- to 10-inch round, ¼ inch thick

Combine 2 cups flour, sugar, and salt in a bowl. Mix the butter quickly into the flour by hand or with the paddle attachment of a mixer until the butter is in small crumbly pieces. Add the water and blend together, gathering the mass into a ball. Wrap in plastic wrap and refrigerate until needed.

Place the pastry on a lightly floured table. If the dough is cold and hard, beat it gently with a rolling pin to soften it. Shape it into a flattened circle. Dust the top with flour, turn over, dust again and roll out the dough into a 9- or 10-inch round to make a tart shell.

Brioche

Use this recipe for the brioche necessary for coulibiac, or bake it in loaves. It can then be sliced and used to line molds or toasted and eaten with smoked salmon or buttered and eaten with tea or coffee.

<table>
<tr><td>2 packets</td><td>active dry yeast</td></tr>
<tr><td>½ cup</td><td>warm milk</td></tr>
<tr><td>2 tablespoons</td><td>sugar</td></tr>
<tr><td>4 to 5 cups</td><td>all-purpose flour</td></tr>
<tr><td>4</td><td>eggs</td></tr>
<tr><td>½ pound</td><td>butter, cut in small pieces, softened</td></tr>
<tr><td>1 teaspoon</td><td>salt</td></tr>
</table>

Dissolve the yeast in the milk with the sugar and leave in a warm place for 10 minutes. Mix in 2 cups of the flour, stirring until the mixture is like thick pancake batter. Cover and leave in a warm place until the sponge has doubled in bulk, about 1 hour.

Mix in the eggs. Add the butter and gradually mix in the remaining flour and the salt. The dough will be dry and firm. Knead the dough with a machine or by hand until it is smooth and elastic, about 15 minutes. Put in a clean bowl, cover, and let rise for 2 hours. Punch the dough down and roll out on a lightly floured surface or divide into 2 equal parts, put in buttered loaf pans, let rise until double in size, and bake in a preheated 375°F oven for 30 minutes.

Crêpes

<table>
<tr><td>¼ cup</td><td>all-purpose flour, sifted</td></tr>
<tr><td>pinch</td><td>salt</td></tr>
<tr><td>2 large</td><td>eggs</td></tr>
<tr><td>½ cup</td><td>milk</td></tr>
<tr><td>2 tablespoons</td><td>butter, melted</td></tr>
</table>

Yield: 10 to 15 crêpes, about 6 inches in diameter

Put the flour and salt in a bowl. Mix in the eggs and then the milk; beat until smooth and the consistency of half-and-half. Add more milk if necessary. Stir in the butter.

Let the batter sit for at least half an hour and stir it just before using.

Heat a crêpe or non-stick pan and brush lightly with butter. Pour in just enough batter to coat the bottom of the pan. Pour off any excess. Cook for 2 to 3 minutes, turn over and cook another minute. Keep cooking crêpes, stacking them on a plate, until the batter is used up. Wrap in plastic film until needed.

Fish Stock

The best fish to use in a light stock for cream and butter sauces are sole, turbot, halibut, and trout. For fish soups and hearty stews, use whatever non-oily fish bones and heads you have: bass, grouper, snapper, haddock, etc. Fish stocks should be brought to a boil as fast as possible, and skimmed and simmered for no more than 40 minutes. The vegetables have to be small so that they cook entirely in this short time. Any leftover stock can be frozen briefly.

5 pounds	fish carcasses
1 cup	celery, finely chopped
1 cup	onion, peeled, finely chopped
2	bay leaves
1 sprig	fresh thyme or ½ teaspoon dried leaves
2 sprigs	fresh parsley
1 sprig	fresh tarragon or chervil, or ½ teaspoon dried leaves
1½ teaspoons	salt
1 gallon	water
1 cup	dry white wine

Yield: 1 gallon

Wash the fish carcasses, removing the gills from the heads and scraping away under water any blood from the backbone.

Put the celery, onion, herbs, and salt in a pot. Add 1 cup of the water, cover, and sweat the mixture over low heat for 10 minutes. Do not let any browning occur.

Add the fish carcasses and remaining water. Bring to a boil over high heat. As soon as it boils, lower the heat to a bare simmer. Skim any scum off the surface, avoiding any floating vegetables or herbs. Simmer, uncovered, for 20 minutes.

Add the wine and simmer another 20 minutes. Remove from the heat, let sit for 5 minutes, then carefully ladle all the stock into a fine strainer over a container. Do not press down on any fish in the strainer. Pour off the last of the stock into the strainer and discard the debris. Immediately refrigerate the stock, uncovered. When it is cold, cover until needed.

Fish Mousseline

The proportions of ingredients for fish mousseline, a puree of fish with cream and egg whites, will vary depending on how you will use it and the type of fish selected. The egg white strengthens the mousseline, and the cream makes it light and delicate. So, if you are using the mousseline to make quenelles, make a stronger one than if you were putting the mousseline in a mold and using it for stuffing another fish.

While petrale or Dover sole is very simple to use and needs little egg white, some other sole give off a lot of water when cooked and will require more egg white: generally, the cheaper the sole, the more egg white you will have to use. Turbot and pike are the easiest to use, requiring very little egg white, and salmon is in between. You could use a combination of fish and sea scallops, or of sole and salmon cut into pieces in the sole puree, or add mushroom duxelles, truffles, pistachios, lobster meat, or shrimp. Always test a piece in salted simmering water before you finish the puree, to check for texture and seasoning.

1 pound fillet	salmon, sole, turbot, monkfish, or bass, skinned, rough-chopped
2 large	egg whites
1 cup	whipping cream, cold salt and freshly ground pepper

Yield: 2 cups

Put the fish in a food processor and finely puree. Add the egg whites and puree again for 2 minutes until the egg whites are fully incorporated. Put the puree through a fine sieve into a bowl set over ice. Discard the debris or save it for fish stock.

Beat in half the cream and leave the puree to sit in the iced bowl for 30 minutes. Whip the remaining cream with some salt and pepper and fold into the puree. Poach a piece of the puree to check for texture and seasoning.

Polenta

Polenta is made from cornmeal, coarse or fine, and for the recipes in this book is cooked in stock or water. Debates rage over whether polenta should be of thick or thin texture but it's really a question of what it is going to be used for. If it is to be sauced with a mushroom ragout, for example, it should be on the thick side. As a bed for grilled little birds, it should be thinner.

The apotheosis of polenta is a version with mascarpone and white truffles, such as I have served at Stars. There is a beautiful photograph of this dish in Giuliano Bugialli's book *Foods of Italy*.

Polenta can be kept in a double boiler for hours. If it thickens too much, add more stock or water. Leftovers can be grilled or fried.

4 quarts	chicken stock (page 220) or water
4 cups	yellow cornmeal, coarse-ground
1 tablespoon	salt
4 tablespoons	butter

Bring the stock or water to a rolling boil. Pour in the cornmeal very gradually in a steady stream. Passing it through a sieve works well. Vigorously whisk the liquid and cornmeal together until all the cornmeal is incorporated and there are no lumps.

Then use a wooden spoon to stir constantly and scrape around the bottom corners of the pot where the polenta will try to stick and burn.

Cook over medium-low heat, stirring slowly and constantly, for 45 minutes. Taste for salt, stir in the butter, and hold in a double boiler until needed.

Grilled Polenta

Spread the polenta out on a buttered sheetpan, cover when cool, cut it in shapes, then grill it over charcoal *very* slowly for an hour, basting it occasionally with herb oil. It becomes crusty on the outside and stays voluptuously soft on the inside.

Pasta Dough

The proportions for this recipe will depend on the type of flour used and the size of the eggs, but 4 ounces of flour to 1 egg plus a yolk is my general rule. Bread flour or good semolina flour is the best. When making pasta by hand, the secret is a long, slow kneading until the dough is like satin.

1 pound	flour, plus extra for kneading
4 large	eggs
2	egg yolks
1 teaspoon	salt
2 tablespoons	olive oil

Put the flour in a bowl, make a well in the center of the flour and add the eggs, the additional yolks, salt, and olive oil. Mix the eggs gradually into the flour. Gather the dough into a ball, dust with flour, and knead it on a lightly floured surface until the dough is dry, elastic, and smooth. Wrap in a towel or plastic wrap and refrigerate for 1 hour.

Cut the dough into pieces and roll out by hand or in a pasta machine. Cut into the shapes you need. To cut the pasta for fettuccine, roll up the dough and cut in ½-inch sections, or put it through the appropriate cutter on the pasta machine.

Green Pasta Dough

Green pasta is made by adding pureed spinach to the above ingredients. Cook ½ pound of spinach in boiling water for 3 minutes. Drain, refresh under cold water, and squeeze as dry as possible. Puree the spinach and add to the eggs in the bowl. Be ready to incorporate more flour than usual when kneading the dough so that it will get the dry, glossy texture necessary for rolling it out.

Tomato Sauce

This sauce can be mixed with olive oil for cold sauces or finished with butter for a hot sauce.

1	onion, peeled, finely chopped
1 tablespoon	olive oil
1 small	bouquet garni (page 127)
4 cups	tomato concasse (below)
4 tablespoons	unsalted butter
	salt and freshly ground pepper

Yield: 2 cups

Sweat the onion, covered, over low heat in the olive oil with the bouquet garni for 10 minutes. Add the tomato and cook, uncovered, over medium heat for 10 minutes. Turn up the heat to high and cook, stirring or tossing constantly, until the tomatoes have just dried out, about 5 minutes. Discard the bouquet, puree the tomato mixture and sieve it. Hold until needed.

To finish the sauce, heat in a double boiler and when hot whisk in the butter until it is incorporated. Season to taste.

Tomato Concasse

The French are economical in culinary terminology: Often one word requires a whole phrase in English. So I have used tomato concasse, an anglicized form of the French term *tomates concassées,* to mean tomatoes that have been peeled, seeded, and chopped. When finishing a sauce with tomatoes, one must use tomato concasse so as not to water down the sauce or fill it with seeds. Grilled tomatoes or ones put in wood or charcoal embers give a particular quality to tomato concasse.

Put ripe tomatoes in boiling water for about 5 seconds. Do *not* overcook or the tomatoes will turn to mush. Plunge them immediately into a bath of ice and water for 30 seconds. Peel off the skin and discard. Cut across the equator of the tomato only, for if you cut through the stem and down you will seal off some of the seed chambers.

Hold the tomato halves cut-side-down and squeeze out the seeds. Dice the tomatoes and put them in a sieve over a bowl to drain. They are ready to use.

Chicken or Duck Stock

5 pounds	chicken or duck parts—backs, wings, feet, necks
5 quarts	water
1 large	onion, peeled, chopped
1 medium	carrot, peeled, chopped
3 stalks	celery, washed, chopped
2	bay leaves
2 sprigs	fresh thyme or ½ tablespoon dried
4 sprigs	parsley

Yield: 1 gallon

Put the chicken or duck parts in a pot with the water. Bring to a boil over high heat. As soon as it boils, lower the heat. Skim off all the scum on the surface of the water.

Add the vegetables and herbs, and simmer, uncovered, for 3 hours. Strain the stock, cool uncovered quickly, and refrigerate, covered, until needed. For rich stock, simmer the stock until reduced by one third.

Beef, Veal, or Lamb Stock

The quantities and procedure are the same as for chicken or duck stock, except that when the meat and bones come to a boil in water, throw out the water and wash off the meat. Put back into a cleaned pot and cook as for chicken or duck stock, but this time for 8 hours.

Fish, Veal, or Chicken Velouté

Flour-thickened sauces have recently gained a bad reputation. Like great courtesans, they seem to come and go. Their recent decline in fashion is the result of years of malpractice. In and of themselves, properly executed, they are light, ethereal, digestible and, in this case, liquid velvet. Veloutés must be simmered for an hour and skimmed constantly. Then they can be enriched with cream or egg yolks and cream, or a flavored butter—tarragon or lobster, or ginger-cilantro, for example. Use a heavy enamel, nickel, or tin-lined pot in which to make the sauce.

3 tablespoons	unsalted butter
4 tablespoons	flour
1 quart	rich fish, veal, or chicken stock
¼ teaspoon	salt
¼ cup	whipping cream

Melt the butter in a saucepan and stir in the flour. Cook over a medium heat for 5 minutes, stirring constantly. Whisk in the stock. Bring to a simmer, skim off any scum, and put the saucepan half off the heat so that it boils gently on one side only. Simmer, skimming constantly on the nonboiling side, for one hour. Add the salt, cook 5 minutes, strain, and stir in the cream.

Shellfish Essence

This recipe works for lobster, shrimp or prawn, and crayfish shells. Crab shells do not give up much flavor or color and are usually too hard to process. This essence is good for using in cream sauces or for mixing with lemon juice and oils for salad dressings. It can also be mixed with butter to make a shellfish butter. If the shells are not cooked, toss them in hot oil for 5 minutes over medium heat or put them in a 350°F oven for 15 minutes until they are entirely red.

4 cups	cooked lobster, crayfish, or shrimp shells
4 cups	fish stock

Grind the shells in a food processor just enough to break them up. Put them in the bowl of an electric mixer fitted with the dough hook or paddle. Add 1 cup of the fish stock and mix on low speed until the shells are completely broken up in small pieces and the stock in the bowl is red-colored, about 40 minutes. (The long mixing time is necessary to break up the shells gradually and extract the full flavor and color.)

Scrape out all the shells and any essence sticking to the sides of the bowl into a saucepan. Add the remaining fish stock, bring to a boil and then simmer for 15 minutes. Strain completely, pressing down on the shells, reserving the liquid and discarding the shells. Hold or freeze the liquid until necessary.

Court Bouillon

This aromatic broth is a poaching liquid for fish and shellfish and, with spices added, for vegetables (as in the preparation called "à la Turque"). For poaching salmon, the white wine can be changed to a young red wine.

1 large	onion, peeled, chopped
1 large	carrot, peeled, chopped
1	leek, chopped, washed
1 stick	celery, chopped
1	bay leaf
1 sprig	fresh thyme
2 sprigs	fresh parsley
1 tablespoon	salt
1 gallon	water
2 cups	dry white wine

Yield: 1 gallon

Put the vegetables, herbs, and salt in a pot with the water. Bring to a boil, skim, and simmer, uncovered, for 20 minutes. Add the wine and simmer another 20 minutes. Strain into a bowl and discard the vegetables.

Shellfish Butter

Use the same method as for shellfish essence, but add 1 pound of room-temperature butter in the last 30 minutes of processing the shells in the mixer. Cook the shells only 5 minutes, strain, and refrigerate the liquid. When it is cold, lift off the butter from the top and use it to enrich sauces or season it and put it on grilled fish.

Braised Sweetbreads

4 large	whole sweetbreads
2 cups	fine mirepoix (page 127)
2	bay leaves
2 sprigs	fresh thyme
4 sprigs	parsley
2 cups	chicken, beef, or veal stock (page 220)
½ cup	dry white wine

Serves 4

Soak the sweetbreads in salty cold water for 2 hours, changing the water whenever it becomes bloody. Drain them and put them in a pot. Add cold water to cover them by 2 inches and bring to a boil. Drain, put them in a colander, cover with ice, and run cold water over them for 5 minutes.

Peel off most of the outer membrane, keeping the sweetbreads as intact as possible. Put them in a pan, put another pan or plate on top, and weight them with some cans or heavy jars. Let stand overnight or at least for several hours.

Heat the oven to 375°F.

Put the mirepoix, bay leaves, and thyme and parsley sprigs in a casserole just large enough to hold the sweetbreads side by side. Cover and cook in the oven for 15 minutes. Put the sweetbreads on the mirepoix, pour the stock and wine over the sweetbreads, and season them lightly. Turn the oven down to 325°F and bake covered for 45 minutes. Remove the casserole from the oven.

Lift out the sweetbreads, brush off any mirepoix clinging to them, put them in a bowl, and strain the cooking liquid over them. Let cool in the liquid.

Herb Oil

If you have herbs from which you have already taken the leaves, bruise the stems of thyme, tarragon, rosemary, and savory, or a combination of them, cover with olive oil in a jar or bottle, and soak for 3 days. If you do not have stems only, chop the herb stems and leaves coarsely and cover them with oil for 2 days or more.

Barbecue Sauce

In Berkeley, California, there is a barbecue place called Everett and Jones' Barbecue, which makes a mouth-watering barbecue sauce. When I was chef at Ventana in Big Sur, I had to produce a barbecue, but was four hours from the nearest good sauce. It was winter, so I had a lot of time to think about how that secret sauce was made. Apple butter came to mind as a possible ingredient, mainly because of the similarity of color and texture. In Ventana's kitchen storeroom were shelves and shelves of cheap canned fruits I had inherited. So one day I started, with Willie Bishop, my old friend and kitchen assistant from Chez Panisse, to throw everything unwanted in a huge pot, including canned catsup and strange bottled sauces. We cooked it for hours, stirring occasionally, and with the help from a little liquid smoke, we produced an honorable version of Everett and Jones' original.

Years later at the Santa Fe Bar & Grill, Steven Vranian rose to the challenge and worked on the recipe again. Here it is. If you like it hot, use smoked chipotle chilies—they are wondrous.

10	tomatoes, coarsely chopped
8	onions, coarsely chopped
3 heads	garlic, chopped
4 to 5	fresh serrano chilies, stemmed, chopped
1 cup	dry red wine
1 cup	vinegar
½ cup	oil
½ cup	Worcestershire sauce
6 to 8 ounces	ancho chili puree (page 30)
½ cup	brown sugar
¼ cup	ancho chili powder
¼ cup	cumin powder
2 tablespoons	dry mustard
1 tablespoon	salt

Heat oven to 350°F.

Put all the ingredients in a thick-bottomed pot and cover. Bake 2½ hours, stirring frequently to avoid burning. Puree in a food processor and then pass through a sieve.

Chilies

Chilies, in both fresh and dried forms, have lent their piquancy and rich flavor to cuisines throughout the world, but have only come into their own relatively recently throughout this country. They are used in many recipes in this book, but because there is often confusion about their correct names I have provided a guide for their identification, opposite. Note: Wash your hands carefully and thoroughly after working with chilies—their strong oils will be highly irritating if they come in contact with the eyes or sensitive skin.

Fresh peppers

 Thai

 Serrano

 Jalapeño

 Fresno

 Pasilla (poblano)

 Anaheim

 Yellow wax

Dried peppers

 Japonés (Japanese)

 Chipotle

 Ancho

 New Mexico

 California

Acknowledgments

FAR NIENTE WINERY, NAPA, CALIFORNIA
Gil Nickel, Larry, Liz, Yvette, Raoul and Mike for the garden and kitchen

FOWLS' FARE, SALINAS, CALIFORNIA
Frank and Bruce, for the hunters' picnic

CLAYTON GRILLO
for the fireplace

RONALD JAMES, SAN FRANCISCO, CALIFORNIA

BARBARA KAFKA, NEW YORK
for the title

KENDALL CHEESE COMPANY, ATASCADERO, CALIFORNIA
Sadie Kendall for the goat cheeses and farm

SUSAN FISHER KING, SAN FRANCISCO, CALIFORNIA

RUSSEL MACMASTERS, SAN FRANCISCO, CALIFORNIA
for the photograph on page 101

EMILE NORMAN, BIG SUR, CALIFORNIA
for the indoor garden and use of his ranch

JOSEPH PHELPS WINERY, NAPA VALLEY, CALIFORNIA
Joseph Phelps, Bruce Neyers, and Craig Williams and guests for the harvest dinner

RON PODELL
for the fireplace

"BARBECUE" BILL ROGERS, OAKLAND, CALIFORNIA
for the grill and unending assistance

JOHN VAUGHAN, SAN FRANCISCO, CALIFORNIA
for photographs on pages 50, 51, 53, 56

CAROLYN WEIL, BERKELEY, CALIFORNIA
for help with the dessert recipes

TOMALES BAY OYSTER COMPANY, CALIFORNIA
Andrew Zorbas and staff for the dock

General Index

American Institute of Wine and Food, inaugural dinner, 206
Asher, Gerald, 59

Balboa Cafe, San Francisco, 141
Balzac, Honoré de, 107
Beard, James, 22–23, 100, 146, 175
Bedford, Sybille, 22, 36, 74
Bishop, Willie, 41
Brillat-Savarin, Anthelme, 107
Budrick, Gerry, 18
Bugialli, Giuliano, 219
Burgundy, 46
    wines, 15, 20

Chaleix, Marie-Claude, 47
Château d'Yquem, 15–16, 184, 191
Cheremetev, Sergei, 15
Chez Georges, 189
Chez Panisse Restaurant, Berkeley, 14, 16, 21, 34, 112, 134, 160, 190
    3rd birthday menu, 18–19
Child, Julia, 36, 84
Core, Philip, 21
Cragun, Richard, 26
Cussy, Marquis of, 134
Czuczman, Oksana, 150

David, Elizabeth, 14, 22, 84, 191
Dessert wines, 191
Diat, Louis, 173
Drinks, personal favorites, 21
Dubois, Urbain, 65
Dumaine, Alexandre, 105

Escoffier, Auguste, 14, 26, 190–91, 194

Fonteyn, Margot, 26
Franz, Mark, 85, 95

Gin and tonic, 21
Goines, David, 18
Grigson, Jane, 157

Kafka, Barbara, 152
Kahn, Odette, 190
Kendall, Sadie, 45, 47
Kennedy, Diana, 119

Lam, Noreen, 123
La Varenne, 104
Lianides, Leon, 17,5
Lur Saluces, Marquis de, 184

McSween, John, 21
Margaritas, 21
Marrakesh, Morocco, 14, 15
Médecin, Jacques, 18

Nignon, Edouard, 134

Olney, Richard, 17, 22, 30, 36, 46, 65, 90, 160, 167, 177, 188
    French Menu Cookbook, 65, 188
    Simple French Food, 167

Palmer, Michael, 26
Perry, Charles, 16
Peyraud, Lucien, 46, 160

Rawlings, Marjorie Kinnan, 202
Rhodes, Belle and Barney, 47

Santa Fe Bar and Grill, Berkeley, 26, 30, 34, 51, 59, 76, 95, 96, 100, 118, 144, 150, 175, 182, 196, 210
St. Ange, Madame de, 188
Sauternes, 184, 188
Sauternes Dinner, 16
Simon, Cathy, 191
Smith, Liz, 175
Stars Restaurant, San Francisco, 60, 77, 89, 100, 134, 172, 179, 209, 219
Stockli, Albert, 38

Tendret, Lucien, 107
Toklas, Alice B., 104, 213
Tour d'Argent, Paris, 112

Ventana, Big Sur, 41, 76
Villas, James, 150
Vranian, Steven, 26, 28

Waters, Alice, 18
Weil, Carolyn, 210
Wines, 15. *See also* Burgundy; Sauternes
    sweet, and food, 184

Youssoupof, Prince, 15

Recipe Index

Aioli (garlic mayonnaise), 36
    and Fennel with Fish Stew, 74
    and Mustard with Grilled Ham Hocks and Rocket, 147
Albacore
    Fish Paillard with Ginger, Garlic, and Tomatoes, 100
Almonds, creams and desserts, 190
Ancho Chili Puree, 30
    Grilled Chicken Paillard with, 118
    and Toasted Chicken Sandwich, 123
Anchovies
    Grilled Swordfish with Rosemary Mayonnaise, 90
    with Roasted Bell Pepper Salad, 167

Andouille Sausage
    with Duck Livers, 118
    in Gumbo, 124
Apples, 189, 191
    Caramelized Tart, 204
    Shortbread with Apricot Sauce and, 202
Apricot
    and Lemon Mousse, 198
    Sauce with Shortbread and Apples, 202
Artichoke(s), 162, 163
    Bottoms Stuffed with Fava Bean Puree, 177
    Lamb Stew with, 148

Artichoke(s) *(cont.)*
    and Rose Peppercorns with Salmon Stew, 88
    Salad with Grilled Prawns, Warm, 176
Asparagus, 162
Arugula. *See* Rocket
Avocado
    and Lobster Salad, Warm, 81
    and Mango Salad, 169
    and Papaya and Rocket Salad, 169

Bananas
    Turtle Cay, with Passion Fruit Sauce, 196

Barbecue Sauce, 222
Basil
    Okra and Tomato Salad, Warm, 180
    Soft-Shell Crabs with Tomato and, 96
Bass. *See* Sea Bass
Bavarian cream (*blanc manger*), 188
Beans. *See* Black Beans; Fava Beans;
        Green Beans
Béarnaise Sauce, 40
    with Meat Glaze, 40
    Mint, or Sauce Paloise, 40
Beef
    fillet of, cooking time, 134
    Fillet, Poached with Vegetables, 153
    Marrow, Brioches with Lobster,
        Poached Garlic, Chervil and, 100
    Marrow with Mushroom Caps, 178
    porterhouse steak, cooking of, 134
    Roast, 16
    shin, braised, 134
    Steak Tartare, 141
    Stock, 220
    T-Bone Steak, Cowboy Style, 146
Beets. *See* Borscht
Bell Pepper(s). *See also* Chilies
    Grilled Vegetable Salad with Texas
        Ham, 165
    peeling of, 167
    Puree, 32
    Roasted, Salad with Anchovies, 167
Berries, pureeing of, 32. *See also names
        of berries*
Bittersweet Chocolate Torte, 210
Black-and-White Ice Cream Soda, 23
Black Bean(s)
    The Cake, 175
    with Ham, Oranges, Lime Cream,
        150
    Soup, My, 175
Black Bean Sauce, 30
    Mark Franz's with Catfish, 95
    Grilled Salmon with Cucumbers and,
        88
    with Stuffed Chilies, 57
Blackberries
    Sauce, White Peaches with Raspberry
        Sauce and, 194
    Summer Pudding, 196
    Warm Berry Compote, 193
Black-bottom pie, 191
Black-Eyed Peas
    Warm Salad, 180
Black Truffles
    and chicken, 105
    freezing of, 17
    with Hamburger, 20
    and potatoes cooked in duck fat, 107
    with Scrambled Eggs, 17
    Sweetbread Ravioli, 59
Blanc manger, 188
Blinis, 15, 20
    of Cornmeal, with Smoked Sturgeon
        and Caviar, 63
Blueberries
    puree, 32
    Summer Pudding, 196
    Warm Berry Compote, 193
Blue Cornmeal Pancakes, 63
Bone marrow. *See* Marrow

Borscht with Pickled Mushrooms and
        Cucumbers, 170
Bouillabaisse. *See* Fish Stew with Fennel
        Aioli
Bouillon, Court, 221
Bouquet Garni, 127
Bourbon Pecan Tart, 209
Braised meats, 134–37, 147, 148
Braised Sweetbreads, 222
Brioches
    basic recipe, 217
    with Marrow, Lobster, Poached
        Garlic, and Chervil, 100
    Saffron, with Pear Glaze, 209
Bündnerfleisch with Vegetable Salad,
        142
Butters
    Chili, with Grilled Sweetbreads, 144
    Cilantro-Lime-Ginger, 34
    Clarified, 216
    classic maître d'hôtel, 34
    Crayfish, with Cream of Corn Soup,
        170
    Montpellier, 34
    Mushroom, with Grilled Sweetbreads,
        144
    Sage and Ham, with Garlic Soup, 172
    Shellfish, 221
    simple *vs.* compound, 34

Cabbage
    My Aunt's Coleslaw, 15
    Salad with Duck Fat, Warm, 110
Cakes, 188. *See also* Tarts
    Bittersweet Chocolate Torte, 210
    Polenta Pound, with Madeira Cream,
        207
Calamari
    Grilled, with Lobster Mayonnaise, 85
    with Sweet and Hot Chilies, Mark
        Franz's, 85
Cantaloupes, with Madeira, 71
Capon with Wild Mushrooms and Mint
        Béarnaise, 130
Caramelized Apple Tart, 204
Catfish
    with Mark Franz's Black Bean Sauce,
        95
Caviar, 15, 20
    Salmon, with Blinis and Smoked
        Sturgeon, 63
Chantilly Cream, 214
Cheeses, 45–47
    aged dry Jack, in Mushroom Caps
        with Bone Marrow, 178
    Fontina, Mozzarella, Parmesan Pizza
        with Tomatoes and Herbs, 18
    Fontina, in Stuffed Chilies with Black
        Bean Sauce, 57
    Goat, 45–47
    in Leaves, Grilled, 53
    with Squash Blossoms, 54
    Raclette with Radicchio, 54
    and seafood pasta or risotto, 58
    Stilton, 47
    White, with Roasted Garlic, 56
Cherries, in Warm Berry Compote, 193
Cherry Chutney, 26, 114
    basic recipe, 28

Cherry Chutney (*cont.*)
    with Raclette and Radicchio, 54
Chervil
    Brioches with Marrow, Lobster,
        Poached Garlic and, 100
Chicken, 104–107, 118–123. *See also*
        Capon
    cooking of, 64
    Forcemeat of, with Ham, 216
    Paillard, Grilled, with Ancho Chili
        Butter, 118
    Salad, with Sweetbread and Pepper
        Coleslaw, Warm, 123
    Sandwich, Toasted, and Ancho Chili,
        123
    Sandwich, Club, 19
    spit-roasted, 107
    Stock, 220
    Velouté, 221
Chili
    with Rabbit, 131
    "The Recipe," 150
Chili(es)
    Ancho
        Butter, with Grilled Chicken
            Paillard, 118
        Puree, 30
        and Toasted Chicken Sandwich,
            123
    Butter, with Grilled Sweetbreads, 144
    Fresh Cherry Chutney, 28
    guide to fresh and dried, 222–23
    Gumbo, 124
    -Mango Salsa, 28, 114
    Mirepoix, 26
    Mission Fig–Mint Relish, 28
    Mussels in Cataplana, 89
    Rabbit, 131
    Salsa, 28
    Stuffed with Black Bean Sauce, 57
    Sweet and Hot, with Calamari, 85
    Tomatillo Salsa, 29
Chocolate
    Paradise, 210
    Sauce, Black-and-White Soda, 23
    Sauce and Sabayon with Pecan Puff
        Pastry, 206
    torte, Viennese, 188
    Torte, Bittersweet, 210
Cilantro-Lime-Ginger Butter, 34
Chutneys
    Fresh Cherry, 28
    Tomato, 29
Clarified Butter, 216
Coach House Black Bean Soup, 175
Coconut Sauce with Mango Mousse,
        200
Cod
    Fish Stew with Fennel Aioli, 74
    My Favorite Fish Soup, 84
    Seviche, 76
    Tarpon Springs Soup, 96
Coleslaw
    My Aunt's, 15
    Pepper, and Warm Chicken,
        Sweetbread Salad, 123
Cornmeal. *See also* Polenta
    Blini with Smoked Sturgeon and
        Caviar, 63

Cornmeal *(cont.)*
Pancakes, Blue, 63
Corn
Cream Soup, with Crayfish Butter, 170
Coulibiac
Brioche pastry for, 217
of Sweetbreads, 156
Country Ham, 23
Court Bouillon, 221
Crab
Dungeness, Grilled, 92
Mixed Shellfish Plate, 99
Soft-Shell with Tomato and Basil, 96
Crayfish
Butter, with Cream of Corn Soup, 170
Cream, with Cucumber Vichyssoise, 173
Salad, with Cucumbers and Dill, Warm, 80
shells of, 72, 221
with Fricassee of Veal, 153
Cream, Tomato, 170
Cream of Corn Soup with Crayfish Butter, 170
Creams, flavored, 188
Chantilly, 214
Chocolate, 210
Madeira, with Polenta Pound Cake, 207
Rum, with Pumpkin Gingerbread, 207
Walnut, with Figs in Red Wine, 195
Crêpes, 217
Cross Creek Tangerine Ice, 202
Crottin de Chavignol, 46
Croutons of Salmon Caviar, with Garden Salad, 165
Cucumber/s
Borscht with Pickled Mushrooms and, 170
Grilled Salmon with Black Bean Sauce and, 88
Salad, with Crayfish and Dill, Warm, 80
Vichyssoise with Crayfish Cream, 173
Currants
Summer Pudding, 196
Custards
basic, flavored, 213
Coconut, 213
Coffee, 213
Pistachio, Orange and Caramel, 212

Desserts, 188–214
Apple Tart, Caramelized, 204
Apricot and Lemon Mousse, 198
Bananas with Passion Fruit Sauce, Turtle Cay, 196
Bittersweet Chocolate Torte, 210
Bourbon Pecan Tart, 209
Chantilly Cream, 214
Chocolate Paradise, 210
Coconut Custard, 213
Coffee Custard, 213
Custard, basic recipe, 213

Desserts *(cont.)*
Figs in Red Wine with Walnut Cream, 195
Fruit Compote, Tropical, 201
Ice Cream, 188
Fresh Plum, 200
Nougat, 213
Lemon and Apricot Mousse, 198
Mango Mousse with Coconut Sauce, 200
Peaches, White, with Raspberry and Blackberry Sauces, 194
Pears in Red Wine with Basil, 193
Pecan Puff Pastry with Chocolate Sauce and Sabayon, 206
Pecan Tart, Bourbon, 209
Plum Napoleon with Sabayon, 203
Polenta Pound Cake with Madeira Cream, 207
Pumpkin Gingerbread with Rum Cream, 207
Raspberry Soufflés with Sabayon, 198
Russian Raspberry Gratin, 195
Sabayon Mousseline Sauce, 214
Saffron Brioche with Pear Glaze, 209
Shortbread with Apples and Apricot Sauce, 202
Summer Pudding (berries), 196
Tangerine Ice, Cross Creek, 202
Three Custards, 212
Trifle, 204
Warm Berry Compote, 193
Dough
for Green Pasta, 219
for Pasta, 219
for Pizza, 19
Duck, 107–118
Breast, with Wild Rice and Mango-Chili Salsa, 114
boning of half-cooked, 108–109
carcass preparation for stock, 108–109
Confit, 113
cooking of, 64
cracklings, 108–109
cutting of when raw, 108–109
fat, rendering of, 113
Fat, with Warm Cabbage Salad, 110
Leg, Grilled, with Endive Salad, 115
Livers, with Andouille Sausage, 118
neck skins, 116
Poached, with Duck Sausage and Horseradish Sauce, 130
raw, cutting of, 108–109
Salad, with Turnip Pancake, Warm, 112
Sausage, Grilled, with Polenta, 116
Sausage with Poached Duck and Horseradish Sauce, 130
Skin Omelet, 110
Smoked, in Stars Gumbo, 124
Smoked, in Warm Pasta Salad with Radicchio, 60
Smoked, with Belgian Endive, 120
Soup, 112
Stock, 220
whole, trussing of, 108–109
Dungeness Crab, Grilled, 92
Duxelles, 50

Eel, Conger
Fish Stew with Fennel Aioli, 74
My Favorite Fish Soup, 84
Smoked, and Grilled Radicchio Salad, 178
Eggplant
Baked, Pasta Salad with Tomatoes and, 60
French-Fried, with Florida Guzpachy Sauce, 182
Japanese, with Grilled Swordfish, 90
and Zucchini Timbale Soufflé, 184
Eggs, 188
Duck Skin Omelet, 110
French Scrambled, with Smoked Salmon, 51
in Hell, Texas Style, 51
Lamb Hash, Noreen Lam's, 52
Poached, with Mushrooms, 50
Rémoulade Creole, 50
Scrambled, with Truffles, 17
Spinach, Sorrel, and Ham Frittata, 52
Elderberry sauce, 198
Endive
Belgian, with Lobster, 78
Belgian, with Smoked Duck, 120
Grilled Vegetable Salad with Texas Ham, 165
Salad with Grilled Duck Leg, 115
with smoked eel salad, 178
Essence of Shellfish, 221
Essences, Hollandaise with, 40

Fava Bean(s), 163
Puree, Artichoke Bottoms Stuffed with, 177
and savory, 79
Fennel, 163
Aioli, with Fish Stew, 74
Fig(s)
Fresh, and Mint Salad, 168
-Mint Relish, 28
in Red Wine with Walnut Cream, 195
Warm Berry Compote, 193
Fish. *See also* Lobster; Shellfish
Catfish with Black Bean Sauce, 95
Mousseline, 218
Paillard with Ginger, Garlic, Tomatoes, 100
poaching liquid for (Court Bouillon), 221
Salmon, Grilled with Cucumbers and Black Bean Sauce, 88
Salmon and Tuna Tartare, 82
Salmon Stew with Artichokes and Rose Peppercorns, 88
"Sausage" with Sorrel and Lobster Sauce, 92
Seviche, 76
soup, 22
Soup, My Favorite, 84
Soup, Tarpon Springs, 96
Stew with Fennel Aioli, 74
Stock, 218
Sturgeon, Smoked, with Blinis and Caviar, 63
Swordfish, Grilled, with Rosemary Mayonnaise, 90

Fish *(cont.)*
Turbot, Poached with Lobster, 94
Velouté, 221
Flatfish, in Favorite Fish Soup, 84
Florida Guzpachy Sauce, 182
Fontina cheese
Pizza with Three Cheeses, Tomatoes, and Herbs, 18
Stuffed Chilies with Black Bean Sauce, 57
Forcemeat, Chicken and Ham, 216
French bream, with Black Bean Sauce, 95
French Scrambled Eggs with Smoked Salmon, 51
Frittata of Spinach, Sorrel and Ham, 52
Fruit. *See* Desserts; Salads; *names of fruits*

Garden Salad with Salmon Caviar Croutons, 165
Garlic
Fish Paillard with Ginger, Tomatoes, and, 100
Fish Stew with Fennel Aioli, 74
Mayonnaise (Aioli), 36
Poached, Brioches with Marrow, Lobster, Chervil, and, 100
Puree, 30
Roasted, with White Cheese, 56
Soup with Sage and Ham Butter, 172
in Warm Vegetable Stew, 167
Garnishes
for Chicken Paillard, 118
for Risotto, 58
Gazpacho, Lobster, 77
Genoise, 188
Ginger
-Cilantro-Lime Butter, 34
Fish Paillard with Garlic, Tomatoes, and, 100
Gingerbread
Pumpkin, with Rum Cream, 207
Glazes
Meat, with Sauce Béarnaise, 40
Pear, with Saffron Brioche, 209
Goat cheese, 45–47
Grilled, in Leaves, 53
Squash Blossoms with, 54
Grains. *See also* Desserts; Dough
Blue Cornmeal Pancakes, 63
Brioche, 217
Cornmeal Blinis with Smoked Sturgeon and Caviar, 63
Crêpes, 217
Polenta, 219
Polenta with Wild Mushroom Sauce, 58
Quick Puff Pastry, 216
Risotto with Prawns, 58
Tart Pastry, 217
Green Pasta Dough, 219
Grilling, with hinged grill, 53
Grouper
Paillard with Ginger, Garlic and Tomatoes, 100
Seviche, 76
for Stock, 218

Gumbo, Stars, 124
Guzpachy Sauce, 182

Haddock
Fish Stew with Fennel Aioli, 74
Seviche, 76
for Stock, 218
Halibut
Poached, with Lobster, 94
Seviche, 76
Stew with Fennel Aioli, 74
for Stock, 218
Tarpon Springs Soup, 96
Ham
with Black Beans, Oranges, and Lime Cream, 150
and Chicken Forcemeat, 216
Country, 23
Frittata with Spinach and Sorrel, 52
Hocks, with Rocket and Mustard Aioli, 147
and Rosemary Stuffing for Roast Pork Loin, 157
and Sage Butter with Garlic Soup, 172
Texas, with Grilled Vegetable Salad, 165
Hamburger, Black-Truffled, 20
Herb(s). *See also names of herbs and spices*
Cream Soup with Sorrel, 172
Mayonnaise, 36
with Squash Blossoms and Goat Cheese, 54
Oil, 222
Pizza, with Three Cheeses and Tomatoes, 18–19
and vegetable stew, 167
Herring, Pickled with New Potatoes, 74
Hollandaise Sauce, 38
variations of, 38
Horseradish Sauce, 130

Ice, Cross Creek Tangerine, 202
Ice Cream, 188
Black-and-White Soda, 23
Fresh Plum, 200
Nougat, 213
Indian pudding, 191

Kidneys
Lamb, Grilled Whole, with Potato Pancakes, 143

Lamb
Chopped Steak au Poivre, 141
Hash, Noreen Lam's, 53
Kidneys, Grilled Whole with Potato Pancakes, 143
left-over and braised, 136–37
and rosemary, 79, 134
Shanks, Braised, 148
Spicy Sausage, Grilled, with Oysters, 146–47
spit-roasted, 134
Stew with Artichokes, 148
Stock, 220

Leek(s), 163
poached, served hot or cold, 162
and potato soup, 160
Lemon and Apricot Mousse, 198
Lime
Cilantro-Ginger Butter, 34
Cream, with Ham, Black Beans and Oranges, 150
Livers
Duck, with Andouille Sausage, 118
Lobster
basic preparation, 72
Brioches with Marrow, Poached Garlic, Chervil and, 100
Gazpacho, 77
Mayonnaise, with Grilled Calamari, 85
Poached Turbot with, 94
removing meat from, 73
Rocket Salad with, 79
Salad with Avocado, Warm, 81
Salad, with Belgian Endive, 78
Sandwich, Toasted, 82
shells of, 72
Sauce, Fish "Sausage" with Sorrel and, 92
Loganberries
Summer Pudding, 196

Macaroni
and Sweetbreads, Timbale of, 65
Madeira, 15, 17, 34
in cantaloupes, 71
Cream, with Polenta Pound Cake, 207
Maltaise Sauce, 38
Mango(es)
and Avocado Salad, 169
-Chili Salsa, Steven Vranian's, 28
-Chili Salsa with Duck Breast and Wild Rice, 114
Mousse with Coconut Sauce, 200
sauces, 26
Tropical Fruit Compote, 201
Warm Berry Compote, 193
Marjoram and zucchini, 79
Mark Franz's Black Bean Sauce with Catfish, 95
Mark Franz's Calamari with Sweet and Hot Chilies, 85
Marrow bones
Brioches with Lobster, Poached Garlic, Chervil and, 100
with Mushroom Caps, 178
Mayonnaise, basic, 36
Black Bean, 36
Garlic (aioli), 36
Herb, 36
Rosemary, with Grilled Swordfish, 90
Rouille, 36
Shrimp Salad with, 78
Meats, 134–57. *See* Beef; Lamb; Pork; Steaks
Minestrone with Artichokes, Sausage, and Pistachios, 182
Mint
Béarnaise, 40
with Capon and Wild Mushrooms, 130

Mint *(cont.)*
  Relish, with Mission Figs, 28
  Salad, with Fresh Figs, 168
Mirepoix, 26, 130
  basic recipe, 127
Monkfish
  Fish Stew with Fennel Aioli, 74
  Mousseline, 218
  Tarpon Springs Soup, 96
Montpellier Butter, 34
Moules à la Marinière, 89
  See also Mussels
Mousse
  Apricot and Lemon, 198
  Mango, with Coconut Sauce, 200
Mousseline
  Sauce, 38
  Sabayon Sauce, 214
  of Fish, 218
Mozzarella
  Pizza with Three Cheeses, Tomatoes,
    and Herbs, 18
Mushroom(s). *See also* Wild
    Mushrooms
  Butter, with Grilled Sweetbreads, 144
  Caps with Bone Marrow, 178
  Chanterelles, Pasta with Rabbit and,
    64
  Duxelles, 50
  Poached Eggs with, 50
  Timbale of Sweetbreads and
    Macaroni, 65
  Truffled Sweetbread Ravioli, 59
Mussels in Cataplana, 89
Mustard Aioli, with Grilled Ham Hocks
    and Rocket, 147
My Aunt's Coleslaw, 15
My Black Bean Soup, 175
My Favorite Fish Soup, 84
My Steak Tartare, 141

Napoleon, Plum, with Sabayon, 203
Noisette Sauce, 38
Noreen Lam's Lamb Hash, 123
Nougat Ice Cream, 213

Oil and vinegar dressing, 32
Okra
  Basil and Tomato Warm Salad, 180
  with Warm Squab Salad, 122
Ollalieberries, in Summer Pudding, 196
Omelet, Duck Skin, 110
Onion(s), 163
  Grilled Vegetable Salad, 165
  Pearl, with Grilled Spiced Shrimp, 99
  and Watermelon Salad, 168
Oranges, Black Beans, and Lime Cream
    with Ham, 150
Oysters, Grilled Spicy Lamb Sausage
    with, 146

Paillard
  Chicken, with Ancho Chili Butter,
    118
  Fish, with Ginger, Garlic, Tomatoes,
    100
Pancakes
  Blue Cornmeal, 63

Pancakes *(cont.)*
  Potato, with Grilled Lamb Kidneys,
    143
  Turnip, with Warm Duck Salad, 113
Papaya
  Tropical Fruit Compote, 201
  Warm Berry Compote, 193
Parmesan cheese
  Pizza with Three Cheeses, Tomatoes,
    and Herbs, 18
  Stuffed Chilies with Black Bean
    Sauce, 57
Passion Fruit
  Sauce with Turtle Cay Bananas, 196
  Tropical Fruit Compote, 201
Pasta, 44–45
  Dough, 219
  Green Dough, 219
  with Rabbit and Chanterelles, 64
  Salad, with Baked Eggplant and
    Tomatoes, 60
  Salad, with Smoked Duck and
    Radicchio, Warm, 60
  seafood, and addition of cheese, 58
  Sweetbread Ravioli, Truffled, 59
  Timbale of Macaroni and
    Sweetbreads, 65
Pastry
  Puff, 217
  Tart, 217
Peaches
  Warm Berry Compote, 193
  White, with Raspberry and
    Blackberry Sauces, 194
Pear/s
  Glaze with Saffron Brioche, 209
  in Red Wine with Basil, 193
Peas, Black-Eyed, Warm Salad of, 180
Pecans
  Puff Pastry with Chocolate Sauce and
    Sabayon, 206
  Tart, Bourbon, 209
Peppercorns. *See* Rose Peppercorns
Peruvian Cream, 188
Pickled Herring with New Potatoes, 74
Pickled Wild Mushrooms with
    Cucumbers in Borscht, 170
Pike, with Mark Franz's Black Bean
    Sauce, 95
Pistachios, Minestrone with Artichokes,
    Sausage and, 182
Pizza, 18
  Dough, 19
  with Three Cheeses, Tomatoes, and
    Herbs, 18–19
Plums
  Fresh Ice Cream, 200
  Napoleon with Sabayon, 203
  Warm Berry Compote, 193
Polenta
  basic recipe, 219
  Grilled, 219
  Grilled Duck Sausage with, 116
  Pound Cake with Madeira Cream,
    207
  with Wild Mushroom Sauce, 58
Pollack
  Fish Stew with Fennel Aioli, 74

Pork
  chops, 134
  loin, roasted and marinated, 134
  Loin Roast, Stuffed with Ham and
    Rosemary, 156
Potatoes
  cooked in duck fat, 107
  and leek soup, 160
  New, with Pickled Herring, 74
  pancakes cooked in duck fat, 113,
    167
  Pancakes, with Grilled Whole Lamb
    Kidneys, 143
Pots de crème, 188
Pound Cake, Polenta, with Madeira
    Cream, 207
Prawns. *See also* Shrimp
  Grilled, Warm Salad of Artichokes
    and, 176
  Mixed Shellfish Plate, 99
  with Risotto, 58
Pudding, Summer, 196
Puff Pastry
  Pecan, with Chocolate Sauce and
    Sabayon, 206
  Quick, 217
Pumpkin Gingerbread with Rum
    Cream, 207
Pumpkins, baking of, 162
Pumpkinseed Sauce with Roast Quail,
    119
Purees. *See also* Sauces
  Ancho Chili, 30
  Berry, with Grilled Squab, 121
  Fava Bean, Artichoke Bottoms
    Stuffed with, 177
  Fish Mousseline, 218
  Garlic, 30
  Raspberry, 32
  Red or Yellow Bell Pepper, 32

Quail, Roasted, with Pumpkinseed
    Sauce, 119
  Warm Salad with Okra, 122

Rabbit, 85
  Braised, with Leeks and Prunes, 127
  Chili, 131
  Pasta with Chanterelles and, 64
  Saddle of, with Black and Rose
    Peppercorns, 127
Raclette, 47
  with Radicchio, 54
Radicchio
  Grilled, and Smoked Eel Salad, 178
  Pasta Salad, Warm, with Smoked
    Duck and, 60
  Raclette with, 54
Raspberries, 190
  Summer Pudding, 196
Raspberry
  and Blackberry Sauce with White
    Peaches, 194
  Puree, 32, 192
  Russian Gratin, 195
  Soufflés with Sabayon, 198
Ratatouille, 90

Ravioli with Black Truffles and
  Sweetbreads, 59
Red Bell Pepper Puree, 32
Red Snapper
  Paillard with Ginger, Garlic,
    Tomatoes, 100
  for Fish Stock, 218
  Tarpon Springs Soup, 96
Red Wine
  Figs in, with Walnut Cream, 195
  Pears in, with Basil, 193
  Relish, Steven Vranian's Mission Fig-
    Mint, 28
Rice. *See also* Risotto
  Wild, with Duck Breast and Mango-
    Chili Salsa, 114
Risotto, with Prawns, 58
Rocket (Arugula)
  and Avocado and Papaya Salad, 169
  Grilled Ham Hocks with Mustard
    Aioli and, 147
  and Lobster Salad, 79
Rockfish, in My Favorite Fish Soup, 84
Rosemary, 134
  and lamb, 79
  Mayonnaise, with Grilled Swordfish,
    90
  Roast Pork Loin Stuffed with Ham
    and, 157
Rose Peppercorns
  with Salmon Stew, 88
  Saddle of Rabbit with Black and, 127
Rouille (red pepper aioli), 36
Rum Cream with Pumpkin
  Gingerbread, 207
Russian Raspberry Gratin, 195

Sabayon, 40
  with Raspberry Soufflés, 198
  and Chocolate Sauce with Pecan Puff
    Pastry, 206
  Mousseline Sauce, 214
  Plum Napoleon with, 203
Saffron Brioche with Pear Glaze, 209
Sage and Ham Butter with Garlic Soup,
  172
Salads. *See also* Salads, Warm
  Avocado and Mango, 169
  Avocado, Papaya, and Rocket, 169
  Bell Pepper, Roasted, with Anchovies,
    167
  Endive with Grilled Duck Leg, 115
  Endive, Belgian, with Lobster, 78
  Field with Squab Mousse, 116
  Fresh Fig and Mint, 168
  Garden, with Salmon Caviar
    Croutons, 165
  Lobster and Belgian Endive, 78
  Lobster and Rocket, 79
  Mango and Avocado, 169
  Onion and Watermelon, 168
  Papaya, Avocado and Rocket, 169
  Pasta, with Baked Eggplant and
    Tomatoes, 60
  Radicchio, Grilled, and Smoked Eel,
    178
  Rocket, Avocado and Papaya, 169
  Rocket and Lobster, 79
  Shrimp with Three Mayonnaises, 78

Salads *(cont.)*
  Vegetable, with *Bündnerfleisch,* 142
  Watermelon and Onion, 168
Salads, Warm
  Avocado and Lobster, 81
  Artichokes and Grilled Prawns, 176
  Black-Eyed Peas, 180
  Cabbage with Duck Fat, 110
  Chicken, Sweetbread, and Pepper
    Coleslaw, 123
  Crayfish, Cucumbers, and Dill, 80
  Duck with Turnip Pancake, 112
  Lobster and Avocado, 81
  Okra with Squab, 122
  Okra, Tomato, and Basil, 180
  Pasta with Rabbit and Chanterelles,
    64
  Pasta with Smoked Duck and
    Radicchio, 60
  Prawns, Grilled, and Artichokes, 176
  Radicchio and Smoked Duck, 60
  Squab with Okra, 122
  Vegetable, Grilled, with Texas Ham,
    165
Salmon
  Caviar Croutons, with Garden Salad,
    165
  Fish Mousseline, 218
  Grilled, with Cucumbers and Black
    Bean Sauce, 88
  for Paillard, 100
  poaching liquid for (Court Bouillon),
    221
  Seviche, 76
  Smoked, serving of, 21
  Stew, with Artichokes and Rose
    Peppercorns, 88
  and Tuna Tartare, 82
Salsa, 26
  basic recipe, 28
  and Florida Guzpachy Sauce, 182
  Mango-Chili, 28
  Mango-Chili with Duck Breast and
    Wild Rice, 114
  Stuffed Chilies with Black Bean
    Sauce, 57
  Tomatillo, 29
Sandwiches
  Black-Truffled Hamburger, 20
  Chicken and Ancho Chili, Toasted,
    123
  Chicken Club, 19
  Lobster, Toasted, 82
Sauce Paloise, 40
Sauces, 26. *See also* Butters; Creams;
  Purees
  Apricot, 202
  Barbecue, 222
  Béarnaise, 40
  Béarnaise with Meat Glaze, 40
  Black Bean, 30
  Blackberry, 32
  Chocolate, 206
  Coconut, 200
  Fish, Veal, or Chicken Velouté, 221
  Florida Guzpachy, 182
  Hollandaise, 38
  Hollandaise with Essences, 38
  Horseradish, 130

Sauces *(cont.)*
  Lobster, 92
  Maltaise, 38
  Mint Béarnaise, 40
  Mousseline, 38
  Noisette, 38
  Passion Fruit, 196
  Pumpkinseed, 119
  Raspberry, 32
  Sabayon, 40
  Sabayon Mousseline, 214
  Tarragon, 93
  Tomato, 220
  Tomato Concasse, 220
  Tomato Hollandaise, 38
Sausage
  Andouille, with Duck Livers, 118
  Duck, with Poached Duck and
    Horseradish Sauce, 130
  Duck, with Polenta, 116
  Lamb, Grilled Spicy, with Oysters,
    146–47
  Minestrone with Artichokes,
    Pistachios, and, 182
Savory and fava beans, 79
Scallops, Sea
  Grilled, with Tarragon Sauce, 93
  Mixed Shellfish Plate, 99
Scrambled Eggs with Truffles, 17
Sea Bass
  Mousseline of, 218
  Paillard with Ginger, Garlic,
    Tomatoes, 100
  Seviche, 76
  Stew with Fennel Aioli, 74
  for Stock, 218
  Tarpon Springs Soup, 96
Sea Urchin Soufflé, 22–23
Seviche, 76
Shellfish. *See also* Fish; Lobster
  Butter, 221
  Crab, Dungeness, Grilled, 92
  Crabs, Soft-Shell, with Tomato and
    Basil, 96
  Calamari with Lobster Mayonnaise,
    85
  Calamari with Sweet and Hot Chilies,
    Mark Franz's, 85
  Crayfish Butter, with Cream of Corn
    Soup, 170
  Crayfish Cream, with Cucumber
    Vichyssoise, 173
  Crayfish Salad with Cucumbers and
    Dill, Warm, 80
  Crayfish with Fricasse of Veal, 153
  Essence, 221
  Mixed Plate of, 99
  Mussels in Cataplana, 89
  poaching liquid for (Court Bouillon),
    221
  Scallops, Grilled, with Tarragon
    Sauce, 93
  shells of, 72
  Shrimp Salad with Three
    Mayonnaises, 78
  Shrimp, Spiced, with Pearl Onions,
    99
Shortbread with Apples and Apricot
  Sauce, 202

Shrimp. *See also* Prawns
    Grilled Spiced, with Pearl Onions, 99
    Mixed Shellfish Plate, 99
    Salad, with Three Mayonnaises, 78
Smoked Duck, with Belgian Endive, 120
Smoked Eel, and Grilled Radicchio Salad, 178
Smoked Salmon, serving of, 21
Smoked Sturgeon with Blinis and Caviar, 63
Smoke-Roasted Squab, 120
Sole
    Fish Mousseline, 218
    Stock, 218
Sorrel
    Fish Sausage with Lobster Sauce and, 92
    and Herb Soup, Chilled, 172
    Spinach and Ham Frittata, 52
Soufflés
    Eggplant and Zucchini Timbale, 184
    Raspberry, with Sabayon, 198
    Sea Urchin, 22–23
Soups
    Black Bean, My, 175
    Borscht with Pickled Mushrooms and Cucumbers, 170
    Cream of Corn, with Crayfish Butter, 170
    Cucumber Vichyssoise, with Crayfish Cream, 173
    Duck, 112
    Fish, 22
    Fish, My Favorite, 84
    Fish, Tarpon Springs, 96
    Garlic, with Sage and Ham Butter, 172
    Lobster Gazpacho, 77
    Minestrone with Artichokes, Sausage, and Pistachios, 182
    Sorrel and Herb, Chilled, 170
Spinach, Sorrel and Ham Frittata, 52
Spit-roasting, 107, 134
Squab
    Grilled, Marinated in Berry Puree, 121
    Mousse of, with Field Salad, 116
    Salad, with Okra, Warm, 122
    Smoke-Roasted, 120
Squash, 162, 163, 165
Squash Blossoms with Goat Cheese, 54
Squid. *See* Calamari
Steaks
    Chopped Lamb, au Poivre, 141
    porterhouse, cooking of, 134
    Tartare, 141
    T-Bone, Cowboy Style, 146
Stews
    Fish, with Fennel Aioli, 74
    Lamb, with Artichokes, 148
    Salmon, with Artichokes and Rose Peppercorns, 88

Stews *(cont.)*
    Vegetable, Warm, 167
Stilton cheese, 47
Stock
    Chicken or Duck, 220
    Fish, 218
    Veal, 220
Strawberries, 190
    Summer Pudding, 196
    Warm Berry Compote, 193
    wild, Soufflé with Sabayon, 198
Sturgeon
    Fish Paillard with Ginger, Garlic, Tomatoes, 100
    Smoked, with Blinis and Caviar, 63
Sugar Syrup, 216
Summer Pudding, 196
Sweetbreads
    Braised, basic recipe, 222
    Braised, in a Sealed Casserole, 157
    and Chicken, Pepper Coleslaw Salad, Warm, 123
    Coulibiac of, 156
    Grilled, with Chili Butter, 144
    Grilled, with Mushroom Butter, 144
    Timbale of Macaroni and, 65
    Veal, with Truffles and Ravioli, 59
Swordfish, Grilled, with Rosemary Mayonnaise, 90
Syrup, Sugar, 216

Tangerine Ice, Cross Creek, 202
Tarragon Sauce, with Grilled Scallops, 93
Tartare
    of Salmon and Tuna, 82
    Steak, 141
Tarte Tatin, 189
    Caramelized Apple Tart, 204
Tarts
    Bourbon Pecan, 209
    Caramelized Apple, 204
    Pastry, 217
T-Bone Steak, Cowboy Style, 146
Three Custards, 212
Timbale
    of Macaroni and Sweetbreads, 65
    Soufflé with Eggplant and Zucchini, 184
Tomato(es)
    Chutney, 29
    Concasse, 220
    Cream, 172
    Fish Paillard with Ginger, Garlic and, 100
    Hollandaise, 38
    and Okra and Basil Salad, Warm, 180
    Pasta Salad, with Baked Eggplant and, 60
    Pizza with Three Cheeses, Herbs, and, 18–19
    Sauce, 220

Tomato(es) *(cont.)*
    Soft-Shelled Crabs with Basil and, 96
    Vinaigrette, 32
Trifle, 204
Tripe, 134–36
Trout, for fish stock, 218
Truffles. *See* Black Truffles
Tuna
    Fish Paillard with Ginger, Garlic, Tomatoes, 100
    Tartare of Salmon, and, 82
Turbot
    Fish Mousseline, 218
    Poached, with Lobster, 94
    for Stock, 218
Turnip Pancake with Warm Duck Salad, 112
Turtle Cay Bananas with Passion Fruit Sauce, 196

Veal
    Fricassee of, with Crayfish, 152
    Kidneys, 134
    Stock, 220
    Sweetbreads with Truffles and Ravioli, 59
    Velouté, 221
Vegetables, 160–85. *See also* Salads
    baby, or *primeur*, 160, 162
    Poached Beef Fillet with, 153
    poaching liquid for, 221
    Ragout, 163
    Salad, with *Bündnerfleisch*, 142
    Salad, Grilled, with Texas Ham, 165
    Warm Stew of, 167
Velouté, Fish, Veal or Chicken, 221
Vichyssoise, Cucumber, with Crayfish Cream, 173
Viennese Chocolate Torte, 188
Vinaigrette, 32
    Tomato, 32

Walnut Cream, with Figs in Red Wine, 195
Warm Berry Compote, 193
Watermelon and Onion Salad, 168
White Cheese with Roasted Garlic, 56
Wild Mushrooms
    with Capon and Mint Bearnaise, 130
    Pickled, with Cucumbers in Borscht, 170
    Sauce, with Polenta, 58
    with potatoes cooked in duck fat, 107
Wild Rice. *See* Rice

Yellow Bell Pepper Puree, 32

Zucchini
    growth stages of, 162
    and marjoram, 79
    and Eggplant Timbale Soufflé, 184